NATIVE AMERICAN STUDIES IN HIGHER EDUCATION

CONTEMPORARY NATIVE AMERICAN COMMUNITIES
Stepping Stones to the Seventh Generation

Despite the strength and vibrancy of Native American people and nations today, the majority of publications on Native peoples still reflect a public perception that these peoples largely disappeared after 1890. This series is meant to correct that misconception and to fill the void that has been created by examining contemporary Native American life from the point of view of Native concerns and values. Books in the series cover topics that are of cultural and political importance to tribal and urban Native peoples and affect their possibilities for survival.

SERIES EDITORS:
Troy Johnson
American Indian Studies
California State University, Long Beach
Long Beach, CA 90840
trj@csulb.edu

Duane Champagne
American Indian Studies Center
3220 Campbell Hall, Box 951548
University of California, Los Angeles
Los Angeles, CA 90095
champagn@ucla.edu

BOOKS IN THE SERIES
1. *Inuit, Whaling, and Sustainability*, Milton M. R. Freeman, Ingmar Egede, Lyudmila Bogoslovskaya, Igor G. Krupnik, Richard A. Caulfield and Marc G. Stevenson (1999)
2. *Contemporary Native American Political Issues*, edited by Troy Johnson (1999)
3. *Contemporary Native American Cultural Issues*, edited by Duane Champagne (1999)
4. *Modern Tribal Development: Paths to Self Sufficiency and Cultural Integrity in Indian Country*, Dean Howard Smith (2000)
5. *American Indians and the Urban Experience*, edited by Susan Lobo and Kurt Peters (2001)
6. *Medicine Ways: Disease, Health, and Survival among Native Americans*, edited by Clifford Trafzer and Diane Weiner (2001)
7. *Native American Studies in Higher Education: Models for Collaboration between Universities and Indigenous Nations*, edited by Duane Champagne and Jay Strauss (2002).

NATIVE AMERICAN STUDIES IN HIGHER EDUCATION

Models for Collaboration between Universities and Indigenous Nations

EDITED BY
DUANE CHAMPAGNE AND JAY STAUSS

ALTAMIRA
PRESS

ALTAMIRA PRESS
A Division of Rowman & Littlefield Publishers, Inc.
Walnut Creek • Lanham • New York • Oxford

ALTAMIRA PRESS
A Division of Rowman & Littlefield Publishers, Inc.
1630 North Main Street, #367
Walnut Creek, CA 94596
www.altamirapress.com

Rowman & Littlefield Publishers, Inc.
4720 Boston Way
Lanham, MD 20706

12 Hid's Copse Road
Cumnor Hill, Oxford OX2 9JJ, England

British Library Cataloguing in Publication Information Available

Library of Congress Cataloging-in-Publication Data

Native American studies in higher education: model for collaboration between universities and indigenous nations/edited by Duane Champagne and Joseph (Jay) Stauss
    p.cm.—(Contemporary Native American communities)
  Includes bibliographical references and index.
  ISBN 0-7591-0124-8 (cloth: alk. paper)—ISBN 0-7591-0125-6 (pbk: alk. paper).
  I. Indians of North America—Study and teaching (Higher)—United States. 2. Indians of North America—Study and teaching (Higher)—Canada. I. Champagne, Duane. II. Stauss, Joseph. III. Series.

E76.6 N385 2002
305.897'0071'173—dc21   2001035761

Printed in the United States of America

∞™ The paper used in this publication meets the minimum requirements of American National Standard for Information Sciences—Permanence of Paper for Printed Library Materials, ANSI/NISO Z39.48-1992.

Contents

Illustrations

Defining Indian Studies through Stories and Nation Building

Introduction

DUANE CHAMPAGNE AND JAY STAUSS

THE GROWTH AND DEVELOPMENT of American Indian/Native American studies at mainstream institutions of higher education has a very brief history, barely spanning four decades. So it is not surprising that there is scant scholarly literature available. For the early work in this area, see Russell Thornton's "American Indian Studies as an Academic Discipline" (1978) and "American Indian Studies as an Academic Discipline: A Revisit" (1981), and Clara Sue Kidwell's "Native American Indian Studies: Academic Concerns and Community Service" (1978).[1] Another handful of articles appeared over the next several decades (i.e., Jaimes [1987], Metoyer-Duran [1993], and Cook-Lynn [1997]).[2] More recently, a special edition of *Wicazo Za Review* (1999) and a chapter by Russell Thornton in *Studying Native America: Problems and Prospects* (1998) address intellectual and institutional issues of American Indian studies.[3] None of these contributions tell the stories of struggle to build Indian/Native studies from the ground up. The main contribution of *Native American Studies in Higher Education* is the rich detail and contextual history that gives life to what most of us know about Indian/Native studies but could only guess from what we heard from one another.

Our volume presents a collection of stories about the formation of American Indian studies in many mainstream university settings. We wanted to know about the particular experiences of trying to develop Indian studies programs at universities and within their local communities. We sent an invitation letter to many institutions asking the people associated with Indian studies programs to tell us their stories. How did Indian studies originate? What relations were created with the Indian community? What financial and administrative relations did Indian studies have with the university administration? What accounted for successes? And what accounted for setbacks? What courses were offered? What was the philosophy for Indian studies? We hoped to identify and document some trends and patterns that could be discussed and used to develop models. The inspiration for the survey came from a study conducted by Susan Guyette and Charlotte Heth in the early 1980s.[4] Guyette and Heth developed a handbook for Indian studies programs and surveyed students, academics, and communities about their needs. They also collected lists of programs and described their general characteristics. We conducted a survey during 1997–1998 and collected information about many of our questions, but we soon decided that much of the information about Indian studies programs was better presented and updated on Internet sites than in print.[5]

Most American Indian studies programs are taught within broader interdisciplinary programs with few, if any, permanent staff. In the United States and Canada, there are thirty programs with majors, about fifty with minors, at least twenty with concentrations, fourteen with master's degrees of various kinds.[6] The most optimistic change since the early 1980s was the addition of two new Ph.D. programs—at the University of California–Davis and at the University of Arizona in Tucson. Otherwise, most Indian studies programs we surveyed offered minors or several general, elective courses, usually with no faculty trained directly in American Indian studies. Many programs focused on student support for American Indian students, but few institutions were willing to allocate funds or develop initiatives to create a major national or international department in Indian studies. While an institution such as Cornell University has a strong Indian studies program for students and encourages Native students to attend the university, its emphasis is on providing multicultural experiences to its student body. The philosophy for building an Indian dormitory house for students at Cornell was to allow students from many cultures to live and work with Indian students. Cornell's administration, however, is not interested in building a nationally recognized Indian studies academic program that focuses on Native issues. Similarly, Dartmouth College has a long record of providing opportunities to Indian students who attend that institution, but the administration, while supporting a well-recognized Indian services program, in the near future most likely will not invest in a department with a degreed undergraduate or graduate program.[7]

The results of our survey led us to concentrate more on the stories and histories of each Indian studies setting. These stories we found very intriguing, and while we hoped to find patterns within the stories, we became even more impressed with the uniqueness of the histories and various strategies adopted by each group in confronting the issues particular to their settings. The case studies we selected were those Indian studies programs in four-year colleges with established academic records and/or those that granted undergraduate or graduate degrees. Not all Indian/Native studies programs are represented, but a broad array of geography, type of institution, departmental status, and other contrasts are represented by the twelve case studies presented in this volume. In many ways, we consider each of these cases a success story. These are programs that have endured, that have developed and deepened their philosophy about American Indian studies and their commitment to students, community, scholarship, and, in many cases, traditional knowledge and language.

We have not included the Tribally controlled community colleges in this collection of essays, but they are certainly worthy of note and are making major contributions to higher education for American Indian students. Some Tribal colleges, such as Sinte Gleska University (SGU) on the Rosebud Sioux Reservation in South Dakota, have created not Indian studies departments, but Lakota studies departments, and SGU requires all students, Indian and non-Indian, to take two years of Lakota language. While non-Indian students balked at first, they soon began to appreciate Lakota culture through language and acquired a new understanding and relation to the Lakota community.[8] While accreditation pressures and finances inhibit many Tribally controlled community colleges from developing Native studies or Tribal studies departments, Indian studies departments in four-year institutions may do well to establish working intellectual and student pipeline relations with Tribally controlled community colleges. University Indian studies programs can help strengthen the curricula and resources of these community colleges and can benefit from sustained contact with Tribal communities and through participation in Tribal higher education issues. We believe that forming intellectual and service partnerships with Tribally controlled colleges are one means for strengthening, focusing, and revitalizing Native Nation building and, at the same time, guiding university Indian studies programs toward upholding the interests, issues, and values of Native communities.

Programs, Departments, and Interdisciplinary Studies

While there are threads of the fabric that bind us together—the political landscape of the 1960s and 1970s, which fostered ethnic studies, or the inter/multidisciplinary and holistic approach—there is also a broad mosaic of differences that enriches the reader's understanding of how, why, and what programs have come to be labeled Indian/Native studies across North America today. There are sharp differences on important issues such as where a program is housed, how it is funded, how important departmental status is, how faculty credentials are evaluated for Elders, what the program's focus is, and so on.

From the variety of stories provided in this volume, it is difficult to select the most important differences or similarities. However, if one focuses on what usually counts in a mainstream institution, then Indian/Native studies programs must grapple with the issue of permanence. Often, seeking permanence means working toward and achieving departmental status. However, at the University of Arizona,

American Indian studies (AIS) has a permanent, state-funded budget, promotion and tenure authority, and control over core faculty resources. Because AIS is a graduate program only (with no B.A. degree), and because it has an interdisciplinary focus, its best organizational fit is in the graduate college as an interdisciplinary degree program (IDP). The University of Arizona provost has argued that AIS should seek departmental status because this ensures a degree of permanence in academia. The counterargument is that the AIS mission is directly related to several of the key elements of the university's mission, such as land-grant responsibilities, diversity, and community outreach, and this, coupled with being in the heart of Indian Country, means AIS has permanence without being a department.

Looking beneath departmental status, one finds control over core faculty resources, promotion and tenure authority, and a continuing state budget at the heart of being considered permanent or institutionalized. The American Indian studies program at the University of Arizona has all the internal, institutional key elements of a department; so the decision to seek departmental status shifts to an external focus. Do funding agencies and foundations that support faculty research and student financial aid make a distinction between programs and departments? Is it important to graduate students whether they are applying for a degree in a program or a department? How important is it to other Indian/Native studies departments and programs that programs become departments? There is little evidence to bring to bear on these questions. The AIS history, particularly in the past decade, seems to indicate that the external considerations may be important in selected instances, but not a predictor of overall success in securing research funding, securing fellowships, or attracting high-quality graduate students. When AIS faculty asked themselves what difference being a department would make in their daily lives, the answer was, very little.

Most Indian studies academic programs are small and interdisciplinary. Many have the permanence of line-item budgets within their colleges or universities, but most do not control significant budgets, nor do they control promotion, hire, or tenure over core faculty members. The American Indian studies program at the University of Arizona is an IDP, but it controls about ten core faculty while maintaining affiliations with another dozen who are in university departments. While not a department, AIS has characteristics of both a department and an interdisciplinary program. It might be a model for every institution wanting to build a national-level Indian studies graduate program. At the University of California–Los Angeles (UCLA), there is no Indian studies department, but an IDP in which all faculties must be housed in the mainstream departments. At UCLA, we now believe, as with the University of Arizona case, that there is need for a core faculty of professors who are dedicated to carrying on the teaching, research, and community work of Indian/Native studies. While appointments in departments will work for many programs and for many individual faculties, the absence of dedicated Indian studies teachers and faculty inhibits sustained support for Indian studies curricula and the development of intellectual agendas. At UCLA, the IDP in American Indian studies receives little financial support, and only in the past few years have faculty been allowed to transfer a portion of their full-time equivalency to the American Indian studies IDP.

A major disadvantage of an IDP that do not have dedicated faculty is there is no control over faculty tenure and promotion. As a practical model, a core group of Native scholars, who are closely associated with interested faculty in mainstream departments through interdepartmental appointments, may be one way to develop a focused Indian studies orientation and provide a curriculum large enough to support majors and graduate programs. However, the challenges of attempting to meet the expedient political and scholarly demands of the home department may limit faculty contributions for the IDP. Maintaining cross-listed courses, including faculty from other units in team teaching, research, and community outreach projects, and including faculty from other units in committee work, all help meet the goal of interdisciplinary education. We would argue that most programs or departments have become more interdisciplinary over the years, and as long as a program or department seeks and maintains a reasonable number of affiliate faculties from other units, then its interdisciplinary focus can remain intact. Not all programs and institutions will have the interest or resources to develop majors and graduate curricula, but linking a dedicated core of Indian studies scholars and associated colleagues in mainstream departments may make such efforts more possible.

The Indian studies faculty at the University of California–Davis, after many years of work, forged a department with a doctoral program.[9] The department has six faculty and has convened some discussions about cooperative efforts with other University of California Indian studies programs throughout the state. There is some discussion of exchanging students, and of developing Internet and distance learning courses. A common dilemma for most Indian studies departments or programs is the lack of faculty and hence limitations on course offerings for students. Increasingly, most Indian studies programs can be contacted through e-mail and have Web sites, and in this way the dissemination of information about programs and offerings is greatly facilitated. New software is making the delivery of courses over the Internet relatively cheap and more interactive. Among the Tribally controlled community colleges, Salish Kootenai College, in Pablo, Montana, won Kellogg Foundation grants to pioneer course development for students who live on reservations without access to a Tribal community college, as well as for students who might prefer to take courses on their own schedule. Several courses have been tested and early results appear promising. Similarly, Northwest Indian College on the Lummi reservation near Bellingham, Washington, has invested heavily in distance learning hardware and course offerings because many of its students attend satellite classrooms not on the main campus.

Distance learning and Internet courses may provide a partial solution to the current chronic issue of too few Indian scholars and not enough course offerings for students in Indian studies programs or in Tribally controlled community colleges. While there may not be any substitute for training more scholars dedicated to Native American studies, Internet and distance learning concepts should be tested to determine whether some courses might prove useful for increasing Indian studies course offerings, supplementing existing courses, and assisting in strengthening and creating undergraduate and graduate curricula and degree programs. It may also be useful to explore distance learning and Internet cross-listings with Tribally controlled community colleges to enrich course offerings at the universities and help extend course offerings for the community colleges.

Ethnic Studies, American Studies, and American Indian Studies

Native Americans remain among the least-understood groups, not only within the general public, but also among university scholars, administrators, and policymakers. Among most contemporary courses on ethnic studies, the central role in Indian communities of sovereignty, self-government, land, and culture is not well covered or well understood. Contemporary American theories of ethnicity do not account for the Native American experience, and therefore Native American history and political status are marginal within that discourse. Similarly, university administrators, while sometimes well meaning, often do not understand fundamental facts about American Indians and generally classify them as a small ethnic group. Issues of Tribal membership and federally recognized Tribes and their rights are little understood by and complicate the task of university administrators.

American Indian studies programs as often small and ad hoc organizations are in danger of incorporation into other disciplines or into ethnic or American studies programs.[10] The reasons for such arrangements are often budgetary or organizational, but such initiatives, combined with a general misunderstanding of Native rights and issues, can lead to administrative structures that may threaten the very future of many Indian studies programs. Ethnic studies and American studies theories often focus on patterns of individual or group assimilation into U.S. society. While an argument could be made for an ethnic studies approach for many urban nonreservation American Indians, the central issues of Native rights, histories, and cultures would be ignored by such an approach. Most scholars and students in Indian studies prefer to focus on issues framed by Native rights, history, and culture.

Indian studies at the University of California–Berkeley took a significant turn when the university decided to form a Ph.D. program within the framework of ethnic studies and in association with faculties from Asian American and Chicano studies. The advantage of this approach was that, with relatively few faculties, the Indian studies program could offer a doctorate in ethnic studies with a concentration in American Indian studies. Many students found this possibility attractive because during the 1980s no other institutions offered a similar doctorate degree. The Berkeley approach was to form small ethnic studies departments with a few faculty members who collectively supported the doctoral degree program. By most accounts, this approach worked reasonably well, although some might argue that the ethnic studies departments were marginalized, ghettoized, and underfunded by the University of California–Berkeley administration.

During the early 1990s, however, with the general U.S. economic recession, the Berkeley administration decided to meet its budget reduction obligations with departmental cuts across the board. Where similar or like disciplines could be joined to share administrative overhead, such unions were mandated. In ethnic studies, the three departments were combined into one department with shared faculty and administrative resources. Thereafter, administration of the Indian studies program was determined by committees composed of faculty from the three formerly independent ethnic studies departments. In this arrangement, ethnic studies views came to dominate course, curriculum, hiring, and retention decisions concerning Indian studies. Indian studies as an independent faculty ceased to exist and became part of an integrated ethnic studies department. Many students could not find courses with Indian studies content and had difficulty finding faculty to work with them on doctoral dissertations. Indian studies, as a discipline, disappeared from the University of California–Berkeley.

The Berkeley example is not an isolated case. Many Indian studies programs find themselves in similar situations, while others are threatened. When Indian studies, as an area of study, is misunderstood by university administrators to be a subdiscipline of ethnic or minority studies, the threat of incorporation into other academic units remains real and may become stronger in the future as mainstream theories of race, ethnicity, and gender gain more attention and theories of Indigenous rights are less widely understood.

Indian Nations and Indian Studies

Establishing the boundaries of Native American studies remains elusive and peripheral to mainstream institutions of higher education. We believe these difficulties derive, to a certain extent, from the applications of mainstream models of scholarship to Native American studies. Most of all, by this we mean that Native American studies is seen as a highly specialized academic discipline after the model of the social sciences. But if one takes this view, then Native American studies makes little sense as an academic discipline and its content defies definition. The problem, we believe, is that Native American studies does not reflect the highly specialized disciplinary structure of U.S. or Western academia. The specialization of academia reflects the social, cultural, and economic specialization and compartmentalization of U.S. or Western European societies. Mainstream academia reflects the goals, interests, values, and institutions of Western civilization—that is, the community that it studies. Applying the Western intellectual experience and categories of discourse and analysis to the study of Indigenous Nations puts the prospective scholar of Indian life at an initial disadvantage. Such modes of analysis may be helpful and illuminating within their own context, but they most often do not address or express the interests, values, and goals of Native communities.

Native American studies does not have to and should not reflect the intellectual specializations and categories of U.S. or Western scholarship. Native American/ Indian studies programs are situated within American universities and colleges and therefore are constrained by the bureaucratic and academic organization of those institutions. Nevertheless, if American Indian studies is going to stake out its own territory and define itself more clearly as an independent discipline, then it must serve the values and institutions of American Indian communities and not the specialized academic disciplines that have developed over centuries to analyze and elaborate upon the history, culture, and policies of Western civilization. The focus of Native American studies must move out of efforts to mimic mainstream disciplines and find its own organization and purpose through analysis, research, policymaking, and participation in Indian communities. Just as Western civilization is the focus and center of most mainstream academic work, American Indian communities, traditions, and values must be the focus of Native American/Indian studies and the center of its scholarship, teaching, and community outreach.

Reflecting Indian communities and their interests and values, we believe, has several implications. The emphasis in American Indian studies should be directed to contemporary Indian communities and only secondarily to the critique of colonial domination. While critiques against historical colonialism and present-day policies are necessary, they should not dominate Native scholarship. Arguments about colonialism are about non-Indian forms of domination over Indian communities. This is part of the history of Indian communities, but puts non-Indian history and policy in central focus, while often leaving the Indian role in history and preservation of community in the background. Putting living Indian communities and Nations in the forefront of the intellectual agenda of Native American studies will establish the foundation of disciplinary development.

Native American studies programs cannot be substitutes for direct living in Native communities. Students should not come to the mainstream university to learn about their culture and community. They need to learn directly from their own culture. This is the inherent strength of Tribal colleges. Some courses such as culture, language, and history may provide students with background about Native cultures in general and their own culture in particular, but they are not and should not be considered substitutes for actual residence and participation in a Native community—especially one's own Native community. Since two-thirds of contemporary Native Americans live in urban areas, many, if not most, do not have direct contact with a reservation-based community. Native American studies courses can provide some help and learning for those students, and many may not have interests beyond taking a few courses to develop an overview and basic understanding of Indian history and culture. Indian studies centers can sharpen students' intellectual skills and knowledge in historical, cultural, and policy analysis. Much of this knowledge is very useful for those who want to work with the associations and organizations that serve Indian Tribes in political and policy arenas, as well as for those who might want to pursue graduate work in the mainstream disciplines. Most Indian studies programs are interdisciplinary, and quite naturally students are exposed to a variety of views from professors trained in several mainstream disciplines as well as from Elders and Indian scholars who often present alternative views. An undergraduate degree in American Indian studies is similar in kind to a degree in the liberal arts. We need to teach our students analytical skills, U.S.–Indian history and policy, and an appreciation and understanding of Native sovereignty and culture to enable them to become critical, informed, and active participants in Native community life as well as in Native issues at the regional and national levels.[11]

Native American/Indian studies programs should maintain active relations with Native communities, both urban and reservation. We do not necessarily recommend that the studies programs become social service centers, although depending on interests of the community, students, and faculty, such efforts are carried on by a variety of studies centers already. One significant role that Indian studies centers can play is in Nation building. Universities and Indian studies centers are often located particularly well to assist Tribes with issues of law, policy, the environment, repatriation, recognition, state–Tribal relations, and other concerns. The advantage of direct engagement with Tribal groups is that the separation of academic and community life is broken down, and students and scholars learn firsthand about a Nation and its important issues and have an opportunity to work directly within the community. These experiences cannot be replaced with textbooks or discussions in the classroom. The ivory tower myth in Western academia is a misnomer; many of the disciplines of today's universities are deeply engaged in legal, cultural, policy, political, economic, and related issues of concern to the United States and the world. In the same way, Native studies programs should be engaged in the issues that reflect Native communities' interests and values.

If Native American/Indian studies needs a central focus, we believe, at least for the moment, that the emphasis should be on Nation building within Indian communities. We use the term *Nation building* here in the broadest possible context.[12] Native American studies should focus on the analysis and policies of Tribal sovereignty, community and cultural preservation, and U.S.–Indian policy. Tribal sovereignty is the right to make culturally informed decisions about major issues within the community. At the present time, and for the past century, Tribal governments and communities have been incorporated into the U.S. state system and are increasingly confronted with a competitive world market, competitive state and federal agencies, and cultural inroads from a variety of sources. Indian Nations will need to meet these challenges in their own ways and under their own terms. Native American studies programs can fulfill their intellectual, research, and community obligations by active engagement and cooperation with Indian Nations working to maintain culture and sovereignty in the contemporary world. Indian Nations are already working to preserve culture, maintain language, revise constitutions, develop Tribally controlled community colleges and schools, create courts, promote economic development, improve state–Tribal relations, and deliver services to community members, to name a few of the many issues being addressed. Just as Indian Nations see their challenges in a community framework, so must Indian studies work within the holistic frameworks of each separate and unique Tribal community. Thus, the intellectual and content matter of the discipline of Indian studies must also be interdisciplinary and holistically focused to reflect the integrated and unique community arrangements of Indian Nations.

Native American/Indian studies should reflect the holistic and community-based culture and sociopolitical organization of Indian Nations; otherwise Indian studies scholars run the risk of advancing overspecialized analyses and solutions that may misinform students and the public and do more harm than good. Indian studies programs should create communities of students, Elders, scholars, administrators, and Tribal members. Student services, student organizations, graduate students, faculty, administrators, and Tribal members should have many opportunities to meet, conduct research, and teach in a continuously interactive community environment. Students should see and interact with scholars and graduate students who will serve as role models and inspire them to seek graduate and professional education. Students should be exposed to active Nation-building projects engaging with local Indian Nations. Students should be trusted with leadership and responsibility. Peer counseling and student peer support groups within a community of scholarly learning, teaching, and service to the community will create environments that foster informed, sensitive, and seasoned scholars, professionals, and good citizens of Indian Nations.

The issue of inclusion of Indian student services in Indian/Native studies programs and departments has both supporters and detractors. There has been some fear that most Indian studies programs are geared primarily toward student services, and those service orientations have often overwhelmed scholarly activities.[13] We argue for inclusion of student organizations and peer counseling, and encouragement of student faculty in regular social gatherings, research, and Nation-building projects. We believe that American Indian faculty and staff share a community responsibility to advise, mentor, and nurture Indian undergraduate and graduate students from across the university, regardless of their majors.

Taking the time to work with large numbers of Indian students or conduct community outreach work can detract from the research agenda. We recommend that research, outreach, and Nation-building projects involve Indian studies students so that teaching on the one hand, and mentoring, research, and Nation building on the other, will mutually support rather than detract from each other, as when they are considered separate, specialized domains of activity. Faculty must balance their community Nation-building efforts with their professional progress, and in Indian studies departments that control faculty promotion and tenure, Nation-building service, student mentoring, and scholarship on the one hand, and promotions on the other, should be considered one and the same. Faculty with interdisciplinary appointments or appointments outside Indian studies will have more difficulties balancing service, research, and writing. Community service and outreach are often not rewarded adequately in mainstream institutions. However, the benefits of faculty, staff, and student involvement in surrounding Indian communities and with Indian organizations should be carefully evaluated by each program or department. At the University of Arizona, the American Indian studies program maintains a full-time professional outreach/community development staff for projects in economic development, human services, and education. These activities, along with internship requirements for graduate students and faculty research/outreach, form the nucleus of ensuring that AIS is meeting its strategic mission commitments and that the Tribes and other organizations are meeting some of their own needs with the help of the University of Arizona. This inclusion of full-time, permanent outreach/community development staff appears to be unique among Indian/Native studies departments, but has proven very useful in institutionalizing AIS at the University of Arizona. The holistic, integrated approach to scholarship, student services, and community development/outreach has worked well at the University of Arizona. The case studies presented in this volume present holistic intellectual and organizational approaches in a variety of regional, university, and community contexts.

Toward World Indigenous Studies

Increasingly in the future it may become important to distinguish Indigenous studies from race, ethnic, cultural, or multicultural studies. None of the latter approaches fully appreciates or emphasizes Indigenous rights of self-government, land, and negotiated relations to state governments. The study of indigenous peoples around the world may well form an independent discipline or domain of study because the issues confronted by the indigenous peoples are often similar. Indigenous peoples around the world have different cultures and different colonial experiences with state systems, but most Native peoples have an understanding of autonomous culture, history, self-government, and territory. Since the 1960s many Indigenous peoples have gathered at meetings with United Nations (UN) agencies and have achieved nongovernmental organization (NGO) status within the UN. The UN has honored indigenous peoples with special meetings, a decade of activities in their honor, and other special recognitions. Indigenous peoples have been actively seeking inclusion of their views and interests in international human rights agreements. Many transnational indigenous peoples have organized throughout North and South America and within the circumpolar regions. Native peoples want to assert their rights to managing local affairs; maintaining their cultures; determining their hunting, fishing, and subsistence relations; and securing more democratic relations with nation–state governments. Most indigenous groups do not wish to secede from the countries they now find themselves living in, but want more local self-government and more democratic relations with their nation–state governments. The activity of indigenous organizations within the international arena derives from similar political situations and interests among the diverse indigenous peoples, and makes an argument for the study of world indigenous peoples as international organizations, or through comparisons as case studies.

Most U.S. Native American/Indian studies programs are small and do not have resources to fully address issues within the United States. Furthermore, the U.S.–Indian treaty history is unique in the world and puts U.S.–Indian relations on very special legal grounds that are only approximated by Canada's treaty relations with its Native peoples, and nowhere else in the world is there a comparable legal arrangement. Nevertheless, the U.S. and Canadian experiences can provide models for policy and Native self-government. Native communities and U.S. scholars could well learn from the experiences of other indigenous peoples. Indian studies at the University of California–Davis has long adopted a hemispheric approach (both North and South America) in its curriculum, faculty, and research. Very recently, the new Native studies department at the University of Kansas has taken a world indigenous approach to its master's program, faculty hiring, and research program. At UCLA, students, visitors, and visiting indigenous scholars from foreign countries such as Japan, Australia, Mongolia, New Zealand, and Finland have all enriched the Indian studies environment with the comparison of indigenous relations in those countries. One visitor to UCLA from Australia was an Aboriginal lawyer who was very interested in the organization of Tribal governments, and the theory of sovereignty, which he wanted to introduce to Aboriginal leaders. Oren Lyons, Onondaga Faithkeeper and professor at the State University of New York, Buffalo, is leading an initiative to establish close ties with several universities in the Caribbean Islands to exchange knowledge, research approaches, and course materials on indigenous relations.[14]

Native American studies programs are beginning to incorporate international issues and establish research and scholarly contacts with scholars in other countries. Opportunities to compare and study indigenous peoples living under a variety of state regimes, with different cultures and colonial histories, will enrich Indian studies and generate greater mutual understanding. In a significant sense, American Indian studies is a subdiscipline of world indigenous studies. Soon, we believe, more scholars will tackle hemispheric and world indigenous issues, and there will emerge opportunities for scholarly journals dedicated to the topic. Native American studies will be strengthened with development of an international discipline devoted to study, teaching, research, community service, and policy analysis about world indigenous peoples. Native American studies scholars should welcome these opportunities, and many departments and programs are already engaged in cooperative work with scholars and communities outside the United States.

Many Stories

The stories we have gathered indicate that there are a few model elements that are absolutely crucial to the development and growth of an Indian/Native studies program or department. One of those few, not surprisingly, is a small but highly committed core of Indian and non-Indian faculty and students who believe in the intellectual and Nation-building agenda of Indian/Native studies. No single organizational model or placement with the university or college structure seems to emerge. An Indian studies program can be located in a college or a department or a research-focused institute and still find success. Sensing and acting on the unique mission and organizational and structural makeup of the particular institution seems to be a key trait. In addition, we would argue that an ideal model includes a strong measure of independence and permanence, as well as significant control over faculty and staff operations and resources. Forming an integrated community of graduate and undergraduate students, staff, faculty, Elders, and Indian Nation members appears as a natural tendency for many programs. Again, these case studies illustrate considerable strength through versatility. The necessary and essential elements of growth and development in Indian/Native studies cannot be clearly listed or easily agreed upon. In many ways the departments and programs reflect the diversity of their institutional university placements and cultures, as well as their relations with local and regional Indian Nations. *Native American Studies in Higher Education* sets down some important stories that should not be lost, stories that need to be handed down and shared with all those interested in developing and building Indian studies programs and departments. Almost four decades have passed since the inception of Indian studies, so it is time we capture this history.

Notes

1. Russell Thornton, "American Indian Studies as an Academic Discipline," *American Indian Culture and Research Journal* 2, nos. 3–4 (1978): 10–19; Russell Thornton, "American Indian Studies as an Academic Discipline: A Revisit," in *American Indian Issues in Higher Education* (Los Angeles: UCLA American Indian Studies Center, 1981), 3–10; Clara Sue Kidwell, "Native American Indian Studies: Academic Concerns and Community Service," *American Indian Culture and Research Journal* 2, nos. 3–4 (1978): 4–9.

2. Annette Jaimes, "American Indian Studies: Toward an Indigenous Model," *American Indian Culture and Research Journal* 11, no. 3 (1987): 1–16; Cheryl Metoyer-Duran, "The *American Indian Culture and Research Journal* and the *American Indian Quarterly*: A Citation Analysis," *American Indian Culture and Research Journal* 17, no. 4 (1993): 25–54; Elizabeth Cook-Lynn, "Who Stole Native American Studies," *Wicazo Sa Review* 12, no. 1 (spring 1997): 9–28.

3. Robert Warrior and Jace Weaver, eds., "Introduction," *Wicazo Sa Review* 14, no. 2 (1999); Russell Thornton, "Institutional and Intellectual Histories of Native American Studies," in *Studying Native America: Problems and Prospects*, ed. Russell Thornton (Madison: University of Wisconsin Press, 1998), 79–110.

4. Susan Guyette and Charlotte Heth, *Issues for the Future of American Indian Studies* (Los Angeles: UCLA American Indian Studies Center, 1985).

5. For example, see: www.richmond.edu/faculty/ASAIL/guide/guide.html [last accessed August 3, 2001].

6. Robert M. Nelson, ed., *A Guide to Native American Studies Programs in the United States and Canada* (Richmond: University of Richmond, Association for the Study of American Indian Literature, 1997). (Also listed electronically on the Web site: www.richmond.edu/faculty/ASAIL/guide/guide.html.)

7. Sergie Kan, personal communication to Duane Champagne, April 11, 1997; Dean of Agricultural College to Duane Champagne, November 1996.

8. Albert White Hat, personal communication to Duane Champagne, August 28, 1998.

9. See chapter 6 in this volume, and Inés Hernández-Ávila and Stefano Varese, "Indigenous Intellectual Sovereignties: A Hemispheric Convocation," *Wicazo Sa Review* 4, no. 1 (1999): 77–91.

10. See Steve Talbot, "Anthropology versus Native American Studies: Theoretical and Ethical Implications," in *The Unheard Voices: American Indian Responses to the Columbian Quincentenary,*

1492–1992, ed. Carole M. Gentry and Donald A. Grinde Jr. (Los Angeles: UCLA American Indian Studies Center, 1994), 133–156.

11. See chapters 3 and 4 in this volume.

12. See chapter 7 in this volume for a discussion on courses concerned with Nation building.

13. Jaimes, "Toward an Indigenous Model," 3–4.

14. Oren Lyons, personal communication to Duane Champagne, December 21, 1999.

Eleazar Wheelock Meets Luther Standing Bear: Native American Studies at Dartmouth College[1]

COLIN G. CALLOWAY

LUTHER STANDING BEAR WAS the first Lakota student to attend the Carlisle Indian boarding school in Pennsylvania, when it opened in 1879. Looking back on the regimented and restricted education he received there, he recalled how Indian students "went to school to copy, to imitate; not to exchange languages and ideas, and not to develop the best traits that had come out of uncountable experiences of hundreds and thousands of years living upon this continent." He lamented the missed opportunities: "while the white people had much to teach us, we had much to teach them, and what a school could have been established upon that idea!"[2]

Eleazar Wheelock never dreamed of such a school. Wheelock founded Dartmouth College in 1769, ostensibly in part for the education of Native American students, but he saw nothing to be learned from Indian peoples and Indian ways of knowing. In his view, Indian students were to be educated in English schools so they could serve as missionaries to other Indians. Today, Dartmouth has a reputation as one of the best colleges in the country; it has a thriving Native American studies program and a demonstrated commitment to Indian education. Heading into the twenty-first century, there may still be opportunity to integrate Standing Bear's vision of learning into the school established by Eleazar Wheelock.

In 1765, in an effort to raise funds for his Indian charity school, Eleazar Wheelock dispatched a Mohegan Indian named Samson Occom to the British Isles. Occom, a former student of Wheelock's and an ordained minister, delivered more than 300 sermons in England and Scotland and raised about £12,000 in private donations. The founding charter of Dartmouth College, granted by King George III, identified as a key part of its purpose "the education and instruction of Youth of the Indian Tribes in the Land in reading, writing & all parts of Learning which shall appear necessary and expedient." But by the time Eleazar Wheelock moved his charity school to Hanover, New Hampshire, in 1770, he was experiencing a change of mind. Some Indians had rebuffed his efforts to recruit their young people, and Wheelock had misgivings about the "fitness" of Indian students to fill the missionary role. In 1771, embittered by what he saw, Occom wrote to Wheelock: "I am very jealous that instead of your Semenary Becoming alma Mater, she will be too alba mater [white mother] to Suckle the Tawnees. . . . I think your College has too much worked by Grandeur for the Poor Indians, they'll never have much benefit of it." Wheelock retorted that "all the Benefit done or proposed to be done to the English is Subservient in the Best Manner to the Indian Cause; and greatly adds to and increases my ability to help the Indians. . . . I hope in God to be able to support a Hundred Indians and Youths designed for Indian Service on Charity in a little Time."[3] But history bears out Occom's disenchantment. By 1775 Wheelock had exhausted the funds raised in England. Only three Indians graduated from Dartmouth in the eighteenth century; no more than seventy-one Indians attended Dartmouth in the years 1770–1865, and in the years 1865–1965, only twenty-eight Indians enrolled at Dartmouth.

Things changed with the inauguration of John G. Kemeny as the thirteenth president of Dartmouth on March 1, 1970. Kemeny rededicated the college to a promise long deferred and reaffirmed Dartmouth's commitment to Native American education. The college began to actively recruit American Indian students. Kemeny, assistant dean Gregory Prince, faculty members James Wright, Jere Daniell, Marysa Navarro, Hoyt Alverson, and William Cook, along with interested students, began plans for a Native American studies program. On May 8, 1972, the faculty of arts and sciences unanimously approved its adoption. It was one of the first Native American studies programs in the United States, following that of the University of Minnesota.

The goal was ambitious: to incorporate into Dartmouth's regular academic curricula a program of courses dealing with the histories, cultures, and artistic traditions of populations native to the Americas. The beginnings were modest: an experimental two-course offering with one half-time faculty member, Michael Dorris, who was appointed chair of the program. In the 1980s, as Dorris devoted more and more time to his writing career, Michael D. Green and Elaine Jahner each took turns at the helm. Native American studies has since grown into a permanent program offering a major and a minor, anchoring five tenured positions, supplemented by regular visitors, and teaching more than fifteen courses each year. The initial course offerings were organized around the study of Native American ethnology, literature, and history. Course offerings now deal with history, culture, religion, government, language, literature, law and policy, archaeology, film, as well as more specialized topics taught by regular faculty and visitors. Currently, core courses include "Indian Country Today," "North American Indian History,"

"Peoples and Cultures of Native North America," "Native American Literature," an introduction to "Native American Religious Systems," and a senior seminar as a culminating experience. Enrollment in Native American courses has more than doubled in the last five years, with some classes reaching 70–75 students, a relatively large number for a college with just over 4,200 undergraduates and a tradition of small classes. The Native American studies program taught a total of 409 students in 2000–2001.

Native American studies at Dartmouth offers a program of study that aims to increase students' understanding of the historical experiences, cultural traditions and transformations, and political aspirations of Indian peoples in the United States and Canada. It also encourages students to explore the intersection of Indian and European histories and systems of knowledge. Students learn about Native American ways of living, organizing societies, and understanding the world, and about their relations with Euro-American colonizing powers. They learn to appreciate how the value systems of different cultures function and to understand the dynamics of cultural change. They examine contact and conflict between Native and non-Native societies and recognize the unique status of Indian peoples in the United States and Canada as Nations possessing certain sovereign powers and distinct legal rights.

Courses in Native American studies at Dartmouth attract students of all ethnic backgrounds. Most courses are cross-listed with other programs or departments. Students who elect to take a major or minor in Native American studies take a number of core courses and explore interdisciplinary approaches to Native American studies. To qualify for a major in Native American studies, a student must successfully complete ten courses in the program; minors complete six courses. Students pursue their own interests and develop an individual program, but they also take certain required courses to ensure that they acquire a shared body of substantive knowledge, gain exposure to crucial ways of critical thinking, and understand the interdisciplinary, or transdisciplinary, nature of Native American studies.

Native American studies at Dartmouth is located within the social sciences division. Faculty members hold joint appointments in Native American studies and a corresponding academic department. At present, faculty hold appointments in anthropology, history, religion, English, and government. Although joint appointments may present administrative problems, and additional hurdles at the time of hiring and tenure, at Dartmouth they have also proved a source of strength to Native American studies. They unite scholars in related fields to a joint commitment in the study of Native America and allow Native American studies to build valuable alliances with other departments, programs, and individuals. Native American studies at Dartmouth does not operate in isolation but sees itself as occupying an important place on the college landscape and representing a significant center of academic life.

In addition to its regular faculty, the Native American studies program and the larger Dartmouth community benefit from visiting faculty and scholars. In recent years, visitors have included Wilma Mankiller, formerly principal chief of the Cherokee Nation, who held Dartmouth's prestigious Montgomery Fellowship in the winter of 1996; Chadwick Smith, formerly principal attorney for the Cherokee Nation and now principal chief; Bernd Peyer, a Swiss scholar who lives and teaches in Germany; Alyce Spotted Bear, former chair of the Three Affiliated Tribes at Fort Berthold in North Dakota; Emma Hansen (Pawnee), curator of the Plains Indian Museum in Cody, Wyoming; Ronald Welburn (Cherokee/Conoy); Thomas Doughton (Nipmuc); Russel Barsh, an expert on international indigenous rights; Vera Palmer (Tuscarora), a Ph.D. candidate at Cornell University; Adrian Tanner, an anthropologist at Memorial University in Newfoundland; Thomas Abler of Waterloo University, Ontario; and Hartmut Lutz from Universtät Greifswald in Germany.

Although funded from the beginning by regular institutional funds, Native American studies has also been supported by private donors and corporate funding, and receives invaluable assistance from the development office on campus in identifying and approaching potential sponsors. In recent years, the generosity of an individual alumnus has allowed the Native American studies program to revive its internship program and to initiate a pilot program that brings a Tribal Elder/mentor to assume an advisory role to Native students on campus. Alumni have also supported plans for a new Native American research center at Dartmouth.

Many Native and non-Native students at Dartmouth participate in term-long internships with a Tribe or Indian organization, and many students have patterned lifelong career goals as a result of their intern experience. Students often identify and set up individual internships themselves, although the program is working to establish several internship programs on a sustained regular basis at selected sites in Indian Country. Some students undertake internships through the Tucker Foundation, which was established in 1951 to "further the moral and spiritual life of the college," and which provides a variety of local, national, and worldwide voluntary services, workshops, and programs.

Dartmouth's Baker Library has supported Native American studies by building up an extensive collection of material relating to Native American history and culture. The Baker Library and Special Collections currently holds approximately 14,000 Native American titles, the majority of which relate to North America, including Canada. The Native American studies program also maintains and supports its own research library where students, faculty, alumni, and visitors can consult more than 4,000 books and a wide variety of periodicals, journals, films, Tribal newsletters, and related materials. The collection is constantly being updated as new scholarly books and periodicals are released.

Native American studies hosts regular symposia on subjects of Native American interest to scholars around the country. Recent themes have included survival and revival in Native New England; new and future directions in Native American studies; the role of traditional knowledge in academia; relations between German people and Indian people over three centuries, in coordination with the German studies department; and Native American and African American histories, in conjunction with African and African American studies and Native American archaeologist relations. The program also holds regular colloquia in which visitors, faculty, and students can share their work and engage in open discussion over lunch.

Dartmouth is preeminently an undergraduate liberal arts college and does not have a graduate program in Native American studies. However, in 1992 the college created the Charles Eastman Fellowship (named after the Dakota physician Ohiyesa, who graduated from Dartmouth in 1887) for Native American graduate students. The fellowship sustains a predoctoral scholar for a full year to complete work on his or her Ph.D. dissertation. Recipients include Christopher Jocks (Mohawk, and currently an assistant professor at Dartmouth), JoAnn Woodsum (Cahuilla), Kevin Connelly (Onondaga), Dennis "Dan" Runnels (Salish, and currently a visiting instructor), Peggy Ackerberg (Potawatomi), Joseph Gone (Gros Ventre), Darren Ranco (Penobscot), Vera Palmer (Tuscarora), and Dian Million (Tanana Athabascan).

Dartmouth's Native American studies program constitutes the academic wing of a number of programs and groups that were established with separate responsibilities but that share a commitment to providing a network of support for Native students at the college. The Native American Program (NAP) was established two years before Native American Studies (NAS). It began in the fall of 1970 as an "Indian program" along with "Indian Americans at Dartmouth" and was always designed to be separate from NAS. It provides Native American student support services and works with students, administrators, campuswide faculty, and programs to ensure the success of Native American students through their four-year residency on campus. Native Americans at Dartmouth (NAD) is the Native student organization. Among other activities, NAD hosts a powwow at Dartmouth each spring. The Native American Council (NAC), composed of members from NAS, NAP, NAD, and other interested individuals, meets four times each term. A Native American Visiting Committee (NAVC) of outside alumni annually reviews all aspects of the Native American programs, reports directly to the provost of the college, and offers regular assistance and support. Dartmouth's Native American Alumni Association includes more than 300 members.

In 2001, Dartmouth matriculated a record number of forty-one Native students from twenty-one states and thirty-one tribes, producing a total enrollment of 120 Native undergraduates. Student graduation rates have grown significantly since the inception of the Native American studies program in 1972. During the first decade of the program's existence, the Native student graduation rate averaged 50 percent; since that time, the rate has risen to an average of 72 percent. Nevertheless, Dartmouth confronts continuing challenges to realizing Luther Standing Bear's dream. As other schools offer new Native American programs, Native American students who opt for an Ivy League education have more choices. The admissions office now has to work harder to attract and recruit Native students, and many NAD alumni are assuming more active roles in pointing good students toward Hanover. Getting students here is not enough, and like some other schools, Dartmouth has implemented new financial aid packages to help make it possible for them to stay here.

Moreover, Dartmouth is still working to provide a comfortable learning environment in which Native Americans, African Americans, Asian Americans, male and female, can concentrate on just being students. Regrettably, but regularly, the Native American community at Dartmouth confronts pockets of resistance and misunderstanding on a campus that was, until the 1970s, almost exclusively a white male institution. The college dropped the Indian mascot as its sports logo in the 1970s, but the issue shows a Rasputin-like refusal to die. Speaking on Columbus Day, 1992, the twentieth anniversary of the Native American studies program, student Nicole Adams, a member of the Colville Tribe and later president of Dartmouth's Native American Alumni Association, urged students to challenge "prejudices that attempt to disguise themselves in the name of tradition":

> Our Native American Studies department is known as one of the nation's best. Over 120 different Indian nations have been represented here. Our graduation rate for Native students is over ten times the national average. Clearly, progress has been made. Yet so often this progress is obscured because we are constantly reminded of just how little understanding people have of such integral aspects of our lives as our religion and cultural beliefs. We are reminded of this when we hear chants of "wah-hoo-wah." We are reminded of this every time we see gross caricatures of our people in every corner of the campus.[4]

Native American students are not just statistics to make Dartmouth look good; they are an essential resource in creating the kind of educational environment that Luther Standing Bear hoped for and that this program aspires to achieve. If students are to make the most of their learning opportunities at Dartmouth, and make maximum contributions to the learning that goes on here, they need a working and living environment in which they do not feel permanently on the defensive. Indian students from communities around the country bring constant reminders to our classes of the complexity and diversity of Indian America. This is not to suggest that all Native students, no matter how removed from Tribal community and culture, are in total possession of some traditional wisdom. Nor do we abandon critical faculties or training in "mainstream" Western academic disciplines because we accommodate Native voices, or automatically discount our research if it runs up against opposing Native viewpoints. But the Indian faculty, students, and visitors who participate in Dartmouth's Native American studies program are the slender threads that remain from a tapestry that was once so rich we can now only imagine it. They connect us to Native American worlds and worldviews that are lost to most of us in modern America, to modern Tribal communities and concerns that seem far removed from a privileged eastern college where it is sometimes difficult to see the forest for the ivy, and to a complex and ever-changing "Indian Country" that exists in eastern cities as well as on western reservations. A steady stream of Indian students is essential to Native American studies and to Dartmouth.

Native American studies continues to pursue opportunities to secure more faculty and increase office and library space. But plans for development do not revolve around bodies and buildings. They center on what kind of program Native American studies is and could or should be. What are its strengths and what qualities will distinguish it from other Native American studies programs around the country? What is its mission and audience? Should a Native American studies program have a clear social and political agenda and concentrate on Native students, or should it try to educate all students about Indian history, cultures, and life? Should Native American studies be part of a liberal arts education for everyone, as it is at Dartmouth, or function primarily to prepare Indian students for leadership roles back home and on the national level? Should it be—can it be—a standardized program, whether taught at an Ivy League liberal arts college, a large state university, or a Tribal college? Are the areas of study and the courses we offer still the most appropriate ones to reflect Native American experiences and issues at the start of the twenty-first century? As exemplified by a conference on "New and Future Directions in Native American Studies" held at Dartmouth in the spring of 1997, different institutions and different individuals have answered these questions in different ways at different times.

In an article titled "Who Stole Native American Studies?" Elizabeth Cook-Lynn complains that the field and its practitioners appear to have lost their way from the vision shared by American Indian scholars in 1970 that Native American studies should be concerned first and foremost with the defense of First

Nation status and indigenousness. Instead, Indian and non-Indian scholars write and teach history, anthropology, literature, biography, autobiography, and demographics, and they share joint appointments, as we do here at Dartmouth, in other departments. In Cook-Lynn's view, Native American studies has been undermined, perhaps even betrayed, by attempts to make it fit American academia:

> The truth is that Native American Studies does not "fit," nor can it, nor should it. Rather, its meaningfulness stems from the fact that it challenges almost everything that America has to offer in education and society. It rejects assimilation in favor of tribal nationhood. It rejects mainstream American conservatism in favor of a new history that acknowledges a horrific period of greed and empire building in America during which genocide and deicide was legalized. It marginalizes equal rights and civil rights in favor of treaty and indigenous rights. It rejects colonization as much as Black Americans rejected slavery. Its principles are indigenousness and sovereignty rather than cultural contact (or colonialism), pluralism, diversity, and immigration. Yet, in terms of the present condition of the academy, indigenous study exists within colonial structures, and the people live with destructive land policies and restrictive economies based on historical racist practices.[5]

At Dartmouth, Native American studies began with a broadly defined academic approach, and the program has always operated within these "colonial structures." Had it pursued a more clearly political agenda, Native American studies on this campus would probably have stifled and died. Instead, it has found room within these structures to breathe and to grow. By including other programs and other individuals who understand, or want to understand, Native American studies, the program has increased its reach and its presence on campus. With Native faculty jointly appointed in other departments, students at Dartmouth College can now encounter Native teachers and Native issues in their "regular classes," without ever setting foot in a Native American studies class. The diversification of Native American studies at Dartmouth might be a sign of vitality and maturity rather than of decline.

Native American studies at Dartmouth has never attempted to exclude non-Native students, faculty, or viewpoints. Indeed, the mission of the Native American studies program depends upon attracting a varied faculty and student body who bring their own perspectives and build upon their individual experiences and understandings. Native American studies at Dartmouth subscribes to Duane Champagne's view that "American Indian studies is for everyone." Despite the failings of some non-Indians in interpreting Indian cultures, Champagne acknowledges there is "room for both Indian and non-Indian scholars."[6] Including both Native and non-Native faculty and students provides the kind of cross-fertilization that Luther Standing Bear wanted and that we want at Dartmouth. Native American studies is not just a counter to the American experience (though it is sometimes that); it is also an essential part of the American experience, and that experience often makes no sense without Indians. In Native American studies at the moment, we have a Mohawk teaching religion, a Houma teaching law, an Anishinaabeg teaching Tribal sovereignty and contemporary issues, a Russian Jew teaching anthropology, a British citizen teaching history, a Tuscarora woman teaching Native American literature, and a multilingual former sea captain from Colville teaching an introduction to Native languages and a freshman seminar. For Native American studies at Dartmouth, to speak with one voice would be impossible. It would also be a terrible waste of opportunities for understanding Native America—and America itself—from a multiplicity of viewpoints and experiences. We try to embrace, not to exclude; we encourage our students not to assign blame but to figure out how things happened and how they were understood and misunderstood.

Located in northern New England's upper Connecticut Valley, Dartmouth does not have a major Native American population base nearby. Because it is a small college, Dartmouth's program will never be as large as those at the University of Arizona, the University of Minnesota, or the University of California–Los Angeles. But Dartmouth does have enduring strengths upon which to build. Increasingly, discussions on these issues return to the issue of academic rigor and intellectual reflection. Native American studies courses must hold their own on this campus in terms of academic challenge, intellectual rigor, and high standards. The program will only progress by maintaining an unassailable reputation and by eradicating any lingering suspicions that it must be a "soft" option, especially for Native students. Native American studies at Dartmouth does not offer courses in "right thinking," nor does it pretend to teach Indian students how to be Indians. Most of our students are non-Indians; Native American studies offers them an introduction to the complex, challenging, and fascinating worlds of Native America and, in doing so, opens some different perspectives on the American past and present. As Devon Mihesuah says, Native American studies has an obligation to eradicate negative, romantic, and distorted stereotypes about Indian people: "The fundamental argument for a good Indian studies program," she writes, "is to educate students who are ignorant about Indians."[7] We do not tell these students what to think, but we do try to give them plenty to think about.

In addition, as evidenced by the network of Dartmouth Native American alumni doing important work at the community and the national levels, Native American studies does help train Native students to be "modern-day warriors" and leaders, arming them with the knowledge, skills, and understandings they need to represent Native peoples and defend Native issues in the twenty-first century. Native American studies now offers a seminar titled "Leadership Resources and Community Development for Native America." By focusing on individual grant-writing projects, senior students have an opportunity to apply the research and writing skills they have developed in college to the kind of "real-life" projects many of them will tackle after graduation.

It would be presumptuous to attach too much importance to the longevity of Dartmouth's Native American studies program. After all, as Carter Blue Clark and Clifford Trafzer point out, "native scholars were quite accomplished in this field of study well before the arrival of Europeans."[8] Nevertheless, at Dartmouth, Native American studies is not just a recent addition to make us look politically correct; it has a thirty-year history and it is part of the culture here. Native American studies in the past has had its share of faculty turnover and loss of direction, the kinds of things that can cause a small program to unravel, or provide an unsympathetic administration with the justification to let it die. Instead, Native American studies today has more faculty, plans for the future, a new Native American student residence, new office space for the program, new offers of financial support from alumni, and new opportunities.

In a characteristically scathing indictment of Western education, the Lakota scholar Vine Deloria Jr. criticizes mainstream colleges for training professionals but not producing people. He may be right. Rather than broadening the mind and feeding the soul, many colleges seem instead to teach the particular skills needed to ensure the marketability of their graduates. Corporate recruiters are active on the Dartmouth campus and some students no doubt see their education at Dartmouth as a ticket to a high-paying career rather than an opportunity for personal growth. But that is not Dartmouth's purpose or intent. At its best, a liberal arts college tries, during a brief four-year period in its students' lives, to challenge their thinking, open their minds, and, perhaps, touch their souls; to prepare them to live full lives, not just to make a good living. The view of education maintained by Dartmouth is very much like that espoused by Deloria: "Education is more than the process of imparting and receiving information, . . . it is the very purpose of human society and . . . human societies cannot really flower until they understand the parameters of possibilities that the human personality contains."[9] That is Vine Deloria speaking, but it sounds very much like Dartmouth's past president James Freedman or current president James Wright, who as a young faculty member helped to get Native American studies started.

Eleazar Wheelock would not recognize Dartmouth today. The place is far more progressive internally than its external reputation as an Ivy League college in the north woods would suggest. The current president is a longtime ally of Native American studies and took office with a renewed commitment to diversity during his presidency. The dean of the college is Native American (James Larimore, Comanche). There are more Native faculty at Dartmouth than ever before, and the Native American studies program continues to find allies on campus. There is much ground to make up, but Native American studies is better placed than it has ever been to offer Native and non-Native students the kind of education Luther Standing Bear dreamed of, and Dartmouth may be closer than it has ever been to turning Eleazar Wheelock's enterprise for English youth into Standing Bear's vision of a truly American school. Nevertheless, in finally venturing down the path that Standing Bear envisioned, Native American studies cannot forget the ways in which it has developed at Dartmouth. Our primary purpose as an academic program is teaching and research, and our efforts in Native American studies should enhance that purpose rather than divert from or dilute it. The school that Eleazar Wheelock created with the money Samson Occom raised for him has grown in recent years to include many different peoples and perspectives. There is surely room for the vision of Luther Standing Bear.

Notes

1. The following colleagues are gratefully acknowledged for their comments on this chapter: Jere Daniell, Bruce Duthu, Michael Hanitchak, Elaine Jahner, Sergei Kan, Deborah Nichols, Dennis Runnels, Ed Simermeyer, Alyce Spotted Bear, and James Wright.

2. Luther Standing Bear, *Land of the Spotted Eagle* (Lincoln: University of Nebraska Press, 1978), 236.

3. Bernd Peyer, "The Betrayal of Samson Occom," *Dartmouth Alumni Magazine* 91, no. 3 (November 1998): 30–37, quotations at 36.

4. Quoted in "Native American Program Enters 3rd Decade," *Dartmouth Life* (November 1992).

5. Elizabeth Cook-Lynn, "Who Stole Native American Studies?" *Wicazo Sa Review* 12, no. 1 (spring 1997): 9–28, quotation at 25.

6. Duane Champagne, "American Indian Studies Is for Everyone," *American Indian Quarterly* 20 (winter 1996): 77–82.

7. Devon A. Mihesuah, "Indian Studies," *American Indian Quarterly* 20 (winter 1996): 99.

8. Clifford E. Trafzer, "Native American Studies," in *Encyclopedia of North American Indians*, ed. Frederick E. Hoxie (Boston: Houghton Mifflin, 1996), 420; Carter Blue Clark, "America's First Discipline: American Indian Studies," in *American Indian Identity: Today's Changing Perspectives*, Publications in American Indian Studies, no. 1, ed. Clifford E. Trafzer (San Diego, Calif.: San Diego State University, 1985), 77–94.

9. Vine Deloria Jr., *Indian Education in America* (Boulder, Colo.: AISES, 1991), 20–21.

American Indian Studies at the University of Oklahoma

2

CLARA SUE KIDWELL

T HE NATIVE AMERICAN studies program at the University of Oklahoma is an interdisciplinary bachelor's degree program. Its curriculum was approved by the State Regents for Higher Education in January of 1994. It currently has approximately fifty majors and has graduated approximately thirty students since its inception. Although the state of Oklahoma is steeped in the history of American Indian Tribes, and the University of Oklahoma has been home to scholars whose work on American Indian issues is nationally recognized, the fact that the university did not establish an academic Native American studies program until 1994 speaks to the particular history of the university and the state as well as to the history of American Indian or Native American studies programs in the country in general.

In 1890, lands that had been the homes of American Indian Tribes in Indian Territory were being opened for white settlement, as part of federal Indian Policy to allot Tribal lands to individual Indians and to assimilate them into American society as farmers. Oklahoma Territory was organized out of ceded Tribal land, and in that same year the territorial government established the University of Oklahoma and two other state universities. A major mission of higher education in the late nineteenth century was to foster the development of agriculture through application of research to solving problems that farmers faced in establishing control of new lands. The Morrill Act in 1862 had provided for the establishment of land-grant universities to undertake this mission, and although the University of Oklahoma was not a land-grant institution, agriculture was prominently mentioned in its original mission statement. The statement was modeled on that of the University of Nebraska, which was a land-grant institution.[1] From its rather humble beginnings on the windswept plains of central Oklahoma, near the Canadian River, the University of Oklahoma rose to a position of some prominence as a regional university.[2]

The Indian Nations in the state of Oklahoma had been moved, sometimes forcibly, from other parts of the country, and the history of the state embodies the ambivalence of federal policy toward American Indians. The Louisiana Purchase, of which Oklahoma Territory was originally a part, was perceived by Thomas Jefferson as a place in which Indians could be removed from the pernicious influences of white society and continue their hunting ways of life. By 1828 it became for Andrew Jackson a place to which Indian Tribes as sovereign Nations could be displaced from American territory. Jackson's nationalism was sorely offended by the presence of foreign (i.e., Indian) governments within American territory.[3]

Although Jefferson saw it as a haven and Jackson saw it as a place of exile, Indian Territory ultimately became the ground for federal policy of assimilating Indians into American society. The Cherokees, Choctaws, Chickasaws, Creeks, and Seminoles, the earliest Tribes to be moved into the territory, had already been subjected to significant contact with white traders, settlers, and missionaries in their eastern homelands. They had established constitutions, legislative bodies, and courts, and missionaries had established churches and schools, and they became known as the Five Civilized Tribes. Their histories would become the subject of scholarly research at the University of Oklahoma, but the passage of the Curtis Act in 1898 effectively dissolved their Tribal governments and their communal land bases, distributed reservation land in severalty, and provided for sale of the excess to white farmers and land speculators.

By 1930 the university had an organization of Indian students and faculty, Okla-She-de-go-ta-ga. Its membership included students and faculty "who have in their veins the blood of the American Indian" and its purpose was "to foster racial pride among the descendants of the original Americans, to preserve tribal traditions and legends, and to further the cause of the education of Indian Youth."[4] This statement points out the paradox of the effects of long years of federal policy—pride in identity and preservation of Tribal cultural traditions were often at odds with nineteenth-century educational practices in mission and Bureau of Indian Affairs schools, where students were not allowed to speak Tribal languages and were kept from participating in Tribal ceremonies.[5] In the twentieth century, they were celebrated at the university.

Mention of the organization disappeared from subsequent issues of the university's *Sooner Yearbook*, but the American Indian presence on campus was again identified with a photo of the Sequoyah Club in the 1935 *Sooner*. The photo caption stated: "There has been an Indian Club in the University of Oklahoma for more than two decades."[6] The club had adopted a new constitution, and the sponsor of the group was Morris Wardell, a faculty member in the history department and assistant to President William Bizzell. Wardell had an interest in Cherokee history, and in 1938 he wrote a well-received book, *A Political History of the Cherokee Nation, 1838–1907*, which was published by the University of Oklahoma Press. One might speculate that the adoption of the name *Sequoyah* for the Indian club was because of that interest. In 1936 the Sequoyah Club played host to the Council of College and University Indian Clubs in Oklahoma, whose primary purpose was "formulating a unified program to encourage advanced education of American Indian youth by means of proper financial scholarships."[7]

Boyce Timmons, a member of the Cherokee Tribe and registrar of the university, became sponsor of the Sequoyah Club and also director of the newly formed American Indian Institute in 1951. He and his wife, Alice, a staff member of the university library's Phillips Collection, were highly visible members of the university's American Indian community. The American Indian Institute was established by the university administration "to preserve Indian culture and provide better educational facilities for the red man—two programs in which the University has been active for some time—conduct research and studies of Indian life and investigate social, economic, political and religious habits."[8] The institute sponsored an annual conference of state Indian leaders beginning in 1954, and at the second conference in 1956, participants proposed the formation of a state board of Indian affairs.[9]

While the university encouraged scholarship through the institute, the Sequoyah Club had become primarily identified with an annual powwow and princess coronation in association with the annual university homecoming football game. In a tradition identified as dating to 1931, members of the club smoked a pipe with members of the Mystic Seven of the University of Missouri (the traditional homecoming rival at the time). During this era of national prominence for the university's football team, events around the homecoming game were of major importance during the school year. The Indian presence at the university had become associated primarily with the primacy of the football team.

In 1948 a controversy erupted over homecoming when members of the Sequoyah Club charged that they had been excluded from the planning of the Union Activities Board, which had decided to select a homecoming queen. They threatened to withdraw from the half-time ceremonies altogether, prompting President George Cross to comment that "They add color and distinction to the ceremonies." Morris Wardell said, "Many people that attend the games consider the Sequoyah club quite representative of Oklahoma University." The Sequoyah Club did not withdraw, the Activities Board proceeded with its election, and a queen and an Indian princess were part of the ceremonies.[10]

The club continued to be associated with football games during the 1950s. Headlines proclaimed "Indian Sign on the Irish" and "Nocturnal Drums to Augur OU Win." The first included a photo of three Indian students putting an

"Indian Sign" on Owen Field to keep Notre Dame from scoring, and the second referred to the powwow before the game.[11] By 1960, however, the Sequoyah Club had disappeared from the *Sooner Yearbook,* which now proclaimed, "Traditionally Pe-et members and members of the Mystical Seven Society from the University of Missouri meet during the halftime of the OU-MU game for a peace pipe and smoking ceremony."[12]

Established in 1910, Pe-et was one of the oldest organizations on campus, but its membership, ten men selected as the outstanding members of the senior class, did not automatically include Indian men. Its mission statement encapsulated the philosophy of the state: "As Oklahoma is the last home of the Indian, it is fitting and proper that at its chief institution of learning memories of the red race should be honored. So, a further object is the perpetuation of old Indian customs and their symbols. Therefore only he who rides the buffalo, outwits the coyote, outruns the turkey, and fights the badger may honor and be honored by Pe-et." The easy displacement of the Sequoyah Club activity by the "tradition" of Pe-et participation at homecoming-game half-time ceremonies indicates the subversion of Indian identity at the university.[13] An elite honor society composed primarily of non-Indian students smoked the Indian pipe while wearing Indian headdresses. What had been an expression of Indian pride was now only a symbolic gesture.

The university's main claim to association with American Indian Tribes during the 1960s was the presence of Little Red as the football team's mascot, along with the miniature prairie schooner pulled by Boomer and Sooner, two Shetland ponies. The juxtaposition of Indian warrior and pioneer settler underscored the history of the state. The tradition of having a band member appear in Indian dress began in the early 1930s when the Sequoyah Club powwow became part of football ceremonialism. By the 1960s an Indian student was being chosen each year as Little Red. He performed a Plains Indian war dance on the field during half time and when the team scored a touchdown. Little Red was never adopted as an official mascot by the university. His presence was simply associated with the cheerleading squad and student-initiated activities.

In the turbulent era of student activism for civil rights and against the Vietnam War during the late 1960s, however, Little Red became the subject of controversy and a cause for Indian student activists. In November of 1969 a group of Indian students who had formed a chapter of the National Indian Youth Council (NIYC) lodged a formal petition with university president J. Herbert Hollomon asking that Little Red's presence be abolished. The petition's signers charged that "This distorted picture of the pseudo-Indian mascot represents the ludicrous, contemptible attitude that the vast Anglo-Saxon community has toward the contemporary Indian."[14]

Public debate raged on the pages of *The Oklahoma Daily,* the student newspaper. An Indian employee at the university denounced the NIYC groups with the strong assertion: "I think you 'people' have stirred up something you should be ashamed of yourselves, to turn against your own race."[15] Sequoyah Club members, however, distanced themselves from the petitioners. Club sponsor Boyce Timmons wrote an article asserting that the NIYC members had "made themselves self-appointed Indian spokesmen for the Indians of Oklahoma without ever asking the Indians of Oklahoma anything about it."[16] And a fifth-grader wrote plaintively, "I missed Little Red Saturday."[17]

President Hollomon referred the petition to the campus Human Relations Committee, which recommended that the university disavow Little Red as a mascot but allow Indian cheerleaders to appear in Indian dress if they so desired. When football season began in the fall of 1970, however, an Indian student let it be known that he intended to dress as Little Red and appear at the opening game; he was promptly slapped with a restraining order issued at the request of the NIYC president. When the student appeared at the following game he was charged with contempt of court under the student constitution. The assistant chief of the Seminole Nation shortly thereafter filed suit in Cleveland County District Court against the NIYC, the American Indian Student Office, and the Student Association General Court, seeking to allow Little Red to appear.[18]

Was Little Red a source of Indian pride, or a degrading stereotype? What did his presence on the football field say about Indian pride and the history of Indians in the state? Opinion was strong, and strongly divided. The debate over Indians as mascots of sports teams rages on in contemporary society, and continues to divide Indians and non-Indians alike, as it did then. Boyce Timmons declared that the protesters had erred in setting themselves up as spokespersons for all Indians in Oklahoma, and Alice Timmons had to have a security guard posted at the door of the university library's Phillips Collection because of their threats to burn all the books there.[19] Despite the uproar, the university administration held to the recommendation of the Human Relations Committee and abrogated any recognition of Little Red as a mascot of the team. Lost in the din were the requests of NIYC students for greater recruitment efforts and an academic Indian studies program.

The basis for such a program could have been found in the scholarship of faculty at the university, who had made major contributions for many years. Edward Everett Dale established a reputation as a historian of the American West and served as a member of the Meriam Commission, whose study of conditions on Indian reservations throughout the country from 1926 to 1928 set the stage for the Indian Reorganization Act of 1934.[20] He also chaired the dissertation committee of Angie Debo, whose doctoral thesis became her first book, *The Rise and Fall of the Choctaw Republic,* published by the University of Oklahoma Press.[21]

Although Debo's first book was well received, her second book, *And Still the Waters Run: The Betrayal of the Five Civilized Tribes*, was more problematic for the university press. Through an investigation of the activities of the Dawes Commission, appointed by the federal government to negotiate allotment of Tribal lands and dissolution of Tribal governments in Indian Territory, the book showed the disastrous impact of allotment on Indian Tribes in the state. Indian peoples, legally incompetent to manage their own affairs under the Indian Reorganization Act, often found themselves at the mercy of white lawyers who were declared their guardians. The book exposed the practices of a number of prominent men in the state who were benefiting from exploitation of Indian peoples and Indian lands, and the university press, upon advice of the university attorney, rejected it for publication.[22] Joseph Brandt, head of the University of Oklahoma Press when Debo's manuscript was rejected, later became head of the Princeton University Press and invited Debo to submit her manuscript there, where it was published in 1940.[23]

Although university officials shied away from the political implications of Debo's scholarship, the university library became a repository for information about Indians. As part of the Works Progress Administration program of collecting state histories in the 1930s, historian Grant Foreman conducted extensive interviews with Indian peoples, and the transcripts of those interviews are now housed as the Pioneer Papers in the university library's Western History Collections. In 1965–1966 the university became one site of the Doris Duke Oral History Project, which funded interviews with Indian peoples from Tribes across the country. The transcribed interviews with members of Tribes in Oklahoma also became part of the Western History Collections.[24]

Despite its resistance to publishing Angie Debo's manuscript, the University of Oklahoma Press became a major publisher of local as well as national scholarship on American Indian topics. Begun in 1932, the Civilization of the American Indian series now encompasses over 220 titles.[25] The university press has a national reputation for its series in American Indian history and literature.

Among the scholars who established University of Oklahoma's reputation as a center for scholarship on American Indians was Oscar Jacobson, first head of the art department and founder of the university museum, who trained five young Kiowa Indian artists in the 1920s and encouraged exhibition of their work in an international exposition in Prague, Czechoslovakia, establishing a tradition of Indian fine art.[26] Anthropologist Morris Opler's studies of the Apaches were widely published in the 1940s.[27] Through the 1960s, Arrell Gibson and Donald Berthrong established a tradition of work in American Indian history.[28] Interestingly, Angie Debo, one of the first Ph.D. students in the University of Oklahoma's history department, never held a regular, full-time academic appointment in a university history department. She had a temporary position at Oklahoma State University, and the bulk of her papers are in the archives at that institution.[29]

Although university faculty contributed substantively to the scholarship on American Indian topics, they would undoubtedly have been skeptical of the notion of an American Indian studies program before the 1970s. Their scholarship was firmly rooted in the academic disciplines and intellectual systems within which they worked. Indian history was primarily the political and military history of the subjugation of Indian Tribes. Anthropology was primarily the search for the commonalities of human society in the study of cultural diversity.

Given the emergence of Native American or American Indian studies programs at major universities in the early 1970s, the history of the state, and the faculty's research interests, it is reasonable to expect that the University of Oklahoma would have established an undergraduate academic program focusing on the study of American Indians. Such was not the case. Boyce Timmons complained to President Paul Sharp that "The University of Oklahoma should be the national leader in all areas of Indian academic and service programs, but has failed to give sufficient support for such activity." He noted that "The thrust and development of Indian projects has been on the basis of an individual interest and concern and not that of institutional policies."[30]

In 1974 an attempt was made to establish a master's degree in public administration "designed for those who intend to participate or who are currently participating in the administration of American Indian Affairs."[31] The degree was to be a joint effort of the political science department and the ethnic studies program, but it never appeared in the university catalog. The university's law college established an American Indian Law and Policy Center and sponsored the publication of *The American Indian Law Review* beginning in 1973. Although several programs during the 1970s and 1980s encompassed aspects of American Indian studies, they had no financial support to develop faculty or programmatic activities. The dean of the arts and sciences college suggested in the mid-1970s to Ruth Hankowsky, a Choctaw faculty member of the communications department, that there might be interest in an academic program, but there were no funds available.[32] Although several other colleges and universities in the state had listings, the University of Oklahoma did not appear in surveys of American Indian studies programs conducted by the Western Interstate Commission for Higher Education and the University of California–Los Angeles.[33]

Financially, the lack of support for a formal program is understandable in a state whose economy and legislature have been dominated by interests based primarily on oil and ranching—activities based on land acquired from Indian peoples. The financial uncertainty of an economy highly dependent on the boom-and-bust cycles of agriculture and oil has had a significant impact on the university.[34] The lack of support is also understandable politically, given the circumstances that led to the establishment of many academic programs for American Indian and other minority students throughout the country during the late 1960s and early 1970s. Political activism inspired by the civil rights movement and opposition to the war in Vietnam led to activism on college campuses and demands for programs that would address issues of representation of "minority" cultures. The NIYC protest over Little Red and the demand for an American Indian studies program was a sign of the times. The state of Oklahoma has always had, however, a reputation for political conservatism and racial segregation.

Political forces within American society mirrored the larger historical context for new university programs. The civil rights movement, which resulted in the Civil Rights Act of 1964, focused on issues of racial oppression of blacks, but it heightened awareness of disparities in economic and educational opportunities for other groups in American society. Opposition to the Vietnam War challenged governmental authority on a broad scale. The film *Little Big Man* (1970) directly equated the massacre of villages at My Lai in 1968 with the massacre of Cheyenne people at Sand Creek in 1861, reflecting anti-war sentiment and sympathy for Indians.

Events in the history of the state of Oklahoma mitigate, however, against civil rights activism. The reality of slave holding among the members of the Five Civilized Tribes and federal pressure for the Tribes to enroll their freed slaves after the Civil War and allotments of Tribal land to freedmen in the early twentieth century contributed to problematic race relationships among Indians, blacks, and whites, and a number of all-black towns were established in the state. Strict segregation prevailed in education, and it was not until 1948 that the Supreme Court of the United States compelled the admission of Ada Louise Sipuel, a black woman, to the university's law school.[35]

The influence of organized religion in Oklahoma instills a sense of respect for authority (65 percent of people in the state declare a religious affiliation and regular churchgoing, the eighth highest percentage in the country),[36] and active political protest is virtually invisible. The moral values and strong family orientation of religious denominations in the state have earned Oklahoma the designation of the "buckle" of the Bible Belt. This influence is significant within the state's American Indian population as well as within its non-Indian population.[37] Despite a long history of Democratic control of the state, by the 1972 presidential election there was a dramatic shift to the Republican Party, and congressional delegations from the state generally represented conservative social and political views in response to student and anti-war activism. In 1999, Oklahoma had the only all-Republican congressional delegation in Congress, although a Democrat was elected in 2000.

The establishment of American Indian studies programs at colleges and universities in the 1970s became a way for society to meet the political demands of civil rights legislation that equal access to higher education be afforded to all people. In Oklahoma, however, the history of the state has promoted a notion that Indians have been fully assimilated into its society. The impact of intermarriage, the allotment of Indian lands in the 1890s, and the dissolution of Tribal governments as a result of the Curtis Act of 1898 seemed to be evidence that Indians were no longer citizens of sovereign and culturally intact Nations but Oklahomans, citizens of the state. The affirmative action initiatives and requirements of federal legislation had little meaning for Indians in the minds of state and university officials.

The programs at the University of Oklahoma that focused on American Indians were the result of personal commitments by university faculty and administrators. Boyce Timmons was among the most influential of these people. As sponsor of the Sequoyah Club and a founder of the American Indian Institute, he fostered both a student social organization that gave Indian students a focus in the university community and a way for the institution to establish a research unit that would be able to address social, educational, and economic issues in Indian communities. The Sequoyah Club sponsored a radio program, *Indians for Indians*, on the university's radio station. It featured interviews, singing, and drumming. The tapes of this program, housed in the university library's Western History Collections, constitute a unique record of Indian performances and opinion in Oklahoma in the 1960s. Alice Timmons, Boyce Timmons's wife, was both a librarian working in the Phillips Collection and a mentor to American Indian students at the university. Using the resources of the Phillips Collection, which became part of the Western History Collections, and receiving research guidance from university faculty, students produced master's and doctoral theses that helped define the history of the state.

The belated establishment of a Native American studies program at the University of Oklahoma is a recognition of the vitality of Indian cultures within the state, a vitality that history and politics have seemed to submerge but that still very much exists. Oklahoma has been a rich ground for scholarship on Indian cultures, but the research has in the past treated Indians as subjects of study rather than participants in the creation of knowledge. The establishment of an academic program at the university has both political and intellectual ramifications. The presence of thirty-nine federally recognized Tribes in the state, the economic impact of Tribal presence on tourism as an industry in the state, and a rapidly increasing number of Indian students at the university have all given Indian peoples increased visibility in the state. The development of academically viable programs at other universities has contributed to the University of Oklahoma's commitment to establishing a Native American studies program.

The academic content of the program depends upon a remarkable explosion of scholarship and literature focused on American Indians. The seminal texts for Indian studies programs in 1970 were *Custer Died for Your Sins* and *Bury My Heart at Wounded Knee*.[38] Both were political statements, new interpretations of history and culture from Indian perspectives. Since then, programs have built upon new scholarly interest in American Indian topics. Arrell Gibson and Donald Berthrong set a certain standard in political and military history in documenting the relations of Indian Tribes on the Plains to the U.S. government, and the Tribes' ultimate defeat, but Francis Jennings established a revisionist paradigm for Indian history with his book *The Invasion of America* in 1975. In the field of literature, N. Scott Momaday, a Kiowa author, won a Pulitzer Prize for his novel *House Made of Dawn* in 1968. Geary Hobson, Cherokee, now a professor of English at the University of Oklahoma, published a major anthology of contemporary Indian literature, *The Remembered Earth*, in 1979.[39]

This new emergence of scholarship on American Indians moved in parallel with the political forces leading to the establishment of American Indian studies programs, but the scholarship has since moved beyond politics to establish new intellectual paradigms for the study of American Indian cultures. Scholars in history and anthropology have recognized that culture is not a static but a changing entity, and the field of ethnohistory has become a new way of examining cultural change in a historical context. Many scholars have rejected the idea that cultures exist on some continuum ranging from "inferior" to "superior," and have abandoned the acculturation theory of the 1940s, the theory that the values of so-called superior cultures will necessarily replace those of so-called inferior cultures.

The people who have fostered the development of a Native American studies program at the University of Oklahoma have been people who are members of the Tribes in the state, people who have had a sense of the history of the state and who have wanted to preserve that history and do something to reverse its impact on American Indian Tribes. They were at work throughout the 1960s and 1970s to ensure that American Indian students had opportunities to attend the university.

The current academic program stemmed from the efforts of two members of the university faculty and staff: Philip Lujan (Kiowa/Pueblo), a faculty member in the communications department, and Dr. Barbara Hobson (Comanche), a counselor and recruiter. Mr. Lujan had been recruited to the university faculty in 1977 to initiate an American Indian studies program and had conducted research on communication styles in several Indian Tribes. The university administration made some limited money available, but the resources to launch a full academic program were not forthcoming. Dr. Hobson and her husband, Dr. Geary Hobson, a professor of English, had come to the university in 1988 with encouragement from then-provost Dr. Robert Hemenway to start a program, but after Hemenway's departure for the University of Kansas, the project languished again. Finally in 1993, with the encouragement of David Young, dean of the College of Arts and Sciences, Lujan and Hobson found the support to develop the academic program and submit it for approval to the state regents. Final approval came in January of 1994.

The program is an interdisciplinary one based on a liberal arts model that encompasses core courses in Native American studies, history, English, anthropology, and art history. The basic philosophical premise of the program is that Indian identity is essential to the concept of Tribal sovereignty in contemporary American society. The interdisciplinary nature of the program allows students to learn about different disciplinary approaches to knowledge. Anthropologists study culture. Historians study changes in human society over time. Literature is an expression of culture, as are aesthetics and performance.

The mission of the Native American studies program is to train students who will be future leaders in Tribes and in organizations that serve the needs of Indian communities. The objectives of the program, as stated in its brochure, are to provide students with basic skills in reading, writing, and analytical thinking, and to instill in them an understanding of cultural diversity through comparison of Native American and other cultural values and issues. The curriculum introduces students to a basic understanding of American history and the role that Native Americans have played in it; an understanding of contemporary social and political issues that affect Native American communities; and an appreciation of the importance of art, music, and dance in Native American life. It further provides students with community-based training that will allow graduates to assume positions in government, education, social services, and Tribal programs; and develops learning skills that will enable graduates to enter academic or professional programs at the graduate level.

The 1997–1999 university catalog listed thirty-five courses applicable to the Native American studies major, while the 1999–2001 catalog lists forty-nine. Twenty-four faculty members, primarily in anthropology, history, English, and art, teach these courses. An especially strong part of the university's offerings is American Indian languages—Creek, Cherokee, Choctaw, and Kiowa—which are offered in three-semester sequences. Students majoring in Native American studies are required to choose from these languages in fulfilling the university's modern-language requirement for graduation, but the courses also attract many students with other majors, as well as many non-Indian students.

As an interdisciplinary program, Native American studies does not control hiring of faculty, but the history, anthropology, and English departments have all strengthened their national reputations in Native American scholarship by hiring new faculty in the past two years. The opening of the university's new natural history museum in the spring of 2000 provides additional opportunities for faculty resources, as well as internship opportunities for students majoring in Native American studies.

The program has received strong administrative growth support from the dean of the College of Arts and Sciences, and it is establishing a national reputation. The growing number of graduates will help build that reputation. Many have been admitted to graduate programs or are working for Indian-related organizations. The Native American studies program, together with the American Indian Institute, still an important part of the university's outreach effort to Indian communities, is making a reality the image of the University of Oklahoma as a center for scholarship on American Indians.

Notes

1. Roy Gittinger, *The University of Oklahoma, 1892–1942* (Norman: University of Oklahoma Press, 1942), 5.

2. Richard Lowitt, "Regionalism at the University of Oklahoma," *Chronicles of Oklahoma* 73 (summer 1995): 150–171.

3. Ronald N. Satz, *American Indian Policy in the Jacksonian Era* (Lincoln: University of Nebraska Press, 1974); Bernard Sheehan, *Seeds of Extinction: Jeffersonian Philanthropy and the American Indian* (New York: Norton, 1973).

4. *The Sooner Yearbook* (Norman: University of Oklahoma Press, 1930), 291.

5. See, for example, Clyde Ellis, *To Change Them Forever: Indian Education at the Rainy Mountain Boarding School, 1893–1920* (Norman: University of Oklahoma Press, 1996), and K. Tsianina Lomawaima, *They Called It Prairie Light: The Story of Chilocco Indian School* (Lincoln: University of Nebraska Press, 1994).

6. *The Sooner Yearbook* (Norman: University of Oklahoma Press, 1935), 342.

7. Morris Wardell Papers, Western History Collections, University of Oklahoma, Norman, box 1, folder 3.

8. Boyce and Alice Timmons Collection, Western History Collections, University of Oklahoma, Norman, box 2, folder 8, newspaper clipping, "Indian Institute Plan Approved," *Daily Oklahoman*, December 15, 1951.

9. Timmons Collection, box 2, folder 10, newspaper clipping, "American Indian Institute Proposes the Formation of State Board of Affairs," [newspaper unidentified], March 18, 1956.

10. Timmons Collection, box 2, folder 7, newspaper clippings, "Dolores Sanmenn (of Meers) Is Named Princess for Sequoyah Homecoming Celebration," [newspaper unidentified, 1948]; "Indians Go on the Warpath Again: Sequoyah Club Says UAB Ignores Homecoming Rites," "Smoking of Peace Pipe—Indian and White Custom Since 1931 to Crown Princess at Halftime," and "Two Queens Too Many for Indians," *The Oklahoma Daily*, n.d.

11. Timmons Collection, box 2, folder 9, newspaper clippings, "Indian Sign on the Irish" and "Nocturnal Drums to Augur OU Win," [newspaper unidentified], September 23, 1953.

12. *The Sooner Yearbook* (Norman: University of Oklahoma Press, 1960), 413.

13. *The Sooner Yearbook* (Norman: University of Oklahoma Press, 1910), n.p.

14. Boyce Timmons, "A Matter of Individual Choice," *The Sooner* 44, no. 1 (October 1970): 3ff.

15. "Leave 'Red' In," letter to the editor from John Aunko, *The Oklahoma Daily*, November 19, 1969, 12.

16. Timmons, "A Matter of Choice," 22.

17. "'I Missed Little Red Saturday,'" *The Oklahoma Daily*, November 19, 1969, 4. See also "Abolish Little Red, Indians Say," *The Oklahoma Daily*, November 14, 1969, 20; "'Little Red' to Get Axed?" *The Oklahoma Daily*, November 14, 1969, 1; "Is Little Red Mascot Wanted? Only His 'Public' to Decide," *The Oklahoma Daily*, November 18, 1969, 1–2.

18. Val Pipps and Connie Burke Ruggles, "Little Red: What Is at Issue?" *The Sooner* 44, no. 1 (October 1970): 1.

19. Alice Timmons, personal communication to Clara Sue Kidwell, August 3, 1999.

20. Institute for Government Research, *The Problem of Indian Administration* (Baltimore: Johns Hopkins University Press, 1928).

21. Angie Debo, *The Rise and Fall of the Choctaw Republic* (Norman: University of Oklahoma Press, 1934).

22. Lowitt, "Regionalism," 163–165; Angie Debo, *And Still the Waters Run: The Betrayal of the Five Civilized Tribes* (Princeton, N.J.: Princeton University Press, 1940).

23. Lowitt, "Regionalism," 163–165.

24. Indian–Pioneer Papers, and Doris Duke Oral History Project, Western History Collections, University of Oklahoma, Norman.

25. University of Oklahoma Press, "The American Indian," fall 1997 catalog.

26. *Oscar Brousse Jacobson: Oklahoma Painter*, exhibit catalog from the Fred Jones Jr. Museum of Art, University of Oklahoma, Norman, November 30, 1990.

27. See, for example, Morris E. Opler, *An Apache Life-Way: The Economic, Social, and Religious Institutions of the Chiricahua Indians* (Chicago: University of Chicago Press, 1941).

28. Arrell M. Gibson, *The Chickasaw* (Norman: University of Oklahoma Press, 1971); Donald Berthrong, *The Southern Cheyenne* (Norman: University of Oklahoma Press, 1963).

29. The Angie Debo Collection, Special Collections and University Archives, Oklahoma State University, Stillwater.

30. Timmons Collection, box 1, folder 1, memo from B. D. Timmons to Paul F. Sharp, August 30, 1972.

31. Timmons Collection, box 1, folder 1, memo from Edmund C. Nuttall, Associate Dean, Graduate College, to Walter Scheffer, Political Science; Dr. Hugh McNiven, Political Science; Dr. Ted Hebert, Political Science; Dr. Jerry Muskrat, Law Center; Mr. Boyce Timmons, American Indian Institute; Dr. Ron Lewis, Social Work; Dr. William Carmack, Speech Communication; Dr. Ruth Hankowsky, Speech Communication; Mrs. Iola Hayden, OIO; Mr. Ralph Martin, Research Administration; Mr. Mark Elder, Research Administration [November 1974].

32. Ruth Hankowsky, personal communication to Clara Sue Kidwell, August 2, 1999.

33. Patricia Locke, *A Survey of College and University Programs for American Indians* (Boulder, Colo.: Western Interstate Commission for Higher Education, 1974); Patricia Locke, *A Survey of College and University Programs for American Indians* (Boulder, Colo.: Western Interstate Commission for Higher Education, 1978); Charlotte Heth and Susan Guyette, *Issues for the Future of American Indian Studies* (Los Angeles: UCLA American Indian Studies Center, 1985).

34. Carol J. Burr, *Centennial: A Portrait of the University of Oklahoma, 1890–1990* (Norman: University of Oklahoma Press, 1990), 35–36.

35. David Levy, "The Week the President Went Fishing," *Sooner Magazine* 18, no. 2 (winter 1998): 26–30.

36. Martin Bradley et al., *Churches and Church Membership in the United States, 1990* (Atlanta: Glenmary Research Center, 1992), 5.

37. See, for example, Jack M. Schultz, *The Seminole Baptist Churches of Oklahoma: Maintaining a Traditional Community* (Norman: University of Oklahoma Press, 1999).

38. Vine Deloria Jr., *Custer Died for Your Sins* (New York: Avon, 1969); Dee Brown, *Bury My Heart at Wounded Knee* (New York: Holt, Rinehart and Winston, 1970).

39. Francis Jennings, *The Invasion of America: Indians, Colonialism, and the Cant of Conquest* (Chapel Hill: University of North Carolina Press, 1975); N. Scott Momaday, *House Made of Dawn* (New York: Harper and Row, 1968); Geary Hobson, ed., *The Remembered Earth: An Anthology of Contemporary Native American Literature* (Albuquerque, N.Mex.: Red Earth Press, 1979).

American Indian Studies at the University of California–Los Angeles

3

DUANE CHAMPAGNE

THE BEGINNINGS OF THE American Indian Studies Center at the University of California–Los Angeles (UCLA) date from the late 1960s during the period of social action and unrest owing in part to the Vietnam War and the civil rights movement. During this period, there was considerable criticism of university curricula, which generally excluded minority-group perspectives, history, and culture. Los Angeles community and student groups pressured the UCLA administration to include more minority students; include more courses relevant to minority perspectives, histories, and cultures; initiate research on minority groups; and recruit minority faculty. Afro-American, Asian American, Chicano, and American Indian student and community representatives requested more admissions of minority students, recruitment of minority faculty, more minority group–focused research, and university outreach to minority communities.

Some American Indian community members and scholars believed that American Indians were not well accounted for in academic courses, and much of the important and badly needed research on Native Americans was not carried out by university faculty.[1] Many felt that the nonminority and non-Indian academic community was not serving Indian research, teaching, and community needs. Indian students and community representatives joined to ask the UCLA administration for an Indian studies center where courses on Indian subjects would be taught, and where faculty could conduct research on American Indian life, history, and contemporary issues. At that time, there were no tenured Indian faculty, although Indian students and community representatives were aided by several faculty who were interested in American Indian issues. In January 1968, UCLA established the American Indian Culture Program, which in 1970 became the American Indian Studies Center (AISC). The goals of the center were to coordinate education, research, and applied programs designed to meet the needs of UCLA American Indian students and American Indian communities.[2]

Between 1968 and 1970, similar activities for organizing minority research centers at UCLA were ongoing among Afro-American, Asian American, and Chicano students, faculty, and community members. All four minority groups, including American Indians, were managed in the same way by the administration, and plans to accommodate the research, academic, and curricula demands of all four groups were combined into a common umbrella organization called the Institute of American Cultures.[3]

Within the university considerable resistance arose against a department of ethnic studies or individual departments, such as American Indian studies or Chicano studies. Issues of departmental status continue to plague relations among current departments, university administration, and the ethnic studies centers. As recently as 1992, several Chicano students and a faculty member went on a hunger strike to gain departmental status, after Chicano faculty spent years lobbying for an undergraduate Chicano studies department through normal academic channels. Most academic departments did not support an academic department for Chicano studies, arguing that topics relating to Chicano studies were already taken up by existing departments, and that Chicano studies did not compose an academic field.

Departments are very strong at UCLA while interdisciplinary programs are comparatively underfunded and considerably less supported than the average department. At UCLA, departments control support staff, organize curricula, have budgets, and are assigned academic full-time equivalencies (FTEs), or a year of salary and benefits for an academic position. The creation of academic ethnic studies departments has always been seen by departments and many faculty as placing additional demands on scarce resources. If the ethnic studies groups formed departments, then they would control budgets, personnel, and faculty appointments. Allowing the ethnic studies groups to form departments allows them to control academic hiring and intellectual production. Efforts to form ethnic studies departments have not gone very far. The strength of the UCLA academic departments and underemphasis of interdisciplinary, ethnic, and multicultural studies are in many ways singular. American Indian studies departments have been organized in a variety of University of California locations, such as Davis and Berkeley. The UCLA case presents an example of ethnic or American Indian studies formation within a university environment of strong and relatively uncooperative academic departments and faculty. Therefore, alternative strategies for construction of an Indian studies program, other than by means of a department, were necessary at UCLA.

University administrators, including UCLA chancellor Charles Young, wrote a grant proposal to create four ethnic studies centers. The proposal was submitted to the Ford Foundation and several hundred thousand dollars were awarded in 1969. The Afro-American, Asian American, and Chicano studies centers started operation in the 1969–1970 academic year, while the American Indian Studies Center started up in the 1970–1971 academic year. The Ford Foundation grant provided five years of funding, and in 1974 the University of California agreed to fund the centers for the following twenty-five years. Every five years the university reviews the four ethnic studies centers with an academic committee of several UCLA faculty and two outside reviewers. In 2000 a fifteen-year review of the four centers took place, and a decision will be made regarding continued funding by the University of California. The AISC did well in the review, and continued UCLA institutional support will be forthcoming for another fifteen years.

Since academic departments were not possible means for organizing ethnic studies centers at UCLA, the centers were formed into organized research units (ORUs), which within the University of California system are organizations that gather together faculty who are interested in a specific research topic. The president and regents of the University of California approved ORU status for the American Indian Studies Center in spring 1971.[4] This achievement was the result of considerable work by faculty, staff, and students. There are about fifty ORUs at UCLA, and they range in research interest from topics in physics and biology to ethnic studies. Some ORUs have budgets and staff, while others have minimal support. After the first five years of Ford Foundation support, the four ethnic studies ORUs received considerably greater financial and staff support from the university than did the average ORU. Unlike departments, however, ORUs do not control faculty appointments and do not organize academic curricula. Most ORUs congregate like-minded faculty, who write grant proposals and carry on research projects through the auspices of the ORU framework. Most ORUs are primarily geared toward research and grant writing, but the ethnic studies ORUs accepted several additional tasks such as student support, community relations, faculty recruitment, publication of academic and policy papers and books, and library services. The ethnic studies centers also were initially charged with developing and staffing student courses.

The strategy to organize the ethnic studies centers as ORUs avoided confrontation over creating departmental status. Especially in American Indian studies, in the early 1970s, there were no full-time tenured American Indian faculty at UCLA, and most likely there would have been little departmental or faculty support for an American Indian studies department. While they do not provide control over faculty or courses, ORUs provide considerable flexibility for pursuing research, student affairs, and community relations projects. The ORU framework allows considerable freedom for faculty and staff to pursue a variety of topics and issues, especially if outside funding is obtained. A major disadvantage of ORUs is that they cannot house faculty FTEs or courses. This disadvantage was severely felt for many years until 1982, when the American Indian Studies Center faculty formed an interdepartmental program (IDP) master's degree curriculum in American Indian studies. The IDP is an interdisciplinary academic unit, with little budget and borrowed faculty from departments, but which can offer courses and degrees.

The four ethnic studies centers were linked together initially through the 1969 Ford Foundation grant and after 1974 through a university unit called the Institute of American Cultures (IAC). While each of the ethnic studies ORUs separately manages its internal affairs, the four ethnic studies centers often cooperate to achieve satisfactory results on issues of mutual benefit and concern with university administration. For a small and politically weak group such as American Indians, there are certain political advantages to this arrangement. The American Indian Studies Center probably would not have emerged without the combined interests and help of the other more powerful ethnic studies centers. Similarly, continued university support for American Indian studies is at least partially dependent on the political visibility and influence of the Afro-American, Asian American, and Chicano communities. Over the years, a cooperative etiquette developed among the ethnic studies centers, especially on issues of mutual interest and concern. Because of the political context associated with the establishment and continuing support of the ethnic studies centers, some faculty and departments carry relatively unfriendly attitudes toward the ethnic studies programs. Despite any academic achievements or justifications for ethnic studies, the centers are often regarded as unwanted stepchildren. This effect has some unifying force among the centers themselves, but mitigates against full participation in some university initiatives, such as formation of ethnic studies departments or openness toward faculty appointments supported by ethnic studies centers.

Early Formation: 1970–1974

The American Indian Studies Center started work on a variety of fronts, including an ambitious research program. While major emphasis was placed on curriculum development, most classes were given as temporary developmental courses outside regular departments, which usually lacked faculty who taught American Indian topics. Only those courses offered by tenure-track faculty in departments remained permanently available to students. While a wide variety of interesting courses were developed, and were well attended by students, most courses were taught by graduate students and temporary lecturers. Nevertheless, the diversity of offerings satisfied the objective for curriculum development, but as yet there was no stable home for such courses. Further compounding the curriculum issue was the unavailability of academic staff or Indian scholars who could move the courses into departments where they could be offered on a regular basis. The center sought to recruit Indian faculty, but found few available. Consequently, the center began nationwide tracking of American Indian graduate students in the hope that some might eventually serve as UCLA tenure-track faculty. There was very little success, however, in hiring Native American faculty before 1975.

Staff and graduate students carried out most center research with relatively little faculty input or guidance. This situation was considered a disadvantage and some projects suffered. Early research projects included a series of bibliographies on materials written about American Indians in fields such as history, education, and literature. Other research projects compiled the texts of U.S.–Indian treaties and legal documents surrounding the laws and effects of the Termination Policy, studied retention and academic achievement among UCLA American Indian students, collected Northern Paiute songs and stories, studied Tlingit art, and carried out research on Bureau of Indian Affairs (BIA) archives. The Ford Foundation grant obligated the center to create a document depository, as well as conduct research and develop faculty. The document project involved many staff in researching BIA documents and collecting treaties, laws, and specific Tribal administrative documents and histories. Several of the early research projects were later published in the center's monograph series.

The Ford Foundation grant required distribution of center research by publication of journals, monographs, newsletters, and other media for academic and community groups.[5] In 1970 the center began publishing the *American Indian Culture Center Journal* and the "AICC Newsletter." The newsletter, which presented national events rather than center activities, was published regularly from 1970 to 1974. The journal solicited and published academic articles about American Indians. Its purpose was "to disseminate scholarly, general and other information as it concerns the involvement of Native Americans in all areas throughout the country."[6] Publication of the journal was irregular, though, owing to budget constraints, lack of staff and student time for editorial work, absence of faculty guidance, and difficulties in attracting a reliable stream of quality manuscripts. While the journal assumed a scholarly format, its content gravitated toward semischolarly and literary articles.[7] Nevertheless, considerable experience was gained, although center staff felt that there were not enough resources and faculty support to produce a more academic journal. In the early 1970s, center staff were not yet sure that producing an academic journal was desirable.[8] Most center staff were not academically trained and most preferred to produce publications with literary, policy, and general readership content. The new periodicals were supplemented by publication of center-sponsored research conducted by staff and graduate students and intended for general and community audiences. Center staff and graduate students edited the journal, newsletter, and book publications. In fall 1973, the responsibility for editing the journal and newsletter was assumed by a single center staff member, who directed much of her effort toward distributing center-sponsored research. Since she had other significant center duties, few new scholarly publications were produced.

In winter 1974, the *American Indian Center Journal* ceased publication after four volumes and was superseded by the *American Indian Culture and Research Journal.* The new journal was intended "to provide a quarterly research forum for scholars and innovators in the areas of historical and contemporary American Indian life and culture. Emphasis will be strongly on the here and now, and on how the past has brought us here."[9] A scholarly editorial board was formed to assist in the solicitation and evaluation of manuscripts. The editorship adopted a regular process of scholarly manuscript review and journal content improved and assumed a more academic orientation. In the first five-year review, the publications unit was assessed as having serious difficulties owing to the absence of quality manuscripts generated from research conducted by center staff and students, and the absence of faculty participation and guidance. Nevertheless, the establishment of the journal and publication of several new monograph series provided valuable experience and laid the foundation for further publication developments in later years.

The center established a library and began the work of collecting documents, books, and other materials relating to Indian history, culture, and contemporary life and issues. In addition the library and center staff carried on bibliographic research projects and contributed to faculty curriculum development and class support. The library provided space for students, faculty, and staff to meet and informally discuss various research and contemporary issues on American Indians.

Student relations involved counseling undergraduate and graduate students. A study of UCLA American Indian student achievement was conducted, and graduate students were tracked. Many graduate and undergraduate students worked on various center research projects and gained valuable research experience. Center staff coordinated activities with the American Indian Students Association (AISA), founded in 1969 soon after establishment of the American Indian Culture Center. In 1973–1974, a three-year review committee recommended that additional funds be made available to the center to expand and organize student counseling for American Indian students. The center's Indian counselor provided culturally sensitive student assistance, coordinated activities among the Indian student organizations, helped UCLA recruit Indian students, and cooperated with academic advancement programs that provided academic assistance to minority and underprivileged students. The student counselor also oriented incoming students, acted as a liaison for faculty, students, and center staff, provided financial aid counseling, and assisted students with selecting majors and making other decisions. During the early 1970s about 200 Indian students attended UCLA. Center research showed that these students, as a group, were not doing well academically. Center student services were designed to provide culturally sensitive help to Indian students to improve student retention and academic achievement.

The center's first four years were occupied with identifying and seeking solutions to balancing community, center, and university objectives and relations. The center established a faculty advisory committee and a community advisory committee. Most center activity was carried out by staff, while faculty provided little support or guidance. Consequently, much of the research and editing was carried out by staff and students, sometimes undergraduates. The absence of faculty participation was in part due to the absence of tenure-track American Indian faculty and departmental demands on those faculty who were American Indian experts. Departments demand full participation from faculty, who are given few rewards, if not career penalties, for extended participation in center activities. Faculty appointments and promotions are evaluated by departments, and, in practice, little credit is given to faculty for participation in center research or activities. The research conducted by center students and staff was often very different from faculty and departmental research interests. The difficulties of gaining consistent and committed faculty support and participation continue to plague all the UCLA ethnic studies centers.

A Period of Reorganization: 1975–1982

In 1975, UCLA assumed financial responsibility and tighter administrative guidance over the ethnic studies centers. The director of the American Indian Studies Center resigned the same year, and a search for a new director of Indian descent with academic and administrative qualifications failed to identify a suitable candidate. The search committee decided to recommend appointment of the only tenure-track American Indian assistant professor at UCLA. The new director, Charlotte Heth, a former UCLA graduate student, was appointed on July 1, 1976. By 1979, Heth had been joined by two more American Indian faculty, although they did not gain tenure. After 1975 the university upheld a policy that the director of the American Indian Studies Center must be a tenured faculty member in an academic department. Since Heth was an assistant professor, she was appointed interim director until obtaining tenure. University administrators and faculty wanted an Indian faculty member to manage the center. The appointment of an American Indian assistant professor, however, was considered necessary to give the center more academic direction in a situation where there were no other tenured or tenure-track American Indian faculty available. Appointment of a tenured non-Indian faculty member was considered undesirable, since most Indian communities will not support a non-Indian director of an American Indian studies program.

The appointment as interim director is a difficult situation to place in anyone's hands. The demands for gaining tenure are usually considered more than enough for most faculty members. The additional demands of managing an ORU still in major stages of transition placed extremely heavy burdens on the new director. The first and former director held the title of Director of Development, and did not have an academic position in the university. Although appointment of an assistant professor was not an optimal choice in several regards, this decision brought greater academic orientation and stability to the center.

After the conclusion of the Ford Foundation grant, UCLA's assuming of funding and administration and the appointment of a new director led to several center reorganizations between 1976 and 1978, and resulted in much of the center's contemporary organization and goals. UCLA required the center to reorganize its administrative positions and provide greater financial accountability. A full-time publications coordinator and a full-time student/community relations officer were hired. These new positions allowed greater attention to student affairs and publications production. The director was supported by a research coordinator, administrative officer, administrative assistant, and secretary, and a full-time librarian managed the center library. The research coordinator was responsible for grant writing, advising faculty and students about research and research opportunities, carrying out research, and publication. Both the director and research coordinator worked closely together to generate research funds, coordinate center research efforts, and carry on a program of scholarly and community-based publications. The director and research coordinator worked well together on many projects, but after a few years the research coordinator left, in part due to overwork.

Although the center received guidance from both a faculty committee and a committee of community advisers, by late 1977 advice from the latter was no longer being sought.[10] In part this decision came about because university demands for research and publication were often very alien and difficult to reconcile with community interests. Community demands were largely focused on service delivery and needs-assessment research that facilitated social service grant writing. The center and faculty were unable to balance community and university demands and decided to provide benefits to the community on their own terms and from within its mandate as an organized research unit. The center did not stop producing books and policy analyses for the benefit of Indian and reservation communities, but it no longer sought community advice through regular meetings with a committee of community members.

The new organizational arrangement united the four ethnic studies centers into a single financial unit under the jurisdiction of the Institute of American Cultures (IAC), which was administered by the vice chancellor for research. By 1977 the IAC provided research funds to the centers, and allowed faculty and students to secure research grants through a competitive review process. The IAC also instituted a program of funding predoctoral and postdoctoral fellowships. The postdoctoral fellowships supported the center's American Indian faculty recruitment goals. Faculty from other universities who engaged in American Indian studies–related work were invited to compete for the yearlong fellowships. Through the postdoctoral fellowships, the university and center reviewed a variety of potential faculty prospects.

The program for faculty hiring also was enhanced with the granting of five institutional FTEs to the center. The FTE could not be used directly by the center, but faculty prospects were hired in departments, after departmental approval. The center passed the FTE to the control of the department, which made promotion and tenure decisions regarding the appointee. The difficulty of hiring suitable American Indian faculty was compounded with the demands of departments for faculty time and participation. Most departments demanded that faculty members fulfill all requirements and obligations in their field, and hence discouraged participation in center research and activities even among faculty who were recruited and appointed through center FTEs. The dual arrangement of departmental and center obligations placed considerable additional burdens on center-appointed faculty members, and left the center with relatively little influence over its own faculty appointments in departments.

The center sponsored research on American Indians, especially research by American Indians and research that benefited the Los Angeles American Indian community, as well as sponsoring the development of an interdisciplinary curriculum for both undergraduates and graduate students; the publication of journals, monographs, newsletters, and other media; and the recruitment of faculty. It also encouraged Indian communities to take advantage of resources available at the university. The center's long-range goals focused on developing Indian leadership, training Indian professionals, seeking Indian solutions to Indian problems, and distributing accurate information about American Indian peoples.[11]

Between 1975 and 1982 the center made considerable progress in grant writing, reorganizing research around external funding and IAC sources, developing a proposal for creating a master's degree program in American Indian studies, and stabilizing the regular production of the *American Indian Culture and Research Journal* and other publications. The center library established relations with the main UCLA library, and circulation and cataloging were emphasized. The center library continued to acquire books and materials on American Indian peoples. The student/community relations officer became a full-time position, with duties of job training for community members, counseling graduate and undergraduate students, and maintaining contact among student, university, and community organizations. Both the library and student relations activities became regularized features of the center. Research became more academically oriented, while considerable research was aimed at solving problems and assisting Indian communities. The center sought to establish itself as a national "think tank" on Indian issues. The journal was issued regularly, and numerous academic, literary, and community-based publications were issued. Center publications took on the character of a small publishing house. Priority was given to publications production, however, as few resources were available for distribution and marketing. Many books were targeted to aid Indian communities by presenting such topics as preserving traditional arts, community-based research, and community language preservation. The center began a series of conferences on American Indian issues, and by 1982 completed six national conferences on a variety of contemporary American Indian issues such as higher education, economic development, and American Indian arts. The conferences served to draw together scholars and community members, who addressed contemporary American Indian issues. Several conference proceedings were published by the center, which continues to organize at least one conference per year.

A major change in curriculum development took place with a proposal to create an American Indian master's degree program at UCLA.[12] Curriculum development had always been a difficult issue for the center, since it could not house courses or faculty. The proposal for the master's degree program was ready by fall 1977, but was not approved until January 1982. Four students were admitted in fall 1982. The master's program provided a liberal arts approach to Native American studies. There are no particular professional skills taught, but extensive work is given on American Indian history, culture, and contemporary issues. A language or linguistics course is also required. Students are encouraged to develop critical faculties and research skills. Many master's students gain greater understanding of Indian cultures and develop improved academic skills before continuing graduate studies in professional or doctoral programs. The master's program offers intensive study in American Indian issues and culture that usually cannot be found in professional or doctoral programs. Those graduates who chose not to continue with more graduate work found employment as Tribal historians, museum curators, teachers, and administrators for Tribal governments.

The master's program is not housed in the center, since the center is an ORU. The master's program was organized as an academic unit, called an interdepartmental program (IDP), which does not house faculty or usually control significant resources or personnel. At UCLA, interdisciplinary programs are formed by a group of faculty who are interested in teaching a particular subject area not offered by departments. The faculty remain in their respective departments, but contribute courses to the IDP curriculum. Students choose courses from a list offered by IDP faculty, but are free to choose graduate courses throughout the university.

As an academic unit, the IDP is not administered by the center, but rather by the dean of social sciences. A faculty advisory committee oversees the IDP and nominates the administrative head, or IDP director. The IDP director expends considerable time advising students and overseeing issues such as recruitment, admissions, and student progress. Since this is a heavy burden, the center supports the IDP by making available the student/community relations officer, who manages much of the IDP's daily routine. A close relationship has developed between the IDP and the center, because the participating faculty are the same people and the IDP carries out the center's goals of developing Indian studies curricula and granting Indian studies degrees.

The decision to take up the master's program was accompanied by considerable discussion and reflected a specific philosophy toward the possibilities and character of American Indian studies education. The faculty decided that the IDP arrangement would offer a master's degree, but not offer an undergraduate major. The advisory faculty reasoned that Indian undergraduate students at UCLA should complete study within one of the mainstream disciplines such as economics, political science, and the like. Consequently, it was not thought advisable to encourage Indian students to earn a degree in American Indian studies. Rather, students were encouraged to take up graduate work in the American Indian studies IDP. At the same time, the suggestion of a doctoral program in American Indian studies was also laid aside, partly for lack of resources, but also in favor of doctoral training in the usual academic disciplines. There was some concern that a Ph.D. in American Indian studies would not be marketable. In effect, UCLA undergraduates were not offered an American Indian studies curriculum. Indian undergraduates felt left out of center activities, in part because there was no course of study in American Indian studies available to them. The decisions not to create a doctoral program or undergraduate major were in part due to the strength of academic departments at UCLA. Both an undergraduate major and a doctoral graduate program would require more faculty and financial resources, and perhaps departmental status, which most likely would not be forthcoming. Nevertheless, the master's program was warmly welcomed and has become a centerpiece for American Indian studies offerings at UCLA.

Program Consolidation: 1983–2000

By the end of 1982, the present organization of the American Indian Studies Center was more or less intact. The following years were ones of consolidating and fine-tuning. Major efforts were made to support the new master's degree program, develop an active research and publication program, enhance the library collection, and continue services to students and the community. Over the past fifteen years, the university annually provided $400,000 to $450,000 in basic financial support to the center. These sums constituted some of the largest and most consistent support for an Indian studies program in the United States. The IAC research grants and fellowships became significant parts of the center research program. Numerous small research grants of $2,000 or less were given to students, and faculty received grants of up to $5,000; predoctoral fellows were aided by stipends of $10,000 and tuition wavers. Many predoctoral fellows finished dissertation work with the aid of the predoctoral fellowship. Postdoctoral fellowships are routinely granted each year with stipends ranging from $23,000 to $29,000. The fellows greatly enriched the center's academic contacts and research activities. Over the years, several hundred publications resulted from the IAC grants and fellowships, and from the appointment of faculty by center FTEs. The postdoctoral fellowship has become a national competition, and attracts considerable interest. Over 300 research grants have been conducted by the center through funding from IAC, external, and UCLA sources. The center remains committed to research and seeking external research funds.

The *American Indian Culture and Research Journal* will see its twenty-fifth volume in 2001. The journal has established itself as a major research resource on American Indian scholarship, and ranks among the finest academic journals in American Indian studies. A recent citation analysis found that it was one of two leading journals most frequently cited in the *Social Science Index* for American Indian subjects.[13] The journal matured with a regular blind review process in which each manuscript is sent to five readers. Center staff maintains a database of over 2,500 scholars, who review manuscript submissions and write book reviews, a regular feature of the journal. Major indices such as *Sociological Abstracts* and the *Social Science Index* carry the journal. In recent years, journal distribution has ranged around 1,000 copies. In general, both the quality and the quantity of published papers are increasing. The publications unit also maintains an active agenda of book publications, and several new books are issued each year.

Since the mid-1980s, the center's publications unit has functioned under a reorganized production process with a heavy investment in desktop publishing equipment and the oversight of a managing editor, who copyedits and typesets the manuscripts. The move to desktop publishing increased efficiency, lowered costs, reduced production delays, and provided considerable control over finished products. After receiving written evaluations from reviewers, a faculty member familiar with academic review processes and the Indian studies field serves as editor and adjudicates the manuscripts. The faculty editor is not responsible for journal or book production, and can focus his/her academic experience and intellectual skills on the review process. The managing editor concentrates on production, while the academic editor focuses on review and acquisition of interesting papers and book manuscripts.

The division of labor between the academic and managing editors has proven very productive. The previous publications coordinator position imposed too many demands on the editor, who was responsible for manuscript acquisition, review and adjudication of manuscripts, copyediting, production, and overseeing sales. In practice, all these activities were too difficult for one person to do well while at the same time maintaining an active and high-quality publication schedule. Hiring a publications coordinator was also difficult, since a candidate needed not only good academic credentials but also good editing and publications skills and a willingness to commit to sales and distribution. Most academics prefer to take teaching and research positions in academic departments. Consequently, the publications coordinator position was often difficult to fill, and successful candidates often did not have strong academic credentials and were highly prone to suffer from mental and physical exhaustion from overwork. The more recent arrangement places some additional workload on a faculty member, but the arrangement has the advantage of allowing the academic editor to spend most of his/her time engaged in manuscript review and exchange with authors and other reviewers. These activities play to the faculty member's strengths, interests, and skills, and provide an experience that is engaging yet not too time-consuming. Similarly, the managing editor does not need to have academic training, but rather editorial skills in English and computer skills in desktop publishing. The managing editor position is thereby easier to fill than the earlier publications coordinator position, which required more skills. Perhaps the most important change created by the faculty editor–managing editor arrangement is that faculty guidance and expertise are introduced into the selection and solicitation of journal and book manuscripts, as well as into the overview of production and the final product.

A persistent difficulty with publications has been the absence of resources for extensive marketing. Many center publications are targeted for reservation and academic audiences and are not intended to have large distributions. In recent years, more attention has been given to producing more nationally marketable books. Nevertheless, publication income barely covers productions costs, and does not cover salaries and overhead. Not unlike a university press, the center's publication program is indirectly subsidized by the university. Staff and overhead costs often run $50,000 over income. A long-range center goal is to put publication on a self-sufficient financial basis. This goal might be achieved with better marketing of center books and the journal.

The American Indian studies library has been consolidated into a reference library serving scholars and students. Efforts to maintain archival materials proved too ambitious, since adequate space and proper environmental controls have not been available to the center library. The library collection consists of over 6,000 volumes and, since remodeling in 1991–1992, is a comfortable and convenient place for study. Most library activity in recent years has concentrated on book acquisition and cataloging a large backlog for circulation. The library and its librarian have proved invaluable resources for completing numerous research and book projects.

The student/community relations officer counsels graduates and undergraduates, recruits students, and manages daily IDP activities. Students are encouraged to visit and study at the center, where space for student organizations and computers is available for study and organizational activities. The student/community relations officer has been encouraged to work more actively on fund-raising for student retention programs and graduate and undergraduate scholarship funds. The Yellowthunder Scholarship fund for undergraduates is currently endowed with over $260,000, and a major center fund-raising objective is student scholarships. Graduate and undergraduate Indian student organizations, as well as the UCLA American Indian Alumni Association, cooperate in center functions and help organize conferences, a gala fund-raising event, and the annual UCLA American Indian Studies Powwow held each spring.

The IDP has matured over the years and now attracts capable students from a variety of backgrounds. Owing to high out-of-state tuition costs in the University of California system, more IDP students are California residents, although some out-of-state and foreign students apply to and enter the program. In 1995 a proposal to create an undergraduate minor was submitted and approved for the IDP. The minor provides an academic program to undergraduates in American Indian studies. During 1999–2000, discussions among faculty and students led to development of an undergraduate major proposal, which was submitted and is currently under review. Professor Carole Goldberg introduced a joint degree program in American Indian studies and law. This program is designed to provide historical and cultural background to lawyers so they can work with Indian communities in a more informed and sensitive manner. Within the last three years, Professor Goldberg introduced the Native American law clinic, which provides legal services to Indian Nations and organizations. The clinic does not litigate cases, but provides student and faculty support for Tribes to write Tribal ordinances, revise constitutions and bylaws, and assist in formation of Tribal courts. This program has gained considerable attention from many of the Tribal governments in southern California.

While the center mission and organizational structure have stabilized, the center continues to face serious problems largely in faculty resources and support. As a research unit, the center does not have enough critical mass in faculty researchers to generate a viable team. The IDP's major problem aside from funding for master's students is the lack of enough faculty to provide the diversity and consistency of course offerings. The activities of the center and IDP would be greatly enhanced by the hiring of only a handful of additional faculty. Consequently, faculty recruitment remains a major goal.

One of the advantages of the center's open-ended community and research mandate is the opportunity to seek grants and funding for many different projects. While the center has always had success in raising funds for book, research, and community activities, recent fund-raising has been very successful and has allowed the center to develop a series of projects that extend directly into Native communities. A grant from the Department of Education allows center staff and faculty to develop legal studies programs for Tribally controlled community colleges. The program is called Project Peacemaker and is designed to create courses and programs to train court advocates, court staff, and paralegals; promote completion of associate's degrees in legal studies; and encourage students to look into law and Tribal law as a profession. We are currently working with four community colleges—Turtle Mountain Community College on the Turtle Mountain Reservation in North Dakota, Salish Kootenai College on the Flathead Reservation in Montana, Northwest Indian College on the Lummi Reservation in Washington state, and Diné College on the Navajo Reservation in Arizona. Through a large Kellogg Foundation grant, the center has partnered with Sinte Gleska University on the Rosebud Reservation in helping with Project HOOP, which is introducing a Native theater curriculum into Sinte Gleska University and helping to develop Native community theater within the entire reservation. We hope to introduce Project HOOP and similar Native theater projects into other Tribally controlled community colleges and Native communities. Other grants and gifts are funding medical education on cancer prevention for Indian women in southern California; federal recognition research for the Gabrielino/Tongva people of the Los Angeles basin; the UCLA–Sundance Institute's Native American Screen Writers Workshop; the Native American Thesaurus project; research on Indian children's needs in Los Angeles County; Tribal–state partnership discussions; research on California Indian economic, legal, and funding conditions; research on Indian health characteristics and needs in Los Angeles County; and other projects. The last several years have produced good fund-raising efforts through private, federal, and foundation sources. This new fund-raising success, and the development of more projects in direct partnership with Indian reservations and the Los Angeles Indian community, creates many opportunities for the American Indian Studies Center to be of service to Indian communities and provide students with opportunities to work and gain experience.

If there is a major flaw in the center's contemporary organization, it is probably the relative inability to consistently support a community advisory committee. Throughout Indian Country, community advisory committees are considered an essential feature of Indian studies centers. Universities, however, often place less value on minority community participation at the advisory level. Until 1977, a community advisory committee was part of the center, and community input and technical service were major center objectives. A community committee was briefly reintroduced in 1990–1991, but no meetings have been held since. Center staff are actively engaged in the Los Angeles Indian community organizations, such as the Los Angeles City/County American Indian Commission, and several staff members are active participants in Los Angeles Indian community powwows and spiritual leadership. Recent successes in fund-raising, aided by appointment of a new development officer shared by all four UCLA ethnic studies centers, have led to development of donor friends who often act as advisers and supporters, for a variety of projects in the community as well as for student scholarship fund-raising. Our research and community activities put the center in regular contact with most of the major Indian organizations in southern California, thereby setting the stage for the formation of a representative and strong community advisory committee that can provide guidance and assistance to center projects and objectives.

Conclusion

Among UCLA faculty associated with the American Indian Studies Center, considerable discussion has taken place over how to organize an American Indian studies program. The UCLA faculty decided not to form an American Indian studies department like the University of California programs at Berkeley and Davis. Departmental status was not possible at UCLA owing to the strength of departments and the underemphasis on interdisciplinary scholarship. Consequently, UCLA faculty opted for creating an organized research unit and providing curriculum through the interdisciplinary program format. The UCLA strategy has some inherent advantages and disadvantages when compared to departmental models.

At UCLA, faculty appointments are made in home departments. The advantage is that once American Indian faculty obtain tenure, they remain permanently within the ranks of the faculty, and cannot be dismissed as part of a department when budgetary crises arise. One fear of the departmental model is that an Indian studies department might easily become a target for budget cuts or underfunding. Having American Indian and other center-associated faculty hired in departments creates a hedge against wholesale loss of Indian studies faculty during times of budget crises or changing political attitudes. Furthermore, departmental appointments allow faculty relatively easy access to the rest of the university, and allow for full status within the academic university community and within their respective disciplines. A primary concern about American Indian studies departments is the tendency for the department and its faculty to become ghettoized and isolated from primary university functions. For example, underfunding and lack of university and faculty support have been a major issue for the American Indian studies department at Berkeley. American Indian studies centers are relatively small organizations, and it is difficult to manage them effectively without support and friends within the rest of the university. Faculty appointments in departments facilitate access to university networks and support services in a variety of contexts.

There are, however, certain disadvantages to the UCLA model. When faculty must be approved by a department, often the intellectual interests of the department do not coincide with those of the center. Candidates who are acceptable to the center are often not acceptable to departments. At the same time, candidates who are acceptable to departments often do not satisfy the center's intellectual and cultural requirements. Consequently, the center often is forced to choose a candidate who is acceptable to a department, but who is less than helpful to the center's intellectual agenda. In the departmental model, this issue is not a problem, since an American Indian department is much freer to choose faculty who will support its research and teaching program. Furthermore, in the UCLA model, faculty appointments in departments engender additional pressures on the appointees for satisfying both the center's and the department's agendas. Thus appointees are forced to take on double duty. Departments want full-time faculty, and since departmental and center intellectual programs often differ considerably, intellectual work performed for American Indian studies is often given little weight in departmental promotions, and tenure decisions. Departments have control over hiring, promotion, and tenure decisions, and therefore have considerable influence over center faculty appointees. Departments often force center appointees to conform to departmental demands, and thus center academic interests and service become secondary. For example, faculty teaching in the American Indian studies IDP is sometimes criticized in departmental reviews because such teaching and service does not contribute to departmental goals. Where there is an American Indian studies department, because faculty are appointed within the department, the faculty do not experience split loyalties and conflicting demands, but are free to carry on the intellectual work and goals of the American Indian studies department. An American Indian studies department has considerable influence over its faculty because it hires, promotes, and grants tenure, and thereby can ensure that the intellectual work and service of an American Indian studies program is carried out.

A great strength of the UCLA model is its inherent integration of its faculty with university departments, and this is thought to promote long-term survivability and continued intellectual exchange and academic inclusion with non-Indian studies faculty and disciplines.[14] The American Indian studies department model has great advantage in the ability to control its own agenda and faculty appointments. Whether the advantages of one model far outweigh its disadvantages is not entirely clear. Strong adherents for both models can be found. The UCLA model was not entirely a free choice, since strong departments at UCLA largely exclude that possibility for American Indian studies departmental status. American Indian studies at Davis and Berkeley apparently did not encounter the same opposition to forming their departments. Hence university departmental and administrative relations may go far toward determining the possibilities for organization of an Indian studies program. Understanding your own university's institutional culture may be the most appropriate knowledge for deciding how to construct viable and productive new programs.

Notes

1. Russell Thornton, "American Indian Studies as an Academic Discipline," *American Indian Culture and Research Journal* 2, nos. 3–4 (1978): 10–19; Jack Forbes, "The Future of American Indian Studies Conference" (paper presented at the conference) (Los Angeles: UCLA American Indian Studies Center, 1994).

2. American Indian Studies Center, "Five Year Review Report, 1975–1980" (Los Angeles: UCLA American Indian Studies Center, 1980); "Formation and Development of the American Indian Culture Center," *American Indian Culture Center Journal* 1, no. 1 (spring 1970): 5–6.

3. "American Indian Culture Center," 5.

4. David S. Saxon, Vice Chancellor, letter to Anthony Purley, Director, American Indian Studies Center, May 28, 1971.

5. "Five Year Report."

6. American Indian Studies Center, "Annual Report: Fiscal Year 1970–71" (Los Angeles: UCLA American Indian Studies Center, 1971), 6.

7. "Five Year Report," 2.

8. "Editor's Introduction," *American Indian Culture Center Journal* 3, no. 1 (fall–winter 1971–1972): 1.

9. American Indian Studies Center, "Annual Report: Fiscal Year 1973–1974" (Los Angeles: UCLA American Studies Center, 1974).

10. "Five Year Report," 5.

11. "Five Year Report," 2.

12. David Draper, "Proposal for an M.A. Degree in American Indian Studies," *American Indian Culture and Research Journal* 2, nos. 3–4 (1978): 20–23.

13. Cheryl Metoyer-Duran, "The *American Indian Culture and Research Journal* and the *American Indian Quarterly*: A Citation Analysis," *American Indian Culture and Research Journal* 17, no. 4 (1993): 44.

14. Wilcomb Washburn, "American Indian Studies: A Status Report," *American Quarterly* 27, no. 3 (1975): 263–274.

Culture, Tradition, and Evolution: The Department of Native Studies at Trent University

4

DAVID NEWHOUSE, DON MCCASKILL, AND JOHN MILLOY

T RENT UNIVERSITY OPENED its doors in 1964 as a small liberal arts and science university located in Peterborough, Ontario, Canada, about one and a half hours northeast of Toronto. Peterborough is a small city of 73,000 people. The university was a project of its leading citizens, who lobbied the Ontario provincial government for a decade for the establishment of a university in their community. Trent is one of the smallest institutions in the Ontario system of seventeen universities. It currently has about 4,500 undergraduate students, 160 graduate students, and 240 faculty members, and has no desire to increase the size of its student population. There are seven Aboriginal (Ojibway and Mohawk) communities located within an hour's drive of the campus. Currently there are approximately 250 Aboriginal students on campus.

In Canada, we continue to struggle with the nomenclature of peoples indigenous to this continent. There is no consensus about the term to be used: *Indian, Treaty Indian, Status Indian, Métis, Inuit* (formerly *Eskimo*), *Aboriginal, First Nation, Native,* and *Indigenous* are all used. The Canadian constitution uses the term *Aboriginal Peoples of Canada* and defines them as including Indian, Inuit, and Métis, leaving room for more. It is in this context that the term *Aboriginal* is used in this chapter.

Beginnings: The Indian–Eskimo Studies Program

Aboriginal issues at Trent University were initially explored and taught under the aegis of the Department of Anthropology. In 1968 the university senate established a working group to examine the possibility of establishing a Native studies program at Trent. A group of faculty under the leadership of Professor Kenneth E. Kidd, an anthropologist noted for his research into Aboriginal societies, undertook a consultation process asking for input from Aboriginal organizations and communities in terms of how Trent University could assist in meeting their postsecondary educational needs. The result was the establishment of the Indian–Eskimo Studies Program in 1969.

Two Aboriginal faculty members were hired and, in 1969, one course was offered, drawing an enrollment of thirty-one students, four of whom were Aboriginal. Thus began the first Native studies initiative in any university in Canada. The program received a significant boost with grants of $204,000 from the Donner Canadian Foundation and $15,000 from the Ontario government for development.

Transformation: The Department of Native Studies

In a desire to effect a broader and multidisciplinary (or interdisciplinary) exploration of Aboriginal issues, and following much debate and discussion about the constraints imposed by the anthropological framework and its ideological implications, the Indian–Eskimo Studies Program was transformed into the Department of Native Studies in 1972. It was a full university department with three tenured faculty members and offered a general (i.e., three-year) bachelor of arts degree in Native studies.

From the outset the department was designed to meet the educational needs of both Aboriginal and non-Aboriginal students. The number of courses grew to sixteen, with enrollment totaling 619 students by 1975. Of the six full-time departmental faculty, five were Aboriginal. Courses in the study of Aboriginal peoples were developed in the areas of art and literature, law, education, urbanization, Ojibway culture, Ojibway language, community development, Aboriginal cultures in Canada, history, politics, and identity. All but two of the courses were taught by Native studies faculty. These two—Aboriginal literature and Aboriginal art— were cross-listed courses offered by faculty of other departments.

In 1972 a five-year plan was developed to set the educational philosophy for the department; it remains in force to this day. The department was to be built upon three interrelated pillars: academic, cultural, and applied. The academic aspect followed the traditional methods of Western scholarly teaching and research. The courses were to reflect the situation of Aboriginal peoples in Canada in a wide variety of areas. They were to provide students with solid intellectual skills of analysis and interpretation as well as prepare them for careers in the Aboriginal community.

The cultural aspect of the department entailed a substantial departure from conventional university norms. The department made the assumption that, in order to help students understand Aboriginal ways of life and thought, it needed to go beyond the traditional university focus on the development of intellectual understanding. The experience the department wanted to offer students was a holistic one—that is, it was to include the mental, physical, emotional, and spiritual aspects of culture as they are integrated into Aboriginal life. The primary cultures that were focused on were those of the two main groups in our territory, Ojibway and Iroquois, although efforts were made to teach about other Aboriginal peoples in Canada, and later an international indigenous peoples component was added with the Native Studies Year Abroad Program.

The department also believed that the cultural aspect should be included in the pedagogy and content of the courses rather than relegated exclusively to extracurricular activities. Thus, in 1973, the department instituted a practice of hiring Aboriginal Elders to teach language and culture courses. They were hired as tenure-track professors, the same as academically trained faculty. The case was made to the university that these Elders, through their skills, wisdom, and experience, possessed qualifications equivalent to those of other faculty. Eventually the department created tenure and faculty promotion criteria to recognize the traditional knowledge carried by the Elders. These criteria were accepted by the university's Committee on Academic Personnel and created a two-track approach to tenure: one based upon the usual academic performance criteria of teaching and research, and one based upon teaching and research in a traditional Aboriginal environment. Trent remains the only university in Canada that will grant tenure on Aboriginal knowledge criteria.

The integration of Aboriginal culture into the Department of Native Studies also entailed pedagogical implications. Some courses, for example, "Native Identity Development," incorporated experiential methods of teaching. This included workshops involving techniques of laboratory teaching associated with personal growth, such as role-playing, trust building, giving and receiving feedback, self-disclosure, and so forth, all related to exploring the individual's identity. The Medicine Wheel was often used as the basis of understanding culture, and Elders were brought in to provide teaching and counseling and to perform sweat lodge, pipe, sunrise, and other ceremonies. Faculty and students were also encouraged to work with Elders in their own territories to develop their own cultural understandings, personal growth, and identity.

Finally, the applied aspect of the department reflected the desire to provide an educational experience that involved students directly in Aboriginal community concerns. A practicum field component was developed in which students would work or carry out research in Aboriginal communities or organizations for a period of time for course credit. Placements were conducted in a variety of settings, including prisons; friendship centers; treatment centers; schools; political organizations; newspaper, television, and film production organizations; environmental organizations; and social service agencies. Students and faculty also became involved in numerous social, political, and environment issues affecting Aboriginal peoples, such as the James Bay hydro-power protests, the mercury pollution of the English river system, the MacKenzie River pipeline hearings, and the Temagame land-claim protests.

Department Structure

Trent University started out as, and remains, a single-faculty university with a dean of Arts and Science to whom department chairs report. The Department of Native Studies, originally headed by one person, is now headed by two chairs. The first is a chair who reports to the dean of Arts and Science and who is also a member of the faculty board, an advisory council to the dean consisting of all the chairs and program heads.

The second is a graduate chair, who reports to the dean of Graduate Studies and Research. The Native studies graduate chair supervises the Aboriginal studies cluster of the Frost Centre for Canadian Studies and Native Studies and is the administrative director of the Native studies Ph.D. program. There is also a supervisor of studies for the Native studies Ph.D. program. This individual, who must be Aboriginal, is responsible for ensuring that students' courses of study include appropriate cultural content and pedagogies. The graduate chair is a member of the Trent Committee on Graduate Studies, which advises the dean of Graduate Studies and Research.

The Department of Native Studies has four standing committees to manage its affairs: administration and finance, student relations, undergraduate studies, and graduate studies. The committees make recommendations to the Departmental Program Committee. Each standing committee consists of at least two faculty members and two students: one undergraduate, one graduate. Staff serve as consultants to the committees. Decisions are made using consensus, avoiding votes whenever possible. The Departmental Program Committee consists of the entire faculty and staff of the department and student representatives. Undergraduate students are represented through the Trent University Native Association, and graduate students are represented through the Graduate Student Association.

Native studies at Trent is an interdisciplinary program. The department has faculty with backgrounds in political studies, critical theory, sociology, history, Aboriginal languages, traditional knowledge, community development, business administration, and environmental and resource studies. The core faculty is complemented by faculty in other departments and programs who have an interest in Aboriginal affairs and issues: economics, administrative studies, politics, women's studies, cultural studies, anthropology, history, environmental and resource studies, and English.

We try to use the principles of the Medicine Wheel (holism and balance) as an organizing metaphor for guiding and organizing our work. Using the idea of holism, we believe that examination of a phenomenon requires looking at it from as many different perspectives as we can. Using the idea of balance, we strive for an intellectual equanimity in our inquiry, not letting any particular discipline dominate. This is proving to be a difficult challenge, however, because the well-established methods of inquiry established by the social sciences are contrary to the relatively new methods of inquiry surrounding indigenous knowledge.

Faculty Complement

The Department of Native Studies has grown from three to eight full-time tenured faculty members and engages approximately eight people on a part-time basis to teach individual courses each year. A varying number of conjunct faculty members are also engaged. The preference is for hiring Aboriginal scholars. It is expected that one full-time faculty complement be added over the next three years. The average department size at Trent University ranges from seven to nine full-time faculty.

The Department of Native Studies currently offers about twenty-five undergraduate courses per year, one master's course per year, and, since 1999, three doctoral courses per year. There are approximately 350 students enrolled as Native studies majors and Native studies joint majors.

Staff Complement

In addition to the faculty complement, there is an administrative staff complement of four members who assist in the carrying out of the academic mission of the department: an academic programs coordinator who heads up the staff and who is responsible for the day-to-day operations of the department, a departmental secretary who provides clerical and administrative assistance to faculty members, a half-time finance officer who maintains the finances and deals with the myriad details relating to the various funding sources, and a half-time graduate secretary who assists the graduate chair in administering the department's graduate programs. There are also three academic support staff who work with students: a Traditional Person in Residence culture adviser, an Aboriginal counselor who provides personal counseling to students, and an academic skills coordinator who helps students improve the skills they need to succeed at academic studies.

Department Vision

Native studies is an interdisciplinary exploration and analysis of the Aboriginal experience. The Aboriginal experience is conceived of in broad and complex terms encompassing diverse geographical experiences (reserve, rural, urban), differing cultural experiences (Anishnawbe, Haudenosaunee, Mikmaq, Haida, etc.), differing relationships to the state (Indian, Inuit, Métis, status, nonstatus, treaty), and differing cultural orientations (traditionalist, modernist), among many other issues. Native studies assists Aboriginal people in better understanding themselves, as well as assisting non-Aboriginal people in better understanding Aboriginal experiences.

Our pedagogy is conceived of in broad Freirian terms, comprising the usual classroom lectures and discussions as well as interactions with traditional Aboriginal people, interaction with Elders who bring Aboriginal knowledge and thought, and exploration of customs, rituals, and language. We try as much as possible in our teaching to provide a holistic learning environment, engaging the body, mind, spirit, and emotions, again in accordance with the principles of the Medicine Wheel. We also try to ensure that the learning remains grounded firmly in contemporary Aboriginal realities. Students have opportunities to study and work with local Aboriginal organizations and to learn through a guided process of reflective experience and reading.

Intellectual inquiry is conceived of in broad terms incorporating both basic and applied research. It may encompass traditional social studies methods such as quantitative and qualitative approaches, archival historical methods, and oral historical methods, among others, as well as participation in traditional Aboriginal spiritual activities by traditional peoples, as these methods can be conceived of as ways of increasing one's knowledge. There is a preference for community-based approaches. Scholarly communication involves a wide range of activities such as community workshops, oral presentations at Aboriginal conferences, and advising Aboriginal organizations and communities, in addition to the usual written papers and books.

In response to student desire to apply their skills and knowledge to an Aboriginal community, a practicum program was designed and introduced in 1973. Those students who so desired could receive instruction in community service and research, and, under the guidance of a field placement supervisor, could work with an Aboriginal organization.

In an effort to increase the number of Aboriginal students studying at the university, the department established a diploma program in Native studies in 1975. Aboriginal students who were unsure whether they wanted to commit to the three-year undergraduate degree or who did not meet the usual admission requirements of the university could take 7.5 course credits over two years and receive a Trent Diploma in Native studies. Students enrolled in the program attended a six-week (now three-week) summer session that focused on improving academic skills and socializing students into the academic milieu, and also took a noncredit course in academic communications in their first year.

The diploma program has proven to be remarkably successful and has brought into the university many students who otherwise would not have attended. About 85 percent of the students in the program have continued on to pursue their undergraduate degrees. One of the unique features of the program is the transferability of credits earned. The courses are regular university courses and hence form a solid base of credits if students transfer to the degree program upon completion of the diploma program.

In 1978 the Department of Native Studies expanded its offerings to include a four-year honors program. The curriculum was also reviewed and a decision made to ensure that students acquired an introductory exposure to and understanding of an Aboriginal culture, either through the study of an Aboriginal language or through courses on culture and community offered in English. Faculty believed that an understanding of the Aboriginal experience would be impossible without first-hand experience of either an Aboriginal language or Aboriginal cultural practices.

Bringing Traditional
Aboriginal People into the Department

During the late 1970s, in accordance with its goal of ensuring that students learned aspects of traditional Aboriginal culture from those who knew it best—Elders—the Department of Native Studies expressed a desire to bring into the university as faculty members and instructors Aboriginal Elders who possessed high levels of knowledge of either Ojibway or Iroquoian traditional rites, rituals, customs, and language. While these people were extremely learned, they did not possess advanced university degrees, the usual qualification for being a faculty member at a Canadian university.

In 1978, Trent University hired two Aboriginal people who had a high degree of traditional knowledge to teach within the program: a traditional Ojibway Elder and a condoled Cayuga chief of the Iroquois Confederacy. Both taught language courses as well as courses that explained and discussed their cultures. It became a formal program requirement that students who wanted a degree in Native studies would have to take a course in one of the two languages or in one of the two cultures. We simply believed that it was necessary for a student to gain an understanding of the philosophical underpinnings of an Aboriginal culture in order to graduate.

At that time, the department members convinced the Committee on Academic Personnel to agree to a set of criteria for the granting of tenure to traditional Aboriginal people. This was a remarkable achievement, and we are still the only university in Canada with a tenure policy for this group of people. The department members were able to convince a group of conventionally educated academics that traditional Aboriginal knowledge was to be valued and, more importantly, that its acquisition could somehow be demonstrated and measured.

In the case of the Ojibway Midewin society, we were able to argue that their knowledge level 1 was equivalent to a bachelor of arts, levels 2 and 3 equivalent to a master of arts, and level 4 a doctoral degree. In the case of the Iroquoian chiefs, we were able to demonstrate that knowledge of the Great Law, the various ceremonies and teachings of the longhouse, and so forth, was equivalent to a doctorate. This is how the university equates levels of traditional knowledge to the achievement of specific degrees of academic knowledge in a particular field.

Trent University has maintained its commitment to the hiring of traditional Aboriginal people within the Department of Native Studies. We currently have four people who have traditional Aboriginal credentials; two of them are tenured, and two are contract faculty. This commitment has made Native studies one of the most interesting programs at the university. It has forced us to ground our work in the Aboriginal community in a way that would not have been possible without these traditional Aboriginal people. Their presence in our midst lends us a credibility and legitimacy that would have been hard to achieve otherwise.

Program Expansion

In 1985 the Department of Native Studies joined the Frost Centre for Canadian Heritage and Development Studies (the site for graduate studies and research in the humanities and social sciences at Trent and renamed in 1999 the Frost Centre for Canadian Studies and Native Studies) and created an Aboriginal studies cluster within its master of arts program. Since that time, approximately half of the theses undertaken by graduate students have been focused on Aboriginal issues and topics. The cluster consists of faculty and researchers from a variety of departments beyond Native studies: history, cultural studies, comparative development studies, psychology, economics, anthropology, English, and politics.

The Native Management and
Economic Development Program

In 1988, again in response to community desire, the Department of Native Studies embarked on a new undergraduate program: the Native Management and Economic Development (NMED) program, a joint enterprise with the administrative studies program. It is designed to educate individuals who are interested in working with or within Aboriginal communities on their development. The program combines administrative studies courses in organization and management, Native studies courses in development, and joint courses in areas where Aboriginal culture affects management the greatest. The program received grants totalling $500,000 from the Donner Canadian Foundation and the federal government's Native Economic Development Fund.

The Native Management and Economic Development venture was also the first effort at formally involving representatives of local Aboriginal communities in academic decisionmaking at the university. Previously the involvement had been highly informal. The Department of Native Studies established the Council of Directors (COD) for the NMED program to steer the program's development and monitor its operations to ensure that it remained relevant to the needs of Aboriginal peoples, as well as to manage the external resources that were brought to start it. The COD consisted of an equal number of Trent administrators and faculty, and Aboriginal community representatives. In the view of Trent, it was an advisory body that would make recommendations to the academic decisionmaking bodies. In the view of Aboriginal community representatives, the COD was itself a decisionmaking body.

Its early meetings were characterized by a high degree of distrust and miscommunication, as each group was unsure of the motives of the other. Trent administrators and faculty were certain that their academic freedom was being infringed upon; Aboriginal community representatives were convinced that the university would take their money and do what it wanted. It took many meetings to break down the walls and develop a sense of joint purpose.

The Aboriginal Education Council

Trent transformed the Council of Directors into the Aboriginal Education Council (AEC) in 1992. The AEC, which consists of an equal number of senior university administrators and faculty, and Aboriginal community representatives, has a broad mandate to steer the university's policies and programs as they relate to Aboriginal peoples. The AEC is a university-wide body whose decisions and recommendations are forwarded to the two main decisionmaking bodies within the university: the senate and the board of governors. The AEC is cochaired by a member of the university and a representative of the local Aboriginal community.

We should note that there was an external impetus to this change. Trent's experience with academic power sharing proved over time to be positive and worthwhile and came to the attention of the Ontario Ministry on Colleges and Universities. The ministry was searching for ways to improve the responsiveness of Ontario's community colleges and universities to Aboriginal peoples' educational needs, and it adopted the Trent model as the central part of its strategy.

The AEC conceives of its relationship with the university as a partnership in which both sides bring to the table ideas, needs, concerns, issues, and resources relating to the role, mandate, and programming of the university as it relates to Aboriginal peoples. From the university side, the AEC's representatives are senior administrators: the president and vice chancellor; the vice president, academic; and a representative of the board of governors. From the Aboriginal community side, the representatives are local Aboriginal leaders. Students, both Aboriginal and non-Aboriginal, are also represented. The AEC meets three times a year. When the AEC is not in session, a small executive committee assumes its responsibilities.

In 1995 the AEC proposed a broad, university-wide Aboriginal action plan for the role of the university in Aboriginal education and in recruitment, retention, and programming for Aboriginal peoples. This plan, officially approved by the university senate, has formed the basis of university actions since then.

Doctoral Studies

Sensing a need both to advance the discipline of Native studies and to educate students at an advanced level in preparation for possible academic careers, discussions began in 1995 within the Department of Native Studies and the AEC about the need for doctoral-level studies. In April 1997 the university senate approved the establishment of a Native studies doctoral program at Trent; it became the first Native studies Ph.D. program in Canada and only the second in North America. In June 1998 the Ontario Committee on Graduate Studies approved the program and allowed it to admit students. The first group of students started their studies in September 1999.

The new Native studies doctoral program was an initiative of one of the cochairs of the AEC. It was developed under the guidance of a committee of faculty from Trent and other universities and representatives of the AEC. The program is intended to bring together, at a graduate level, Aboriginal and non-Aboriginal students to study at an advanced level the historical, cultural, and contemporary situation of Aboriginal and Indigenous peoples.

The doctoral program is interdisciplinary in nature and is based upon the integration of Indigenous and Western academic knowledge. It combines traditional academic, cultural, and experiential pedagogies through a partnership between the university and Aboriginal communities. Aboriginal scholars, including Aboriginal Elders, are central to the program.

The Native studies doctoral program was developed in partnership with the Aboriginal community through the Native Studies Ph.D. Council. The council, which has the responsibility for guiding, directing, and steering the program, consists of Elders from Aboriginal communities, Aboriginal and non-Aboriginal academics from a variety of disciplines, and graduate students. It continues the practice of partnership formalized with the COD program and the NMED program a decade and a half ago.

Into the Field

Extending the learning environment beyond the classroom has always been an important activity for Native studies. Students are encouraged to become involved in Aboriginal communities in both informal and formal ways. The Department of Native Studies encourages students to engage in practice with local Aboriginal organizations and to receive credit for this experience.

The department has also offered courses off campus in Aboriginal communities, for example, in Winneway in northern Quebec; in Six Nations of the Grand River in southern Ontario; in Tyendenaiga, a local Mohawk community; in downtown Toronto in collaboration with the local friendship center; and in Moose Factory, a Cree community near James Bay.

On a larger scale, the department offers three off-campus activities that have proven to be highly successful for students: a Thailand Year Abroad Program, which provides students with an opportunity to work with the Hill Tribes people of northern Thailand; the Pangniurtung Bush School on Baffin Island in Nanavut, which focuses on understanding Inuit culture and landscape; and the Mohawk Valley Field School in upstate New York, which focuses on traditional Iroquoian culture, language, and longhouse spirituality. Approximately twenty students enroll in each of these off-campus academic activities. The Thailand Year Abroad Program is a full-academic-year activity.

Members of the AEC and the Department of Native Studies sensed an opportunity for another collaborative effort at the university, this time with the Environmental and Resource Studies Program. The resulting Indigenous Environmental Studies Program started in the fall of 2000. The program of study consists of courses in Native studies and environmental resource studies coupled with practicum assignments in the upper years of study. It was developed in response to requests from the AEC.

Reflections on the Development of Native Studies

Native studies at Trent has been in development for thirty years. It has evolved from a small program located within the Department of Anthropology to a full university department in its own right, offering a full range of degree programs. It has evolved from a single disciplinary focus to a multidisciplinary focus, encompassing most of the social sciences and humanities at Trent and soon, some of the natural sciences. This development has required tremendous effort on the part of many people and has also entailed considerable risk for a small university in starting a new discipline. That risk appears to have paid off.

The creation of an academic program and a departmental structure within an existing university engenders unique challenges for all concerned, especially for those who desire to bring something as different and unknown as "Indigenous knowledge" into the university. Native studies has always been a unique program at Trent University and has endeavored to maintain its uniqueness. This uniqueness has been based upon the attempt to create within the university a community that is reflective and supportive of Aboriginal ideals of community. This means bringing together a group of people who respect one another, who are willing to debate but unwilling to see that debate turn ad hominem, who challenge the status quo through their scholarly activities, and who are willing to accept pluralism as the basic premise of society. Native studies is also unique in its desire to balance the number of Aboriginal and non-Aboriginal faculty, believing that dialogue between the two groups in society is important for social change. Faculty members have had to become highly skilled university politicians adept at promoting and advancing what has become the dual mission of the department: to further the discipline of Native studies as a whole through highly innovative programs of inquiry, both applied and basic, and to support the development of Aboriginal peoples through advocacy, research, and teaching.

At times, the relationship between Native studies and the rest of the university is reflective of the mainstream relationship between Aboriginal peoples and mainstream society: two solitudes who are somewhat suspicious of each other, with each wishing that the other could be more like itself. University administrators want Native studies to be like other disciplines and departments, while Native studies desires recognition of its differences and supportive action to nurture those differences. One of the unique features at Trent, however, has been a desire to break down the walls between the solitudes. Native studies could not have survived and grown at Trent without the support of the many people who devoted significant portions of their research, writing, and teaching time to Aboriginal issues. The development of friends in high places helped immensely in creating and maintaining a place for Native studies.

Native studies has two primary constituencies: an academic constituency and a community constituency. Balancing the needs and demands of the two makes for a difficult challenge. One is forced always to confront the utility and relevance of one's own work using the differing values of these two constituencies. The academic constituency was initially suspicious of the discipline itself, as it often is of new initiatives, wondering about its goals, its theoretical frameworks for inquiry, wondering about academic standards for its courses and programs, raising questions about the content and construction of Aboriginal/Indigenous knowledge, and taking its time in accepting this new interdisciplinary program as one of its own, much the same way as it has done with other new interdisciplinary studies programs. Over its thirty-year life, however, Native studies has garnered a great deal of respect for the work it does, and has become an important and valued resource at Trent.

Most Native studies programs at other universities are also young, usually less than twenty years old, and it has been hard to establish new Native studies programs in Canada. The traditional disciplines have been reluctant to move aside to create room for a Native studies program, seeing it as an interloper having little if any intellectual rigor. At the same time, declining public financial support for universities in general has made it difficult at times to garner the necessary resources to develop fully the three pillars of a Native studies program. It is a constant struggle within a competitive environment to obtain sufficient resources to do what needs to be done and to mount quality programs.

Trent's experience in the establishment of a Native studies program and department has not been without challenge and debate within the university. The singular advantage that Trent's Native studies program has enjoyed is its founding early on in the establishment of the university (within its first five years). This early action has provided the department with a foundation of resources and a place within the university's decisionmaking and resource-allocating structures and processes. The singular disadvantage is that the ability of the program to raise outside funding for its activities causes some difficulty in obtaining and maintaining a level of university financial resource commitment consistent with student enrollment and community programming requirements. Yet despite the financial turmoil that the university experienced, it has consistently and constantly provided a level of support for Native studies that is enabling rather than disabling.

The Department of Native Studies has also maintained a high level of community support because of its cultural focus. It was one of the first in Canada to act upon the desire for a cultural focus for its programs. The incorporation of traditional Aboriginal Elders who taught both language and culture helped the university to remain at the forefront of the cultural developments that were under way in Ontario in the 1970s and 1980s. Students who attended the university in the early years of Native studies found a community that was very supportive of their cultural aspirations and faculty who acted as advocates and supporters of their own desire to study their own cultures and languages. One of the early debates was whether or not some Aboriginal traditions should be taught in the university. Indeed, the early Elders who participated in the academic programming were initially criticized by their own communities. This continues to be debated within some quarters.

Around the core of Native studies, we have begun to see the establishment of a series of programs in specific areas: teaching, health, economic development, management, environment and resource studies, language, law, journalism, fine arts, and literature, to name a few. These programs attempt to build upon the core knowledge of Native studies and offer something that is more relevant to Aboriginal peoples and, as we like to say in Canada, more culturally appropriate. These developments are important and necessary, but they bring to the forefront the importance of the need for more attention to the question of Indigenous knowledge/thought. As these programs continue, we see more and more questions about Aboriginal perspectives and their definition. What does it mean to talk about politics from an Aboriginal perspective, or about economic development from an Aboriginal perspective, or about health from an Aboriginal perspective? There is an urgent need to think through Aboriginal theoretical perspectives on health, politics, development, and the whole range of subjects and then use this knowledge as the basis for informed and thoughtful critique, discussion, and action.

There are eleven Native studies programs in Canada. The faculty in these programs is generally a mixture of Aboriginal and non-Aboriginal people. Most programs strive to have a balance of both. Within the Aboriginal faculty, these people are generally reflective of the cultures within the area. For example, in the Atlantic provinces, Mikmaq; in Quebec, Cree; in Ontario, Iroquoian and Ojibway; in the West, Cree; and on the West Coast, various Pacific Northwest Nations. Maintaining a cultural balance then involves a number of different dimensions: Aboriginal and non-Aboriginal, as well as the dimensions reflected by cultural groups within the Aboriginal community.

The Aboriginal community raises questions about the nature of the Native studies enterprise, wondering what its motives are and how it will use the knowledge that its members generate, trying to figure out if the discipline is friend or foe, asking about its relevance both to the contemporary labor market that their children will enter and to their cultural development agenda, questioning the background and character of those who teach their children and research their communities and experiences. A considerable amount of time needs to be invested and effort made to ensure that the relationship that one develops with Aboriginal peoples and communities is respectful and does not duplicate the older type, based upon the anthropological model, that dominated until recently.

The job of the Native studies professor is a complex one. One cannot retreat to the relative safety and distance of the university, engaging in only teaching and research. The job has several dimensions: researcher, teacher, writer, speaker, advocate, and fund-raiser, all the usual aspects of the job for principal professors in other programs. The complexity is that it is carried out in two worlds and in front of two audiences, each of whom is asking a different set of questions about its worth.

Funding for Trent's Native studies operations is provided from two sources. The first and smallest part consists of the departmental operating fund that is provided to each department based upon its size and programming needs. This funding amounts to approximately $7,000 per year. In addition, the university provides resources for an academic programs coordinator and a departmental secretary.

The Department of Native Studies has been highly successful at raising money for programs, either from private donors or from government sources. This amounts to approximately $400,000 per year and far outstrips the resources provided from the university's operating budget. When we succeed in bringing in huge quantities of resources to fund our own programs, our colleagues then look at us with envy and question whether we should be getting as much as we do from the university's operating budget. It takes consistent effort to convince others of the additional costs of the Native studies programs.

In Canada, there are discussions under way concerning the establishment of an Aboriginal Peoples' University. The relationship of this new institution to existing universities will need to be worked out. It will be interesting to see the shape of Native studies within this university if it is established. If such a program exists, will they call it Native studies? Native studies is an aspect of a liberal arts education. It creates a critical consciousness rather than a set of concrete applied skills demanded by the contemporary labor market. One of the challenges facing Native studies departments will be balancing applied and critical skills.

There have also been significant attempts across the country to consult Aboriginal peoples about the academic mission of Native studies programs, and some power sharing over the nature and shape of these programs is beginning to take place. These last efforts have been difficult, as universities do not like to share any power over academic programs. In Ontario, the government in effect bribed the universities into offering Aboriginal peoples more control. To those universities that were willing to establish Aboriginal Education Councils with real powers, the government offered increased operating grants. In this day and age of diminished public support for universities, this was a real incentive. It has taken about five years of operations for these councils to convince the universities that the sky was not falling.

These developments could be seen as stemming from the Canadian government's adoption of a policy of Indian control over Indian education in 1973. The initial effort was at the primary and secondary school levels and only recently has moved to the postsecondary level. It seems like a logical next step, and an appropriate one to take at this time. Yet it is unclear how the policy of Indian control over Indian education can be applied to universities that pride themselves on their independence from political guidance and control.

The issue of power sharing, of giving Aboriginal peoples an influence over the shape and content of programs directed at Aboriginal peoples, proved to be a controversial one. Many were concerned about academic freedom. Some members of the university senate were convinced that Trent's Aboriginal Education Council was going to have the authority to tell them what to teach. One of the most interesting discussions we had was based upon a situation that arose in an anthropology class. The professor wanted to teach the Bering Strait theory. He wondered if he would be allowed to teach it, given the opposition to it by many Aboriginal peoples. The council discussed it and decided that it would not interfere with the course offerings or classroom behavior of individual professors. The council simply asked that other theories and views be presented as well. The expected challenge to academic freedom did not occur.

In the university senate, during the debate about the establishment of the Aboriginal Education Council, one of the members said to the university vice president: "You are asking us to give some of our power to this Council. The Co-Chair of the Council has said that if the Council has power, it will use it. I find this situation untenable." The vice president responded: "We are entering into a partnership. If it is to be a real partnership, then both parties will have power and both parties can use it. We are interested in a real partnership."[1] That is indeed the challenge: What is a real partnership, and how does one make it work?

Students in Native studies encounter an intense, personally challenging world unlike any other that they encounter in the university. Students who are not of Aboriginal origin find their assumptions about Aboriginal peoples constantly challenged and so find that their own worlds are challenged as well. In many cases, they find a sense of community that is not present in other academic departments. Students of Aboriginal origin also find their experience challenging, as they find that their assumptions about their world, about themselves, and about non-Aboriginal peoples are simultaneously challenged and reinforced. Both groups learn to engage in a constructive dialogue after many difficult starts.

The student experience illuminates one of the fundamental dilemmas of the Native studies enterprise. As a university, we are challenged with the twin tasks of passing on human knowledge gained from the past while challenging that knowledge and creating new knowledge for a better understanding of the human experience. When we apply this idea to Native studies and to the current cultural development agenda of Aboriginal peoples, which admittedly is also a political agenda, we can see that, in one sense, we have to assist in the transmission of Aboriginal cultural knowledge and simultaneously challenge it. It creates a wonderfully complex world, but one that needs to be discussed on a regular basis to ensure that one gets the balance right. For it is balance that is part of the traditional Aboriginal worldview.

The issues that confront Native studies evolve from its dual mandate. One set of issues surrounds the web of relationships that the department exists within and focuses on how to maintain that web in a respectful fashion. The second set of issues surrounds the nature, methods, and ends of Native studies and focuses on the future direction of the discipline itself. Taken together, these issues are:

1. How to maintain a respectful relationship with Aboriginal communities who wish students to receive specific skills appropriate for high-quality participation in the labor market while still incorporating a critical dimension into the discipline?
2. How to balance the need for academic freedom (of inquiry and expression) with the desire of Aboriginal communities for increased control over the process and content of education?
3. How to create and maintain a dialogue between Aboriginal and non-Aboriginal faculty over issues such as voice, power, and identity?
4. How to assist Aboriginal students in succeeding and achieving at the university?
5. How to move the discipline forward to incorporate what has become known as Indigenous knowledge, as requested by many Aboriginal peoples?

Extending the Rafters: The Future of the Discipline

A university can play a vital role within the Aboriginal community. It can make a significant contribution to the reestablishment of a place of pride and dignity for Aboriginal people on this continent. In general, one of the fundamental roles of a university is to help us understand ourselves—that is, to explain us to ourselves, to help us understand our place within the universe, to generate knowledge about ourselves and our world. In this role, a university also has a responsibility to pass on the knowledge of previous generations to a new generation, who can then build upon it or discard it, as it must at times. Universities then are important institutions for cultural development. It is here in the relative safety of the university walls that individuals can challenge the accepted wisdom and explore ideas that may not be well accepted outside this place.

Much of the earlier work in Native studies is what we would call "Indianism," with respect to Edward Said.[2] By this, we mean that Native studies is an explanation of the Aboriginal world through non-Aboriginal eyes and words, or an explanation of how Aboriginal peoples came to occupy this place on the margins of North American society. This intellectual project is a worthwhile and important one. We believe that understanding how this marginalization occurred is important and critical to helping ensure that it doesn't happen again.

We reviewed the last decade of the *Canadian Journal of Native Studies* to see what has been published. In our view, the journal indicates the thinking of the leaders of the discipline and reflects the work of members thinking, researching, and writing in this discipline. Most of the articles we saw in our review were attempts by outsiders to explain Aboriginal peoples or to understand a certain aspect of Aboriginal society or culture. Here are a few samples:

1985: "The Fur Trade and Early Capitalist Development in British Columbia: North American Indian Nationalism and the Decline of Sacred Authenticity"

1986: "Faces and Interfaces of Indian Self-Government"

1987: "The Construction of Dependency: The Case of the Grand Rapids Hydro Project"

1988: "Economic Development and Innu Settlement: The Establishment of Sheshatshit"

1991: "Profile of Aboriginal Youth in a Community Drug Program"

1992: "Attitudes towards Aboriginal Self-Government: The Influence of Knowledge, and Cultural and Economic Security"

1994: "Dances with Affirmative Action: Aboriginal Canadians and Affirmative Action"

1996: "Alternative Perspectives on the Over-representation of Native Peoples in Canadian Correctional Institutions: The Case Study of Alberta"[3]

These are excellent articles. They increase our understanding of Aboriginal situations and Aboriginal identities. To some extent, however, they all are examples of Indianism. They attempt to explain Aboriginal peoples. But for the most part, they are not the voices of Aboriginal peoples or explanations posited using Aboriginal ideas.

We need, however, to move beyond these explanations and this type of inquiry. This type of inquiry, while helpful in many respects, does not always help us develop communities based upon Aboriginal ideas. And that is what we hear people say they want to do. They want to use Aboriginal ideas as the basis for Aboriginal communities. This requires a new intellectual project to be added to the discipline. Using a metaphor of Iroquoian people, we need to extend the rafters. If universities are going to be relevant to the rebirth that is commonly assumed to be under way, then this new intellectual project must be based upon Indigenous knowledge.

What we need to do then is to create a place within the university for traditional Aboriginal knowledge. We must also then create a place for the methodology by which that knowledge is constructed or uncovered. Some of these methods are extra-reasonable—that is, they may involve activities such as dreams, fasts, and other ceremonials. They may also involve the expression of knowledge

through song, dance, art, and similar activities. For traditional Aboriginal knowledge, the accepted methods of expression may go beyond things such as written
essays and papers.

This also means that we must create a place within the university for traditional
Aboriginal people. The tradition within the university is that one teaches what one
is knowledgeable about, and that teaching is based upon one's own inquiry and its
findings. If we wish to bring traditional Aboriginal knowledge into the university,
then we must also bring in those who are competent to create it and who can also
evaluate the level of knowledge of others.

Creating a place for traditional Aboriginal knowledge within the university is
indeed a complex undertaking. It involves bringing in a body of knowledge, the
methods by which that knowledge is constructed, and those who can construct the
knowledge and who are in a position to transmit it through teaching. This is not
something that many universities are willing to do, because it involves the accreditation of those who have not undergone the usual initiation of graduate school.
Yet we could argue that the tests for a traditional Aboriginal researcher and teacher
are even more rigorous than those confronting a graduate student.

We also face discrimination about what can be brought into the university for
examination and analysis: given the complex, interwoven nature of Aboriginal
spirituality and knowledge, we are also confronted with the desire of the university to examine and know everything. Some traditional Aboriginal knowledge is sacred and open only to those who have properly prepared for it. What happens
when the unquenchable thirst of the university confronts a solid "No, I will not
reveal this"?

There is an intermediate position that is quite tenable, given the nature of the
university. We have started to talk of "Aboriginal thought" as a compromise and
as a way of trying to lend credence to the intellectual life of Aboriginal peoples.
By this we mean that we must begin an exploration of Aboriginal knowledge,
philosophies, ideas, concepts, notions, in order to develop them and make them
relevant to contemporary life. For example, if Iroquoian people are interested in
making the Great Law a central part of their contemporary life, we must develop
a body of Great Law scholars who think about the Great Law and its philosophic
underpinnings in contemporary terms. What type of social contract does the
Great Law envision? Can this contract be translated into contemporary terms?

We have been engaged in a debate at Trent about the establishment of a Ph.D.
program in Native studies. In 1997 the university senate approved the program as
an academic program of the university. It has taken twenty-seven years and much
effort to get here. At the heart of this program is this new intellectual project. It
had its beginnings about two decades ago with a fundamental programming decision that occurred in the early 1970s. That decision placed an exploration of

Aboriginal culture at the center of Native studies. At some point, it had to move into the thinking that resides within the culture.

One of the issues that we face in establishing this new program, and that is also beginning to emerge in our master's program as well as with our senior undergraduate students, is the issue of methods and knowledge construction. It surfaced most recently in a letter that a faculty member sent to the president of Trent. It says: "This is the challenge that we face: can we successfully incorporate some of the traditional forms of creating knowledge within the academy? Do we need to develop a new method of testing candidates? We need somehow to create new methods that permit us to somehow gain an understanding of the veracity of the knowledge that is created."[4]

The creation of methods is only one part of the emerging new paradigm. The second is the codification and development of what we have come to call "Aboriginal thought." If we are going to contribute to the renaissance that is occurring around us, then we must find some way to contribute through methods that go beyond looking at social or political phenomena such as urbanization, modernization, and integration. We must begin to play a role in advancing Aboriginal thought. What we mean is that we must somehow document Aboriginal thought in all its forms and help translate it into forms that people can read about, integrate into their own thinking, and then use as the basis for conducting their daily lives.

The project must also be more than documentation and translation. It must be a development project, in which we engage the ideas, think about them, expand them. In a sense, we need to develop our own philosophical conversation about our own ideas based upon our own worldviews. For example, in Canada we are in the midst of the development of a new set of institutions of self-government. There is much questioning about the role of government within Aboriginal communities. Much of that debate is occurring around Western ideas of government. Virtually none of the debate centers on traditional Aboriginal ideas of governments and their roles and responsibilities, as evidenced by our review of articles in the *Canadian Journal of Native Studies*. Perhaps it is too early in the development of our discipline to devote much time to this project. Perhaps the presence of the traditional Aboriginal people in our midst will spur us on.

The challenge before the university is to try to move to accommodate these traditional Aboriginal forms of knowledge creation. The challenge for Aboriginal people working within the university is to try to take these traditional methods and explore them in a way that is respectful and that contributes to their further development. We have made some headway, but there is still more to be done. We still need to develop a language that is mutually understandable. We need to find ways of bringing traditional Aboriginal knowledge-keepers into the university and treat them with respect while at the same time learning how to question them.

Notes

All dollar amounts stated in this chapter are in Canadian dollars.

1. Trent University Senate, February 1993.

2. Edward W. Said, *Orientalism* (New York: Pantheon, 1978).

3. See *Canadian Journal of Native Studies* 5, no. 1 (1985): 27–46; 6, no. 1 (1986): 43–62; 7, no. 1 (1987): 57–78; 8, no. 1 (1988): 1–25; 11, no. 1 (1991): 25–48; 12, no. 1 (1992): 75–93; 14, no. 1 (1994): 77–100; 16, no. 1 (1996): 15–36.

4. Fred Helleiner, Department of Geography, personal communication to Vice President, Academic, March 1997.

American Indian Studies at the University of Arizona[I] 5

JAY STAUSS, MARY JO TIPPECONNIC FOX, AND SHELLY LOWE

T HE GROWTH AND DEVELOPMENT of American Indian studies (AIS) at the University of Arizona (UA) has two separate but intertwined stories. One story is related to the UA land-grant mandate, the other to the multiple visions of UA Indian and non-Indian faculty, staff, and students, who have been committed to American Indian studies at UA for over three decades.

The land-grant story began with the placement, over one hundred years ago, of the UA in the heart of Indian Country in the Southwest. The Morrill Act, which passed Congress July 2, 1862, created one land-grant university in each state. This act enabled each university to obtain federal funds for its schools of agriculture and mines. What is now called the state of Arizona is home to twenty-one federally recognized Indian Tribes with a combined population of over 250,000. Twenty-five percent of the land in Arizona is held in trust for the Tribes. The land-grant mission, focusing on agriculture and serving the needs of rural people, ensured the intertwining of histories for both the UA and Indian Tribes in Arizona. The UA's Department of Anthropology built its national reputation as a top-ten department researching Indian archeology sites. The Department of Anthropology's focus was on using Indian informants to publish research in academic journals and presses. There was no concern for ensuring that Indian peoples or communities would benefit from the research. No programs were developed to help bring Indian students to the UA. No one stepped forward to advocate for an American Indian studies department. Perhaps, the beginning of American Indian studies would have been different if a department other than anthropology had taken the initiative, but in this early period Indians were clearly the property of anthropology and not any other department.

The other UA American Indian studies story began with the vision of Professor Edward P. Dozier, a Tewa from the Santa Clara Pueblo, in collaboration with faculty such as Edward Spicer in anthropology, and staff such as Emory Sekaquaptewa; Arlene Hobson, Indian studies adviser; and Gordon Krutz, coordinator of Indian programs. A Ford Foundation grant funded to the anthropology department in 1971 laid the foundation for the eventual development of AIS by the faculty, staff, and students, and for a gradual reversal of the pattern of exploitation of Indian Tribes and individuals that permeated the first eighty years of university–Tribal interaction. The major focus of the Ford grant was on hiring Indian faculty and staff as role models and increasing the number of Indian students at the UA. It has taken the past three decades to develop American Indian studies into a nationally recognized academic program. While the UA sits in the heart of Indian Country, its major focus has not been on serving Indian communities or Indian students. The university developed into a Research One higher education institution with world-class programs such as astronomy, optical sciences, and space and planetary sciences. Today the UA is a public, land-grant research university. It is a top-twenty research institution with an average student enrollment of 35,000 (7,000 graduate students). There are over 2,000 faculty and 6,000 staff at the UA. There are over 750 Indian students, about 160 of whom are graduate students. This chapter describes the history and growth of AIS within the UA, and also provides an analysis of this program's development as a case study for development of American Indian studies in other institutions of higher education.

The Land-Grant Story

As part of its land-grant tradition, the UA has, from the time it first admitted students, been involved in teaching, research, and service involving Indian Tribes and Indian peoples in Arizona. In 1893 the Arizona Territorial Legislature approved housing the Arizona State Museum (ASM) at the university. The mission of the ASM was to investigate and restore Indian sites, preserve and display cultural objects, and interpret these findings as part of the Indigenous historical past of Arizona. In 1915 the museum appointed Byron Cummings as director. Cummings became widely recognized for his work with Hopi and Navajo people in the interpretation of early Arizona Indian history.

In 1915, Andrew E. Douglas developed a new technique in tree-ring research called dendrochronology. Douglas's breakthrough made it possible to date Indian habitations. This technique greatly enhanced anthropologists' abilities to explain Tribal migrations. University explorations of Snaketown, an ancient Hohokam site located on the Gila River reservation, resulted in significant publications on an "ancient people called Hohokam." This project also led to major publications interpreting the history of an array of Arizona precontact life ways and relationships with Mexican Indian societies, and highlighted the development of sophisticated Indigenous irrigation systems particularly adapted to the Desert Southwest environment.

The College of Agriculture and Cooperative Extension, for over eight decades, worked with Arizona's Tribal communities through training and research in plant development, range management, and irrigation practices. Genetic research with selective cattle-breeding programs has involved several Tribal herds in Arizona. The development of arid land grasses provided cattle feed for Tribal herds.

The first Native American graduate from the UA was Christine Garcia (Tohono O'odham) in 1930. As a student she was involved in various student organizations, such as the Home Economics Club and the girls A Club, and also took part in the hockey and baseball teams. After graduation, Garcia taught home economics for several years at Bureau of Indian Affairs schools in Sacaton and Phoenix before venturing to New Mexico to teach at schools in various Pueblo communities. A caring and dedicated teacher, Christine continued serving and helping people even after retirement, through involvement in Head Start and the Elderly Medical Program. She died at the age of seventy-seven.

The Bureau of Applied Research and Anthropology (BARA) was founded in 1952 as the Bureau of Ethnic Research, within the anthropology department. Under its director, William Kelly, an anthropologist known for his research in social change and the application of anthropology in problem solving, BARA focused on American Indian societies.

In 1958, President Harvill appointed an Indian Advisory Committee (IAC) charged with leadership for university–Tribal relations. The IAC met regularly, but little evidence remains of the work accomplished. Certainly, no initiative was taken by this presidential committee to develop Indian programs on campus until a decade later, when an Indian professor took over as chair of the committee. Edward Spicer chaired the first committee and Edward Dozier, the first American Indian to earn a doctorate in anthropology in the United States, became chair in 1968.

The Lilly Foundation funded the IAC, and using these external funds the position of a part-time Indian student adviser was created in 1959. The first part-time Indian student adviser was Edward Parsee, who served in that capacity from 1959 to 1963. Parsee's successor, Vi Former, served from 1963 to 1969. Both were non-Native. Before then, Indian students were advised through the anthropology department. In 1968, Gordon Krutz, a non-Indian, was hired as coordinator of Indian programs to assist with university-wide program development. This created the Office of Indian Programs (OIP). The early focus of the OIP was to reach out to Indian Tribes in Arizona and help maintain good relations between the UA and Indian Tribal governments. The OIP was housed in the anthropology department. In 1969, Arlene Hobson, a non-Indian, was hired as the first full-time Indian student adviser and was housed in the Dean of Students office. At this time, this position was possibly the first of its kind in the United States. Hobson was instrumental in encouraging a network of American Indians both on and off campus, which eventually led to the development of an American Indian alumni group in 1984. In 1985 the first Native American was hired to fill the position. Joshua Mihesvah (Comanche) served until 1989. Vivian Juan (Tohono O'odham) followed from 1990 to 1992, Debiallison Nalwood (Navajo) served in the interim from 1993 to 1995, and Bruce Meyers (Chippewa-Cree) was hired in 1995.

In 1968 a proposal for the development of a formal American Indian studies academic program was begun by Professor Dozier. At the time, he was a member of the board of directors of the Ford Foundation. In 1969, Dozier was offered a position as chair of the Department of American Indian Studies at the University of Minnesota. Because of health concerns he declined the offer and remained in Tucson, where his advocacy for an American Indian studies program continued until his untimely death in 1971. In 1970, Professor Dozier became the first chair of the American Indian studies program.

Multiple Faculty, Staff, and Student Visions

Two months after Dozier's death, the University of Arizona received a five-year, $500,000 grant from the Ford Foundation to establish the AIS program. Emory Sekaquaptewa (Hopi) was selected to serve as chair of the AIS committee in 1971. Under the Ford grant, the university committed itself to expanding Indian faculty and staff; increasing library materials; increasing Indian and Indian-related publishing, including publishing on American Indian bibliographical materials; increasing scholarship aid to Indian students; improving recruitment with direct contact to high schools within a radius of 125 miles from Tucson; improving retention by expanding Indian student counseling services; providing special educational programs such as the Summer Workshop in Linguistics and Ethnohistory and the Arizona State Museum Educational Extension Program; and continuing its already well-established research and service programs through such offices as the Bureau of Ethnic Research (now BARA), the Cooperative Extension Service, and the Office of Indian Programs. In 1970 there were about 300 students who self-identified as American Indian. In addition, fifteen anthropology courses already existed that could be cross-listed with American Indian studies. The grant was for five years (at $100,000 a year), and the president of the university agreed to match this with over $700,000 of university money.

The Ford Foundation grant establishing AIS was administered by the Department of Anthropology in the College of Liberal Arts. The major way the university provided a match to the Ford grant was through the hiring of new American

Indian studies faculty. The grant paid 100 percent of a faculty member's salary in year one, then the department paid 20 percent in year two, 40 percent in year three, 60 percent in year four, and the entire salary in year five. Four departments from across the campus hired faculty under this grant, but anthropology also hired individuals as AIS faculty. By 1975 the anthropology department had four AIS faculty members, and the English, political science, and sociology departments each had one AIS faculty member. Of the seven original hires, only one, Jay Stauss (Jamestown Band S'Klallam), was American Indian. The other hires were Gerald Levy, Susan Phillips, Richard Diebold, Joyotpaul Chaudhuri, Larry Evers, and E. Adamson Hoebel. An undergraduate minor was developed by AIS, and Indian-related courses throughout the curriculum were expanded in this early phase of development of the AIS program. The Ford Foundation, though, terminated the grant.

The lack of Indian faculty hires and internal conflicts over the use of funds were instrumental in the discontinuance of the Ford Foundation grant. Questions and concerns were raised by both faculty and staff about the use of Ford Foundation resources, in particular, to benefit the Department of Anthropology and not American Indian studies. There was considerable scholarly work, service, and especially advice for Indian students going on outside the anthropology department. Indian students, in particular, were concerned that few Indian faculty role models were hired under this grant and none were hired in anthropology. The clash between the anthropology department's focus on producing scholarly articles and other faculty's interests in serving Indian communities and nurturing Indian students was paramount during this period. Ironically, some of the faculty eventually hired after the grant was terminated by Ford included Vine Deloria Jr. (Lakota), Tom Holm (Creek/Cherokee), N. Scott Momaday (Kiowa), and Ofelia Zepeda (Tohono O'odham).

Beginning in 1976, AIS, under its new chair, Jay Stauss, initiated a reorganization of the program aimed at developing "interests and intellectual skills for Indian and non-Indian students toward interpretation and appreciation of Indian life." The foremost goal of the program was reformulated to stress leadership training for undergraduate Native Americans. Then, in 1978, Vine Deloria Jr. was hired in the political science department and was affiliated with AIS and became its director.

Deloria Jr. envisioned the future of AIS in the graduate arena. He argued that what was needed to meet the needs of struggling Indian Nations and communities was a cadre of well-educated Indian graduate students. The heart of their graduate education, Deloria Jr. believed, should be federal Indian Policy. Deloria Jr. was also well aware of the failed promises of the 1971 Ford Foundation grant, which had focused its resources on undergraduate activities. Since he held a tenured professorship in political science, he persuaded his colleagues to create a concentration within the political science M.A. program to produce federal Indian Policy graduates. This program began in 1979 and laid the groundwork for the more broadly conceived, freestanding M.A. in American Indian studies, which was later approved. Deloria Jr.'s struggles to develop AIS graduate programs and the university's failure to provide support eventually played a major role in his leaving for Colorado. Deloria Jr.'s program, the first of its kind in the United States, was also funded with major support from the Ford Foundation.

Small Steps and Slow Growth

In 1982 the AIS program significantly broadened its teaching, research, and service mission within the university with the formal approval of an AIS interdisciplinary M.A. program. The AIS master's program was the first freestanding degree program of its kind in the United States. It coordinated from across the university core graduate-level courses required for a master's degree, and was housed in the dean's office of the College of Social and Behavioral Sciences (SBS). At this time, Robert Thomas (Cherokee), a well-respected Indian scholar, was hired as director of the program. Thomas was not granted tenure by anthropology, an effect symbolic of the continued clash between anthropology and American Indian studies, and his position had to be held in the dean's office. The first graduates under the political science M.A. program were Anna Lee Townsend (Shoshone-Bannock), 1981; Marlys Mae Duchene (Sioux-Sisseton), 1982; and David Eugene Wilkins (Lumbee), 1982. The first graduates under the American Indian studies M.A. program were Richard Martin Wheelock (Oneida), 1984; Karen B. Ziegelman (non-Indian), 1985; and Steve Andrew Pavlik (non-Indian), 1985. The number of graduates with an M.A. in American Indian studies began to accelerate by the mid-1990s. There were seventeen graduates in 1995, eighteen graduates in 1996, and nineteen graduates in 1997. As of 2001, the program has more than 160 graduates.

By 1984 a minor in American Indian studies at the Ph.D. level was approved by the graduate college. Curriculum development for the AIS program continued to demonstrate considerable growth and innovation throughout the 1980s as American Indian studies classes were designed and offered in such diverse areas as political science, history, literature, and languages. Whereas anthropology had the most courses in AIS during the 1970s, today Indian policy, law, and literature courses are the most prevalent feature of the curriculum.

In 1986, Ofelia Zepeda took over as director of AIS, replacing Emory Sekaquaptewa, who was serving as interim director after Robert Thomas resigned from the position. Zepeda, while on tenure-track as an assistant professor in linguistics, was half-time director of the program from 1988 to 1991. Under

Zepeda's leadership in 1986–1987, in a joint effort with the law college, a naturally respected Native American law professor, Robert A. Williams Jr., was recruited to the university and law courses were permanently cross-listed with AIS. In the academic year 1987–1988, course offerings were again expanded, including the new cross-listed law classes. AIS faculty members were significantly involved in university service at this time as academic advisers, committee members, and chairs. They also devoted significant amounts of time in public service to the Tucson Indian community and to Tribes and Indian peoples throughout the state. In 1991, when Zepeda returned to the linguistics faculty, Jay Stauss returned to AIS and was named interim director. He became permanent director in 1992.

The years that the master's degree was housed in SBS (1979–1994) were characterized by slow development and growth. AIS was in direct competition with a significant number of large and prestigious departments, such as anthropology, psychology, and sociology. University budget decisions were driven either by national prestige plus department size or by the teaching of large numbers of graduate or undergraduate students. AIS was a small, poorly funded program in a college loaded with powerful departments. Requests for additional resources from Stauss, Deloria Jr., Thomas, and Zepeda fell on deaf ears. The program had no college or university administrator who was a strong supporter or advocate.

Prior to 1991, AIS was operating with a half-time director, with 1.0 full-time equivalency assigned to the program, and with a core of committed faculty from across the university whose attachment to the program was based on courtesy appointments. There was a 1.0 staff line, $4,900 in operations, limited and variable support for graduate students from the graduate college, and a small amount of other competitive funding within SBS. The program was housed in four small, temporary offices borrowed from political science. About sixteen to twenty-five graduate students were enrolled in any given semester. The program had never undergone an academic program review (APR) since its inception as an interdisciplinary M.A. program in 1982. Academic program reviews are mandated by the Arizona Board of Regents (ABOR) for each academic program every seven years. It's a double-edged sword. A unit can gain some new resources or find that it is in deep trouble. AIS used the academic program review as an avenue to highlight need, which had never been met by the college. A self-study report was prepared and in May 1991 an internal review team report was issued. In April 1992 an external review team report was completed. As a result of the APR process and negotiations surrounding the offer of the permanent director's position to Stauss, who moved from an administrative position as associate vice president for affirmative action, AIS was provided a broad array of new resources. These included a permanent, full-time director (Stauss), three new faculty lines, retention of a vacant line in SBS, an increase in operations from $4,900 to $12,000, and a commitment to finding new space.

These new resources signaled an important milestone in the development of AIS. In 1992–1993, many of the APR goals began to unfold. Most significantly, the first draft of the Ph.D. proposal was completed, new brochures were developed and distributed, advising/mentoring policies were developed and implemented, and the M.A. degree was revised. A Strategic Plan was developed (the first ever). AIS goals included securing approval for a Ph.D. degree, finding financial support for AIS graduate students, investigating the feasibility of a baccalaureate degree, discussing the pros and cons of securing departmental status, hiring additional Indian faculty and staff, finding ways to meet Tribal education needs from across the state, and helping to provide services to Indian students from across the campus. In addition, in 1993 the university assessment team awarded AIS with an "exceeds criteria" appraisal in a university-wide internal evaluation of all university departments and programs—this during a period of fiscal restraint, and during an assessment that resulted in several academic programs being terminated.

Large Steps and Rapid Progress

In 1993–1994, a series of extraordinary milestones occurred in AIS. One of the most significant challenges a program faces is how to offer its core curriculum when it does not control faculty resources. Although AIS had the benefit of very dedicated faculty with courtesy appointments across the campus, the director's main job was to keep making the rounds with departments to ensure the continuity in curriculum. A strong recommendation from the APR external faculty review committee was that AIS be allowed to hire new faculty to alleviate the problem. The review committee recommended "a substantive program of enhancement of administration, curriculum, faculty, staff and infrastructure."

The review team's recommendations played a major role in decisions that central administrators made in subsequent years. The provost authorized the program to develop a core faculty through transfers and new hires by granting promotion and tenure authority. Three faculty transferred full time into AIS: Tom Holm from political science, Michelle Taigue from English, and Mary Jo Tippeconnic Fox from an administrative position as associate vice president of student affairs. Two other faculty were recruited for the fall, one as a full-time tenured associate professor (K. Tsianina Lomawaima) and one as a half-time assistant professor on tenure-track in linguistics (Mary Willie). Student enrollment doubled. New space was acquired in the Harvill Building.

A specific strategy AIS implemented at this time was the development of courses to meet general education requirements for undergraduate students. Although AIS is an interdisciplinary graduate program with no undergraduate degree, the faculty created several courses to help educate undergraduates. This effort resulted in permanent graduate teaching assistantships being assigned to AIS. These assistantships helped fund new and continuing graduate students. The student credit hours generated from general education courses also helped AIS when negotiating with the central administration in each new budget cycle.

By 1994–1995, AIS became American Indian Studies Programs (AISP), moved from SBS to the graduate college, doubled its graduate student body from about twenty-five to fifty students a year, revised the Ph.D. proposal, and began negotiations to incorporate the Office of Indian Programs into the unit. Outreach and community development activities increased, and two new undergraduate courses were developed. In 1994 the Office of Indian Programs merged with AISP to provide for more efficient delivery of educational, economic, and community development services to American Indian Tribes in Arizona. The office assists American Indians in obtaining educational opportunities; provides technical assistance and resource identification; assists with self-determination efforts; and helps sponsor legal research and assistance to American Indian Tribes, organizations, and individuals. These activities provided a means for fulfilling the university's commitment to providing service activities to American Indians located in Arizona under the land-grant mandate.

Indian studies AISP committed significant staff funding to help hire a full-time director for the Indian Language Development Institute. This nationally recognized program provided a vital link for AISP students to the crucial area of language maintenance.

In 1996–1997 the Ph.D. proposal passed the Graduate Council. The doctoral program is an interdisciplinary program with the goal of preparing students to conduct basic and applied scholarly research from a cross-cultural perspective; develop innovative theories, methodologies, and research tools appropriate for and useful to sovereign Tribes; and train candidates to assume leadership and policy-making roles in higher education, Tribal communities, the state, and the United States. Students are required to include three of the four concentrations within their program of study: American Indian law and policy, American Indian languages and literature, American Indian societies and cultures, and American Indian education. After this broad interdisciplinary foundation, candidates specialize in research related to one of the concentrations. In addition, a faculty recruitment was under way, which resulted in the hiring of Eileen Luna as a full-time, tenure-track assistant professor specializing in American Indian law and policy.

A successful National Indian Education Association (NIEA) conference was held in Tucson with significant AISP faculty and staff leadership. The M.A. program was again revised to require more core courses, and financial aid/application procedures were strengthened. The program also strengthened its relationship with the College of Law by sharing a half-time appointment with Rob Williams.

Approval of the Ph.D. degree took two years. The Graduate Council, comprised of faculty from disciplines across the university, had to be convinced of the "scientific rigor of an interdisciplinary degree." This same hurdle was faced by all interdisciplinary proposals. The strategy used to gain approval was to form a small subcommittee of the council and work closely with that small group. When the proposal came up again a year later, the subcommittee reported all questions had been answered. After the Ph.D. proposal passed all campus committees, it was sent to the other two universities in Arizona (Arizona State University in Tempe and Northern Arizona University in Flagstaff) for review and comment. The other universities had been informed about the proposal and were, in general, supportive. However, when the proposal reached the Arizona Board of Regents, one representative raised the question, "Why wasn't this a joint degree between all three universities?" The proposal was nearly tabled until both provosts from the other two universities reaffirmed that the UA had a two-decade history in American Indian studies graduate education, which they lacked, and neither had any plans in the area of American Indian studies graduate education. It turned out that keeping a close watch on the proposal all the way to the ABOR stage was crucial. Usually, curriculum matters were passed on a consent agenda, with no discussion. Having the UA provost, the ABOR staff, and the other two institutions fully briefed was instrumental in the eventual approval of the degree.

The first class of Ph.D. students, four females, began their studies in the fall of 1997. They supplemented a class of fifty-five students seeking M.A. degrees. In the fall of 1998, two more female candidates joined this core group. Then, in the fall of 1999, five additional Ph.D. students, including the first two males, joined the program. By the fall of 2000, the total number of Ph.D. students was fourteen, of which ten were Native. By the fall of 2001, the program had its first graduate and sixteen enrolled. In a decade of fiscal restraint for higher education and academic program elimination at the university, AISP had commitment and support from key central administrators, which resulted in significant program growth. The implementation of the Ph.D. program and two new faculty hires, along with a half-time transfer, positively impacted the quality of the program. The two faculty hires were Luci Tapahonso (Navajo), who joined AISP as a tenured full professor with a shared appointment in English, and Bob Martin (Cherokee), who was full time in AISP. The transfer of Nancy Parezo, a non-Indian, who became a tenured professor in AISP with a shared appointment in the Arizona State Museum, added strength to the core faculty. Parezo later transferred fully into AISP. Manley Begay (Navajo) joined the faculty the fall of 2000. Full-time and shared appointments equal 10.3 full-time equivalencies, with an additional thirteen faculty having nonfunded adjunct appointment.

In 1997, AISP completed its second comprehensive academic program review. A team of external and internal reviewers reported:

> The team finds that the American Indian Studies program has developed very rapidly in the past five years into the premier American Indian Graduate Program in the country. Its faculty are nationally known; it is attracting a high quality pool of American Indian and non-Indian graduate students. Its graduates are contributing significantly to Indian communities by finding jobs with Tribal organizations and groups serving Indian people, as well as by being admitted to doctoral programs or other professional programs. The Ph.D. program has strong potential to contribute to future scholarship in American Indian studies by training future teachers and researchers.

Today, AIS is an interdisciplinary program housed within the graduate college. Its permanent and affiliated interdisciplinary faculty numbers twenty-six, of whom eighteen are Indian. AISP has promotion and tenure authority and a solid base budget, which is a continuing and permanent funding from the state. In effect, it operates as a quasi department, without the department title. The program is institutionalized and helps meet one of the most important mission areas of the university: outreach, research, and service to Indian Nations and communities. There is no other institution of higher education in the country that has eighteen Indian faculty working together in an American Indian studies degree program. Other institutions may have more Indian faculty, but their faculty are usually scattered across the university and have no reason to work together or to work with Indian students in a degree program.

Conclusion

What can we learn from the University of Arizona case study? When the American Indian studies program began in 1971 it had significant outside funding from the Ford Foundation, a small but committed faculty with courtesy appointments, and a handful of students. However, university funds and commitment did not immediately materialize. It was two decades later that the program took off. There are only certain times when new resources have traditionally been available to a program at UA. Routine budget cycles usually resulted in a net loss, especially given inflation. At UA, new resources were committed when there was an external review, when a new chair/director was hired, or when a new academic program was implemented.

The initial key ingredients for accelerated growth included a mandated academic program review, the hiring of a new, permanent director, a vice president who took an interest in the program, and the hard work of a committed American Indian faculty and staff. The results of the first APR yielded a permanent, full-time director, new faculty resources, an increase in the operations budget, and a commitment to finding new space. The organizational move out of social and behavioral sciences and into the graduate college was important. The recommendations of prestigious reviewers from peer institutions outside the university provided the director with the evidence to acquire new program resources from permanent, continuing funds.

The next crucial program development facilitator occurred when the provost extended promotion and tenure authority to AISP even though it was not a department. In addition, a core of four faculty was brought together through internal transfers from across the university. The provost bartered these transfers with departments, leaving the AISP director's relationship with other colleges and departments intact.

The development of the first Ph.D. degree program in American Indian studies in the United States provided increased resources from the central administration for student support. The incorporation of a community development and outreach component into the academic program was also a successful strategy. Having full-time staff working with Indian Nations and communities heightened the awareness of American Indian studies as an academic program. Graduate students were also provided increased avenues of experience in working with Indian communities as part of their academic careers.

As the past three decades of growth in AISP come to an end, the faculty are, again, discussing the pros and cons of acquiring departmental status. The merits and challenges of developing an undergraduate major will also have to be revisited to address the growing interests and needs of Indian students and communities across the Southwest. The most significant drawback of acquiring departmental status is the fear that, once again, AISP will be without a strong central administrator or collegiate dean advocate. The program, even given unprecedented growth, would still be a very small department in competition with much larger and often resource-rich departments. If AISP becomes a department, it will have to move out of the graduate college and vice president for research division and join, again, one of the colleges. The most likely candidates are humanities or social and behavioral sciences, but neither is a perfect fit. In humanities, the program would be in resource competition with another new interdisciplinary program, comparative cultural and literary studies, where a number of M.A. graduates from AIS go for a Ph.D. In social and behavioral sciences, there are several large, nationally recognized departments.

One of the greatest challenges for AISP is staying competitive. There is growing national interest and commitment in courses, degrees, and programs, and competition for the scarce Indian faculty member is accelerating. AIS has enjoyed three decades of outstanding Indian and non-Indian faculty associated with its programs. The faculty today includes: Barbara Babcock; Manley Begay (Navajo); Stephen Cornell; Larry Evers; Joe Hiller (Lakota); Mary Jo Tippeconnic Fox (Comanche/Cherokee); Robert Hershey; Tom Holm (Creek/Cherokee); Jennie Joe (Navajo); Hartman Lomawaima (Hopi); K. Tsianina Lomawaima (Creek); Eileen Luna (Choctaw/Cherokee); Robert Martin (Cherokee); Teresa McCarty; Barbara Mills; N. Scott Momaday (Kiowa); Nancy Parezo; Alice Paul (Tohono O'odham); Emory Sekaquaptewa (Hopi); Jay Stauss (Jamestown Band S'Klallam); Richard Stoffle; Luci Tapahonso (Navajo); Robert Williams Jr. (Lumbee); Mary Ann Willie (Navajo); Melanie Yazzie (Navajo); and Ofelia Zepeda (Tohono O'odham). Student interest continues to grow, especially at the graduate level. AISP still needs nurturing, as would any smaller and newer program or department in today's highly competitive environment.

AISP has demonstrated a historical commitment to meeting the needs of Indian students across the campus, regardless of their academic interests. The principle involved is that both Indian graduate and undergraduate students can benefit from separate cultural and academic activities when they are brought together in meaningful ways. AISP has recently supported the development by two new B.A. degrees in American Indian studies at its sister institutions, Arizona State University and Northern Arizona University.

The University of Arizona has moved in the late 1990s in the direction of combining and centralizing resources for minority students. Recently, a multicultural student center was brought together in the student union. Individual resource centers were not disbanded, but activities and major events are now more highly centralized and coordinated. One motive, of course, is to save on program costs. American Indian studies has always taken the stand that we are not a "minority" group, but the targeted services provided are directly related to the university's land-grant commitments and its direct relationship as a state agency with each of the federally recognized Tribes in Arizona. Centralized services tend to blend groups and confuse rights and responsibilities that only Indian Tribes and their members have, as established by treaty and law. The AISP strategy to counter this trend has been to build a larger, more comprehensive set of programs that can stand alone. The academic program is combined with community outreach and student support programs that reach the entire campus and state.

Finally, as the University of Arizona enters the new millennium, the two original American Indian studies stories have come together. Institutional commitments promised over thirty-five years ago finally materialized in the early 1990s.

AIS has matured into a nationally recognized leader in the field, having substantial, permanent institutional support and an integral role in the university's mission. The program has tenured faculty and permanent staff and operations. Community development and outreach efforts are based on Tribal requests. Graduate students are involved with Tribal communities. AIS has over 160 M.A. graduates largely working throughout Indian Country. A 1997 alumni telephone survey revealed: "Nearly one quarter of respondents were candidates or graduates of Ph.D. programs, 20% were teaching college, 10% were enrolled in law school, another 10% were working in public education administration and the remainder in a variety of positions with Tribes, consulting on Indian issues or closely related professional appointments." In 2001, American Indian studies graduated its first Ph.D. The future success of American Indian studies will be significantly judged on these students' accomplishments and, especially, their contributions to strengthening American Indian Nations, Tribes, and communities.

Note

1. The history presented in this chapter benefited greatly from an academic program review self-study written in 1990 by Professor Rob Williams. In addition, Shelly Lowe interviewed eight former administrators involved in the development of Indian programs at the University of Arizona and incorporated those findings into this history. Finally, excerpts from the 1998 academic program review survey of alumni, carried out by Dan Ferguson, a graduate of our program, are also included.

A Hemispheric Approach: Native American   6
Studies at the University of California–Davis

JACK D. FORBES, WITH STEVEN JAMES CRUM, INÉS HERNÁNDEZ-ÁVILA,
GEORGE LONGFISH, MARTHA J. MACRI, VICTOR MONTEJO, AND STEFANO
VARESE[1]

NATIVE AMERICAN STUDIES at the University of California–Davis (UC–Davis) focuses upon the Indigenous peoples of the Americas, that is, upon the peoples, Nations, Tribes, and communities whose ancestors have lived in North, Central, and South America from earliest times. Native American studies is interdisciplinary in its approach to the world of American Indian peoples, offering a comprehensive and comparative perspective. This unique hemispheric approach is built around the concept of an interdisciplinary and holistic approach to the history, culture, art, literature, and society of American Indian peoples, with some comparative study of other Indigenous peoples. It is also built around the concept of the study of all Indian groups, including Indian refugees and immigrants from Mexico and Central America as well as Indian groups still residing on reservations and in traditional homelands in all parts of the Americas.[2]

Native American studies at the University of California–Davis began with one faculty member in the fall of 1969. Today it is an independent department, one of the few in the United States, with eight permanent tenured faculty, two active emeritus professors, and several lecturers, part-time instructors, visiting fellows, and researchers. When the Davis program began, it was forced to begin life as part of a larger department, as is the origin of most Native studies units. Early plans were quite ambitious, envisioning a comprehensive program with attention given to Maya literature, Quechua language, and other aspects of Meso-American and South American Indigenous life. But although its plans called for a hemispheric orientation, the program's initial focus was largely upon the United States, with some attention to other areas when dealing with ancient American origins, with the Plains region, or with the Southwest.[3] A *Handbook for the Development of Native American Studies* was published in 1971, exposing many persons to such hemispheric concepts, as well as to a Native American chronology that was hemispheric and that utilized Maya calendar-dating along with European calendar-dating. By the mid-1970s, a bit more attention was being paid to Canada and an experimental course was taught on "Native Peoples of Mexico and Central America." However, the small size of the faculty prevented the full development of a hemispheric approach at that time.[4]

Native American studies faculty also had to confront the power of European intellectual colonialism, which had almost always sought to "package" Indigenous Americans as "Canadian Indians," "Alaskan Eskimos," "Mexican Indians," "Guatemalan Indians," and so forth. In other words, intellectual colonialism sought to force upon Native peoples a colonial mentality, an acceptance of being placed in separate little boxes by the processes of Euro (Yuro) conquest and administrative subordination. Of course, the Yuros attempted to develop colonial administrative systems in each "nation-state" so that the "Indians" would be dominated by a particular bureaucracy controlled by a specific state. D'Arcy McNickle was one of our early Native writers who began to break this colonial pattern by including the history of both Canadian and U.S. Tribes in his seminal historical works.

McNickle was a Cree from the Salish-Kutenai area, where many groups are intersected by the U.S.–Canadian boundary. He knew that a genuine Native historiography could never be subservient to the Yuros' way of carving up ancient homelands. As Native American studies has matured, many of us in the field have realized that it is foolish to divide up our peoples in a colonial way.

The Davis program started to become seriously hemispheric in the late 1980s when Stefano Varese, a Peruvian scholar, was employed to develop courses relating to Meso-America and South America. He was soon joined by Martha Macri (Cherokee), a specialist in Native writing systems, languages, and Maya hieroglyphic and linguistic-cultural studies. Varese and Macri were joined by Dr. Inés Hernández-Ávila, whose dual Nez Perce and Chicana-Mexicana background and bilingual capability takes her often across frontiers in her scholarship and creative writing, and Jack Forbes (Powhatan-Delaware), who also has done writing and research about northern Mexico and the rest of the Americas, and incorporates that material into his courses.

Davis launched a revised major in 1989–1990 that allows students to specialize in either North America, Meso-America, or South America. This is also true of the Ph.D. program, where students may focus on any of these areas or may undertake joint doctorates in combination with such fields as Spanish, English, comparative literature, geography, anthropology, history, sociology, and education. The Native American Studies (NAS) program officially became a freestanding department in the spring of 1994. One of the reasons for this accomplishment was the excellence of the faculty in terms of their creative, scholarly, and leadership capacities. Well-known are national leaders such as David Risling (Hoopa-Karuk-Yurok), scholars such as Steven Crum (author of *The Road on Which We Came: A History of the Western Shoshones*), teachers such as the late Sarah Hutchison (Cherokee and a counselor of numerous former students), George Longfish, a major artist (Seneca-Tuscarora), and the others already mentioned.

The Davis faculty are well-known for their historic focus on the community. That tradition continues. The Carl N. Gorman Museum, long headed by artist George Longfish and then by Theresa Harlan (Laguna), reaches out to the Native art world as well as to local school children and the general public.

Native American Studies as a Discipline

Most of our present fields of study in higher education are relatively recent, and moreover, many are the result of compromises, consolidations, conquests, and separations that have occurred during the past century. Especially in the social sciences and humanities, the boundaries that have resulted are often arbitrary and not always logical. This is particularly true when seen from the perspective of people within the non-European or colonized society.

First Americans, traditionally, tended to look at the world of knowledge and wisdom in a holistic way, integrating theory and practice, aesthetics and philosophy. Wise men were known as those of the red and black ink in ancient Mexico—poets, philosophers, and historians combined. Traditional Native American studies, if we can speak thusly, revolved largely around the search for knowledge and wisdom that could be used in the life of the people. The core of this knowledge was concerned with the elucidation of harmony and appropriate behavior, behavior that might lead to the proper functioning of the human-animal-plant–world relationship. But Native American studies was greatly changed with the Spanish invasion from Chile north to Virginia, an invasion that forced original Americans perhaps for the first time to become concerned with the preservation of their identity and legacy. Thus at that time we find many Native American scholars composing books that treat the history, culture, religion, society, and conditions of the Native peoples.

A premier example of such a scholar is Felipe Huaman Poma de Ayala, a Quechua-speaking "Inca" man of unmixed American ancestry who devoted many decades to carefully studying the situation of Perú (Tahuantinsuyu) in the period before and after 1600. When in his sixties, Poma organized his research into a book (ca. 1613), which he titled *Crónica Nueva y Buen Gobierno* (New Chronicle and Good Government). This remarkable book is certainly a pioneer example of Native American studies. Holistically, Poma combined history, ethnology, sociology, political economy, the analysis of colonialism, and sociopolitical planning into a comprehensive account. Of course, Poma's *Crónica* was not "interdisciplinary," since the concepts of "discipline" as applied to a particular methodology and "interdiscipline" as applied to a combination or intersection of methodologies are both extremely modern. Moreover, with the exception of "history," none of the "fields" mentioned above actually existed as separate entities in the early 1600s.

Poma's work was comprehensive because he apparently believed that the oppressed position of the Native peoples could only be brought to an end by exposing the historical background; the means of subjugation; the social, political, and economic conditions; and a possible remedy, all in the fullest manner (especially as regards the crimes of the conquest and the corrective measures needed). We see here the concept of combining theory with action and of having scholarship inform application directly. In so many ways, Poma's *Crónica* agrees with the modern thrust of Native American studies, that is, in the use of all appropriate data, of all relevant evidence, including wonderful drawings, to clarify a subject area, as well as in the desire to make such a clarification in an area that will be useful to the community, to the human "objects" of study.[5] Interestingly, Poma's work was suppressed and remained unpublished for about 300 years. That also marks a similarity with the work of modern Native American scholars, who sometimes have difficulty in obtaining publication, especially in the "mainstream" journals of academia. It is also similar to the situation of hundreds of Indigenous texts that still remain inaccessible.

Many other Native writers, such as Garcilaso el Inca, attempted to push Native American studies forward in the period after 1520. Garcilaso wrote his "History of Perú" by combining historical, ethnological, and sociopolitical data into a valuable synthesis. Many Mexican authors also wrote books about their particular nations, regions, or cities, again using a holistic or comprehensive perspective. In Guatemala, Quiché scholars prepared a written version of the ancient *Popul Vuh*, while in other Maya-speaking regions various accounts, such as the *Books of Chilam Balam* and the *Annals of the Cakchiquels*, were written, often with the view of preserving historical and prophetical knowledge.

As the Spanish Empire tightened its grip on autochthonous American societies, the early scholarship was often suppressed and Native American intellectual life went underground. In any event, one can see that Native American studies is not really a "new" field of study but rather a very old subject simply suppressed by colonialism and specifically by the "underdevelopment" (oppression) of Native societies. Huaman Poma marks a good beginning for this discussion of Native American studies because his comprehensive approach is the hallmark of what we ought to be doing today. To do this, most of us have to partially unlearn what we were taught in white-dominated fields in order to learn new methodologies and comparative perspectives. Let us illustrate further:

A few years ago, Sam Gill wrote a book on the "Mother Earth" concept, wherein he argues that white people actually popularized (or even invented) the Mother Earth idea in the nineteenth century. Gill does this, in part, by ignoring First American beliefs in Mexico and Peru, as well as by overlooking many groups in Canada and places such as California. Gill basically ignores the kind of thorough research into ethnographic, linguistic, historical, archaeological, and oral-traditional evidence that one would need in order to be able to deal with the history of such a concept, but above all, he ignores the hemispheric approach necessary to deal with ancient American ideas.

Likewise in the post-1492 period, as with a subject such as the evolution of the Native cowboy, it is easy to forget about the life of Native Americans within the Spanish Empire or the Mexican Republic if one is trained in the field of United States history. Generally speaking, the latter field views Indians primarily as an attribute of the expanding western U.S. "frontier" or from the narrow perspective of the U.S. government's policy toward Native Americans.

Hopefully Native American studies as a field will force us to learn Spanish, or French, or Portuguese (or Quechua, Navajo, or Maya), or whatever languages are needed for a comparative and comprehensive approach to the Native American story and one not limited by the boundaries of the particular colonial system under which a given group happens to fall. But the Native American story cannot be fully told without also utilizing the data to be derived from archaeology, ethnology, folklore, and a score of other approaches that have something to say, something that can be ignored only at our peril as scholars.

The truth is that in so many problem areas it is almost meaningless to look at a Native American issue from a narrow perspective. For example, we might want to study the issue of crime or criminalization in Native American societies. Sociology is the European field that usually looks at crime, but criminology also exists as a separate field in some countries. In any case, the normal sociology method seems to focus upon statistical data provided by governmental agencies' records, such as police reports, arrest records, court records, and so forth. Quite clearly, quantitative data of that kind might be a first step, but such data will tell us very little about Native American criminalization.

Certainly it is also necessary to utilize ethnographic and qualitative data to shed light upon the human beings behind the statistics. It is also necessary to utilize political economy data to comprehend the poverty, colonial structures, lack of employment, lack of self-determination, and other sociopolitical and economic factors involved. The schools must also be examined to shed light upon educational failure or upon cultural bias or racism in school settings. Time-depth evidence, such as provided by archival material and oral interviews, should also be part of the picture, since criminalization is a historical process moving through time. Dr. Luana Ross's book *Inventing the Savage: The Social Construction of Native American Criminality* exemplifies this holistic approach. This work was published while she was at Davis.[6]

The Native American studies approach, we would argue, focuses upon the problem to be solved, not only in the sense of an intellectual problem, but also in terms of a social problem that can be ameliorated through acquiring knowledge. Thus we would study the problem of Native American crime not as a sociological problem, not as an anthropological problem, not as an educational problem, not as an historical problem, not as a psychological problem, but as a human problem that in the end cannot usefully be divided up.[7]

As Native American studies scholars, we might not be satisfied with a statistical study based upon records of arrest and commitment, we might not be satisfied with a study of the employment rates or poverty rates in the community, we might not be satisfied with an ethnographic account of Native American "felons" or of crime in a particular community, we might not be satisfied with a history of reservation police forces and judges, and we might not be satisfied with a compilation of relevant federal, state, and reservation statutes. Ultimately, to answer the needs of Indian peoples, we would want a comprehensive, multi-methodological, problem-focused discipline. Native American studies should be that discipline.

Contemporary Conditions
Supporting Native American Studies

During the last five decades throughout the whole hemisphere, Indigenous peoples of the Americas have experienced a dramatic process of territorial, demographic, socioeconomic, and cultural transformation. Due to globalization and other pressures, First Nation peoples have increasingly lost control over their lands and resources and have been constrained to live in marginal rural areas and city ghettoes.

For those Indians who have remained in their territories, the struggle to defend their historical right to lands and resources has resulted, most of the time, in precarious arrangements that do not guarantee conditions for their autonomous and self-sustained development. In certain areas of Central and South America, the expropriation of Indian lands has been accompanied by military occupation and the establishment of authoritarian regimes. Population studies in various countries of the Americas indicate, however, that deliberate assimilation policies implemented by governments throughout the years have consistently failed. Census analyses of the region show that the majority of Indigenous ethnolinguistic groups have increased in absolute numbers, despite systematic attempts to distort census counts.

Substantial transformations have occurred, nevertheless, in the sphere of Indian peoples' spatial mobility and location. Although uprooting and forced migration constitute old and well-known experiences for Native peoples of the Americas, during the last few decades the phenomenon has become massive and has acquired a transnational character. The constant flow of Indigenous peoples from Mexico, Guatemala, and Central and South America to the United States has grown considerably as a concomitant manifestation of the endemic economic and political crisis that has afflicted Latin America's social life during this century. The internationalization of capital, the explosive urbanization of rural societies, the invasion of Indigenous lands, and the environmental deterioration of certain areas of Latin America have produced important phenomena of economic deportation and political expatriation that are increasingly affecting the Indigenous peoples of the Americas.

Today, Purepechas, Mixtecs, Zapotecs, Chinantecs, Tzeltal and Tzotzil Mayas, Nahuas, and other Indigenous peoples from Mexico, as well as Kanjobal, Quiché, Mam, Kakchiquel, and Ixil Mayas from Guatemala, Miskito from Nicaragua, Quechuas from Peru, and Mapuches from Chile, are living and working in the United States. They are here as unrecognized political refugees, migrant workers, or economic deportees. Massive movements of Indigenous peoples are not limited in any way to the United States; they are also occurring between Latin American countries. The Guajiros are disregarding the frontier between Colombia and Venezuela that has cut in half their historical territory; the Quechuas and Aymaras are mobilized along the border of Peru and Bolivia; the Shuar and Aguajín are moving across the frontier of Peru and Ecuador. Substantial demographic transformations are taking place also within the various national territories of Latin America, where large numbers of Indigenous peoples are cyclically or permanently leaving their rural communities to seek economic improvement or simply survival in urban areas.

In the United States since the 1950s, the legislated policy of Tribal termination and relocation programs aimed at Native Americans on reservations has led to a series of important demographic changes that are transforming the vast majority of American Indians from rural peoples to urban dwellers. One of the last manifestations of this induced urbanization process is currently occurring in Alaska, where Native Americans from "bush" villages are being relocated to regional centers. A new inter-Tribal ethnic identity has thus emerged in the cities and is finding its expression through Pan-Indian activities, ethnopolitical discourses, and the reconstruction of renewed forms of cultural, intellectual, and artistic expressions.

All these movements across national frontiers, socioeconomic and regional borders, and rural–urban territoriality, however, do not seem to generate a weakening of the ethnic boundaries and cultural identity of each Indigenous group; on the contrary, they have produced an intensification of the Indigenous ethnic allegiance. At least in one well-documented case, that of the Mixtec farmworker migrants in California, Oregon, and Washington, expatriation from Mexico has resulted in a series of strong cultural organizations through which their consciousness is stressed while traditional Indigenous forms of self-help and mutual assistance are adapted to the new social environment. Very seldom does distance from ethnic territory seem to entail an abandonment of Indian cultural values; rather it suggests the adapted renewal of some of these ethnic characteristics in an effort to endure the burden of an exile that is perceived as temporary.

Different forms of Indian ethnicities have survived five centuries of colonial efforts to eradicate them by assimilation. Economic, social, political, and cultural conditions of domination have changed through time and space, as have the adaptive mechanisms of survival and resistance implemented by Indigenous peoples. Native peoples today are a dynamic manifestation of a long historical process in which pre-Columbian and colonial matrices are equally recognizable as foundations of adaptive social and cultural strategies. In conclusion, we are witnessing a process of constant readjustment and cultural creation that allows each Indigenous society to reproduce itself and to continue to exist as a social entity differentiated from the surrounding non-Indian community. At the same time, a more generic Indian identity is being generated, and it is manifested by a vivid sense of sharing a common history of colonial oppression and contemporary discrimination, as well as by a unique spiritual orientation toward life and the world.

These new forms of Indigenous ethnicities with their complex demographic dynamics, socioeconomic structures, and ethnopolitical processes, and with their intellectual expressions, artistic creativity, and unique cultural configurations, constitute the main subject matter of the multidisciplinary study program of Native American studies at UC–Davis.[8] Native ethnicity, cultural diversity, and the understanding of the complexity of interethnic relations are particularly relevant for the increasing sociodemographic transformation of California within the frame of the Pacific Rim, which is becoming a distinctive region that calls for analytical paradigms that transcend national frontiers.

To deal with the phenomena of the growth and survival of Native American peoples, a new discipline is emerging, one that is also very old but that has been silenced by several centuries of European dominance. The Department of Native American Studies at UC–Davis is a leader in the evolution of this field of study (as it has been for some twenty years despite small size and program status).[9]

Development of Native American Studies in the United States[10]

Native American studies in white-dominated colleges and universities in the United States emerged in 1969. Native Americans and other minority groups, under the banner of the Third World Movement, were successful in introducing their university-based academic programs in various postsecondary institutions, principally in California at first.

Also in 1969, the Special Subcommittee on Indian Education of the Committee on Labor and Public Welfare released its well-known report *Indian Education: A National Tragedy—A National Challenge*. It made some important higher education recommendations, including one specifying that colleges and universities should include Native American studies courses. Here was a radical shift on the part of one segment of the federal government, for it was now advocating cultural pluralism and moving away from its age-old policy of assimilation for Native Americans.

Thus the year 1969 represents a watershed in the history of Native American studies, for it marked the beginnings of many Native-oriented courses to be offered in established U.S. colleges and universities. This is not to say that the idea of Native American studies started in 1969, as the concept has been around for a long time in this country. Sarah Winnemucca advocated an Indian teacher's college in the nineteenth century, while in 1912 Fayette McKenzie, a professor of sociology at Ohio State University and a visionary who helped organize the Society of American Indians in 1911, advocated the teaching of Native courses, including Indian history. In 1913 he called for the creation of an endowed chair of Native studies with emphasis on sociology. Some years later, Lakota thinker Chief Standing Bear, in his *Land of the Spotted Eagle* (1933), wrote about an "Indian School of Thought." This unique type of school, if established, would train students as Native scholars, and offer them courses in Native arts, languages, and philosophy. Firmly convinced that Native American culture had something to offer white America, Standing Bear stressed: "America can be revived, rejuvenated, by recognizing a native school of thought. The Indian can save America."[11]

But as late as 1959 and 1960, Native-oriented courses were almost nonexistent. In this earlier period there were at least three university-based "Indian" programs: the American Indian Institute (1951) of the University of Oklahoma, the Institute of Indian Studies (1955) of the University of South Dakota, and the Institute of American Indian Studies (1960) of Brigham Young University. Yet these early programs, dominated by non-Indian scholars with limited Indian input, made little or no effort to establish Indian-oriented courses. In fact, the University of South Dakota, over thirty years ago, was the only postsecondary institution to offer a minor in "American Indian" studies (there were no majors). Unfortunately, this program included only one existing Indian-oriented course, "North American Indians" (Sociology 163).[12]

In 1961, Jack Forbes developed a formal proposal for an "American Indian Studies" program on the Northridge campus of California State University

(CSU). This proposal took advantage of existing courses from both anthropology and history. It was not adopted, but at the same time Forbes began introducing Native materials into his courses, using works such as *Black Elk Speaks* and *American Indian Prose and Poetry*. Shortly thereafter, Forbes developed a proposal for an independent "American Indian University" instead, setting up the American Indian College Committee with Carl Gorman and Mary Gorman. The university proposal took some ten years to be realized, and in the meantime Forbes moved to the University of Nevada–Reno, where he introduced a course on "The Native in North American History." It was perhaps one of the first Native American courses in a history department outside Oklahoma.[13]

When the Third World Liberation Front student strike erupted on the UC–Berkeley campus in 1968, Forbes was working nearby at the Far West Laboratory for Educational Research and Development. He soon became an adviser to the Indigenous students and prepared many proposals, including one for a "College of Ethnic Studies," which was to include a Native American studies department. Forbes was selected by the Third World groups as their candidate for chairing the new unit (a department, not a college). He was offered a full professorship in anthropology and the chair position in ethnic studies, but he eventually turned down the offer to accept a full professorship at the Davis campus in anthropology and applied behavioral sciences with the prospect of developing a large Native studies unit. Forbes selected Davis over Berkeley because the leadership of the California Indian Education Association (CIEA) believed that Davis, with its agricultural and applied tradition, and with its central, rural location, would be preferable for California Native students. Forbes took a large cut in pay to make that choice and for many years it was not at all clear that the choice had been a wise one.

The organization of the CIEA, led by David Risling Jr., and its powerful influence in the years from 1967 through 1969, were major factors in the appearance of Native studies at UC–Davis, UC–Berkeley, CSU–Long Beach, and elsewhere. The CIEA at its first statewide conference in 1967 adopted proposals for introducing Indigenous curricula into higher education:

> The conference participants strongly recommend that California's colleges and universities strengthen their programs in California Indian history and culture, develop special programs for teachers of California Indian pupils, establish more scholarships for Indian students, ...
>
> One or more California state college or university campuses should be strongly encouraged to develop a center for Indian studies in order to provide special training for teachers, Indian leaders, social workers, et cetera.

The grassroots delegates from throughout California were anxious to see changes soon:

> *The California Indian Education Association now believes that it is time to begin implementing the above recommendations.* The Indian people of this state have waited more than a century for justice and the time for action is now.

The CIEA members lobbied the California legislature and were able to obtain passage, by an overwhelming majority, of a state-senate resolution calling upon the University of California to develop one or more major centers for Indian studies and research.[14]

The formation of United Native Americans (UNA) in the San Francisco Bay Area in 1968 was also instrumental in advancing the cause of Indigenous studies. Many of the leaders of UNA, such as Jack Forbes, were also CIEA activists, and student members of UNA were leaders of the Native students in the Third World strike at the University of California–Berkeley (as well as at Alcatraz later).

During this same period (1967–1969), CIEA and UNA members shared ideas with leaders of the National Indian Youth Council who had come to set up their headquarters with the Far West Laboratory, where Forbes, Melvin Thom, and others had discussions about the future of Native higher education (discussions initiated in Nevada somewhat earlier). Forbes succeeded in developing contacts with Senator Robert F. Kennedy and his staff person on the Senate Subcommittee on Indian Education, Adrian Parmeter. As a result, Forbes was able to get the subcommittee to support the idea of Native studies in higher education (as noted above) in its final report. He was also able to arrange Kennedy's visit to the Stewart's Point Reservation and to speak with him privately on various aspects of Native education, in addition to the public testimony the subcommittee gathered. The report of the CIEA's conference of 1967 was published by the subcommittee, giving national distribution to its recommendations.

Subsequently, the CIEA specifically called upon the University of California to develop the Davis campus "as a center for the development of American Indian Studies and as a center for the recruitment of Indian students." The resolution also called for an "American Indian Research Institute" at Davis (now the Indigenous Research Center of the Americas), and requested that a "major program for the training of teachers, health personnel, agricultural personnel, and attorneys for working with Indian communities be developed on the Davis campus."[15]

The process of persuading the University of California to allocate resources to an ethnic population whom for a century it had largely ignored (except as subjects for anthropological cataloging) took a lot of political work. But between the UNA and the CIEA there was a large cadre of Native activists and educator-activists who were exceptionally successful in those years.

Historical Development of the Department

In July 1969, Jack Forbes was hired at UC–Davis, half in anthropology and half in applied behavioral sciences, the latter in the College of Agriculture and Environmental Sciences. He had obtained promises of support for the development of Native American studies and for increased recruitment of Native students (there were only five in 1968–1969). After many meetings and the preparation of numerous position papers, he was able to secure a secretarial position, filled by Jeri Kemp (Comanche), and several faculty positions. In addition, space was acquired in a two-story wooden building that, although old, was replete with a kitchen stove and sink and areas for student meetings, dinners, art studios, and a small exhibit space. As a unit, Native American studies began as a program within applied behavioral sciences, which also housed the infant Asian American studies unit and a community development unit. The early faculty, after Forbes, were David Risling Jr. (coordinator, then director), Carl N. Gorman (Navajo), Kenneth Martin (Assiniboine), and, a bit later, Sarah Hutchison, aided by Wilbor Wilson (Choctaw) in avian science. George Longfish joined the faculty in 1973, the same year the Carl N. Gorman Museum was established as a vital component of the program.

In the exciting first year of 1969–1970 we enrolled 422 students in twelve courses, including a graduate seminar on Indian ethnohistory taught in anthropology. By April 1970 we had nine nonteaching staff, including part-time student assistants, and we had a center featuring "an Indian cultural exhibit (four rooms) with paintings, historical-cultural informational units, and artifacts. The center also includes an Indian student center, art workshops, a Native American community services office, and the beginning of a volunteer Indian legal service program. . . . Outdoor exhibits, including a tipi and two 'wickiups,' are also located at the center."[16]

Many courses were developed in 1969–1970, and the major was submitted in 1970, although its approval was held up for several years as the campus Committee on Courses sought to put the brakes on "ethnic" studies programs. In 1974 a freeze was imposed on all new "ethnic" studies courses, which Forbes responded to by noting that it must apply to European ethnic-focus courses as well. In June 1974 the major was resubmitted, but in the meantime we had had many students majoring in Native American studies as a focus within applied behavioral sciences. In 1975 the independent Native American studies major became established.

Howard Adams (Cree-Métis) from Canada served in the program from 1975 through the 1980s. In the late 1970s we developed a "History of the Americas: A Field of Concentration in the NAS Major" in an effort to encourage hemispheric work, although we still had insufficient faculty to fulfill our objectives.[17] After active participation in the creation and continuance of the Native American studies program, three of our faculty retired: Adams (1987), Sarah Hutchison (1987), and David Risling (1989). Forbes then replaced Risling as director and oversaw the move to the College of Letters and Science.

David Risling garnered many national honors during his stay at Davis. He was appointed by three U.S. presidents to the National Advisory Commission on Indian Education during the 1970s, served as a founding board member of the Native American Rights Fund, served as founder-president of the California Indian Education Association, as founder-chair of the board of the California Indian Legal Services, and still serves on the board of the Association on American Indian Affairs. A David Risling Scholarship Fund has been established on campus, and in 1992 he was honored with the university's Distinguished Public Service Award; a large conference room was named in his honor in 1994.

The initial growth of Native American studies was quite rapid, but by 1973 a backlash took place at UC–Davis, as noted, and although we were finally able to get our major approved in 1975 (after several years of stonewalling on the part of conservative faculty) and to complete the hiring of Adams, we were to remain at 4.5 faculty for a number of years. Many struggles ensued subsequently, including a serious battle to obtain security of employment for Risling, Hutchison, and several other non-white lecturers in 1976–1977. But the deepest threats to our existence occurred in the 1979–1986 period, when our major was temporarily suspended and personal attacks were mounted against several of our faculty. Things reached such an impasse that most of our space was taken from us, our unsold publications were put out for dumping, and our library was given away, saved only by Risling's hard work. The able and wise leadership of Dave Risling and the courage of the majority of the other faculty enabled us to face such severe harassment and prejudice. In 1985 we attempted to transfer to the College of Letters and Science, to no avail. The Department of Applied Behavioral Sciences eventually had proven to be a very dangerous environment for us, being located in an increasingly hostile college (agriculture) under hostile administrators. Our faculty positions were greatly desired by other specialties, and we constantly had to fight against being cannibalized.[18] An ethnic studies task force investigation in 1986–1987 (which ultimately brought in off-campus minority scholars as advisers) helped frustrate the plots against us, and a new chancellor (Theodore Hullar) and vice chancellor (Carol Cartwright) finally changed the atmosphere for the better in 1988–1989.

In 1989, Native American studies moved out of the Department of Applied Behavioral Sciences (and the College of Agriculture and Environmental Sciences) and into the College of Letters and Science, as an interdepartmental program. A new major had to be developed for the A.B. degree, with North, Meso-, and South American tracks, and the transition of faculty, both new and old, had to be managed. The new included those mentioned above: Inés Hernández-Ávila, Stefano Varese, Steven Crum, and Martha Macri. Both Professors Crum and Macri were hired after having been in residence as UC President's Postdoctoral Fellows with Native American studies, with Jack Forbes as their mentor.

The 1970 plan for Native American studies had included a call for an Institute of Native American Research and Development. We were able to house several projects, including one that led to the founding of D-Q University, a Native-controlled Tribal college, in 1971–1972. But our faculty never received credit for our applied research in the community, and indeed, several of us were punished for our work with D-Q University specifically. Ironically, one of the reasons that we had originally chosen to affiliate with applied behavioral sciences had been our belief that the department, with its history of community involvement and work with cooperative extension, would support our applied research programs. But, it seems, that was not to be the case with us. Later, with Hullar as chancellor and a new college-home, we were finally able to establish an organized research program, which was given seed money from the Office of Research for four years beginning in 1991. That was an active period for us, and we were able to create a graduate group in Native American studies with campuswide support. With their sponsorship in 1992 we submitted our first proposal calling for a graduate program in Native American studies. We were advised to first create a designated emphasis in Native American studies as a way to transition into the full graduate program. Our designated emphasis was approved by the graduate group and was accepted for joint Ph.D. degrees by the anthropology, Spanish, comparative literature, geography, history, and sociology departments. In the spring of 1993 we offered our first graduate seminar under the NAS name (and the ethnohistory seminar Forbes had been offering in anthropology for many years was transferred to the department).

Also in 1991, Forbes began preparing the documents supporting an independent departmental status. With strong support from key administrators, the proposal moved forward step by step and was approved by the Office of the President in the spring of 1994, making us the only Department of Native American Studies in the country, with Jack Forbes as chair.

In 1994 our organized research program became the Indigenous Research Center of the Americas (IRCA), directed by Professor Varese, and we applied for a four-year Rockefeller Foundation grant in the humanities, which was awarded.

Under this program, outstanding Native intellectuals from all of the Americas have been able to spend time at Davis, interacting with the academic community and pursuing their projects. Scholars and artists have included: Florentino Laime (Quechua), Brent Michael Davids (Mohican), Beth Brant (Mohawk), Ana Uriarte (Peruana), Hulleah Tsinhnahjinnie (Navajo-Muskogee), Felipe Molina (Yaqui), Rudy James (Tlingit), Javier Galicia-Silva (Nahua), Maria Eugenia Choque (Aymará), Victor de la Cruz (Zapotec), José Narciso Conejo Quinche (Quichua), and Joann Marie Barker (Lenápe).

Professor Forbes retired in 1994; however, he served for an additional year as chair and has continued to play an active role in the teaching and research program of the department. He mentors several graduate students and teaches for Native American studies on both the Davis and Berkeley campuses, and is also continuing with his own research, lecturing, and writing. Martha Macri served as chair in 1995–1996 and again in 1999–2000, providing excellent leadership. Inés Hernández-Ávila served as chair for two years, from 1996 to 1998, accomplishing a great deal, including the finalization of our successful Ph.D. proposal. Professor Victor Montejo is the current chair and a very prolific scholar, poet, and writer.

In 1995–1996 we were able to hire two new junior faculty: in 1995, Prof. Luana Ross (Salish), a sociologist who focuses on Native American criminality and deviance, and in 1996, Prof. Victor Montejo (Jakaltek Maya), who is a creative writer and anthropologist with a specialization in Maya communities. Both Professors Ross and Montejo were awarded tenure in 1997. (Unfortunately, Professor Ross recently left us to join her husband at the University of Washington.) Professor Montejo was a UC President's Postdoctoral Fellow with us during 1994–1995. Dr. Zoila Mendoza, a Peruvian scholar and authority on dance and music (especially of the Andes), joined us in 1999–2000. Dr. Anne Dannenberg (Cherokee) taught our lower-division literature courses as a lecturer for several years, with great success. Dr. Joann Marie Barker joined us in fall 2001 as an assistant professor. We have been successful in bringing in more UC President's Postdoctoral Fellows than any other department (to our knowledge), recently sponsoring Peruvian scholar Prof. Tirso Gonzalez, who works in environmental studies with an emphasis on biodiversity and Native intellectual property rights. By July 1, 1997, all of our junior tenure-track faculty had been promoted to associate professors with tenure. Three of our faculty, Prof. Inés Hernández-Ávila, Prof. Steve Crum, and Prof. Luana Ross, have also been Ford Foundation/National Research Council Postdoctoral Fellows. Professor Forbes has been a Social Science Research Council Fellow, a Guggenheim Fellow, the Tinbergen Chair in the Netherlands, and was awarded the John Adams Chair in the Netherlands for 1999–2000. He has won the Senior Fulbright Award, the American Book Award for Lifetime Achievement in 1997, and the title Nonfiction Writer of the Year from the Wordcraft Circle of Native Writers for 1999.

Mention should also be made of the guest faculty who have served with us, including: David Wilkins (Lumbee), Anthony Garcia (Apache), Victoria Bomberry (Muskogee-Lenápe), Annette Reed-Crum (Tolowa), Richard O. Livingston (Cherokee), Hulleah Tsinhnahjinnie (Navajo-Muskogee), Steve Talbot, Susan Lobo, Troy Johnson, and many others. Dr. Louis Owens (Cherokee-Muskogee) joined us in 2000–2001 with a joint appointment in English, bringing our total tenure-track faculty up to eight. Now, with Dr. Barker, it is nine, plus two active emeritii.

The Departmental Philosophy

Native American studies at UC–Davis has emerged as a discipline with several objectives. First, it bridges the humanities and social sciences through the study of the history, languages, philosophy, and values, society, politics, ways of life, and development through time of Indigenous peoples of the Americas. Second, it develops concrete insights into the civilizational unity (hemispheric/land-based commonality and history of cultural exchange and influence) of Native American peoples as well as the specific diversity in which this fundamental unity is expressed throughout the hemisphere. Third, the field develops research capabilities and critical intelligence, and fosters an understanding of the broad human experiences in which Native American life and thought serve as the vehicle for analysis, comparison, and synthesis. Fourth, the hemispheric focus fosters the student's understanding of Indigenous creative thinking and illustrates how, in Native American life, the aesthetic and artistic approaches are an integral part of the cultural whole.[19] Finally, the field of Native American studies is more than an academic chronicler of Native cultures and histories. From the very beginning we planned to hire faculty and staff who could work for the direct benefit of Native communities. We argued for theoretical scholars, practicing artists, and "persons with broad practical experience in Indian affairs, tribal management, Indian legal practice, Indian community development, etc. . . . This is because the thrust of Indian Studies is not primarily to study the Indian community but to develop practical programs for and by the Indian community."[20]

Our department has been and is actively involved in the preservation and development hemispherically of Native peoples and their communities. It is, in fact, this definitive commitment to Native Nations and communities that contributes to the charge of the University of California as a land-grant institution. Our departmental proposal argued that in order to accomplish its mission, Native American studies would need to respond to the enormous changes taking place in the hemisphere in a uniquely Indigenous manner. As Professor Varese has written:

The intellectual challenge for Native American Studies is enormous but solvable, since the object is not to re-write the various disciplines that have hegemonized that scene of Western hermeneutics of Indian societies, but rather to recuperate the principles that sustain Indian cultures and consolidate a heuristic which can serve the learning and problem-solving needs of the Indian societies of the Americas. The question of offended academic territorialities provoked by an imaginary threat to the scientific monopoly of established disciplines or to the professional labor market will certainly rise. The answer is not to be found in a millimetric negotiation over the disciplinary boundaries (conventionally artificial anyway), but rather in the uniqueness of Native American Studies as an intellectual, scientific, cultural, and pragmatic domain of the Indians of the Americas.[21]

Implementation of Philosophy

Among the other basic elements of the philosophy of the department are these objectives: (1) excellence in research and creative work, illustrated in part by the creation of an organized research program in Native American Research and Development, now the Indigenous Research Center of the Americas; (2) excellence in undergraduate teaching for majors, minors, and students seeking general education; (3) excellence in advising with close attention to individual student needs; (4) excellence in extra-classroom activities, including the operation of the Carl N. Gorman Museum and work with the Native American Student Union, American Indian Science and Engineering Society, Staff of American Indian Descent, D-Q University, and "Native American Culture Days"; and (5) excellence in graduate education, in working with existing Ph.D. programs as well as in developing our own Ph.D. in Native American studies.[22]

As noted earlier, we began to develop a small exhibit space in 1970, but it wasn't until 1973, with the arrival of George Longfish and the establishment of the Carl N. Gorman Museum, that any real development occurred. Longfish, recognized as one of the top Native artists in the country, served as director and curator of the museum for twenty-three years, along with being a full-time faculty member in Native American studies. The reputation of the Gorman today is solidly established not only locally but nationally, in that about 90 percent of the Native artists recognized at the national level have had their work exhibited here. Combining his responsibilities as artist, faculty member, and curator, Longfish, and his successor Theresa Harlan, developed a professional exhibit space for Native artists that allowed them to be advocates of modern/contemporary Indian art, to exhibit the work, and to meet the artists. Longfish and Harlan were able to identify and give recognition to Native artists, fostering relationships with them and among them, while also, in the larger sense, contributing to the building of the community of Native artists as we know it today in (particularly) the United States and Canada. Through his selection of exhibits Longfish also actively supported the hemispheric perspective that distinguishes our program. In his twenty-three-year history with the museum, he installed approximately 150 exhibits in the Gorman. Through Longfish's research and creative work, he has played a critical role in the establishment of the field of contemporary Native American art, and from an academic standpoint vis-à-vis our program, he has ensured that this field is a major component of the evolving discipline of Native American studies. Longfish stepped down from the directorship of the Carl N. Gorman Museum in the spring of 1996, but has recently resumed that role.

Theresa Harlan succeeded Longfish as curator and made the Gorman an even stronger center of exhibitions, seminars, poetry and fiction readings, and film. The museum has enhanced our course offerings immeasurably by creating a space for the visual arts; our faculty often take their classes to the Gorman to relate their lecture or presentation to the artwork being exhibited. At the opening receptions and through special programming associated with each exhibition, students and the general public have the opportunity to meet and hear presentations by the artists themselves. The monographs produced by Harlan for exhibitions place the work of these artists in relation to current art and cultural studies criticism. Another positive aspect of the Gorman is the programming that occurs on weekends, whereby members of the Native community and other persons can come together for events such as "Ancestral Memories: Sharing Memories and Stories of Native Survival," which took place in the winter quarter of 1997. A winter 1999 program that featured the work of Claudia Bernardi, focusing on her work as a forensic anthropologist and artist investigating the massacres of Maya people in Guatemala, drew a very large audience, who were exposed to the interface of visual art and moral struggle.

In 1970–1971 we began offering coursework in the Navajo language, taught by Carl Gorman. Recently, we have been able to revive our Native-language teaching program, using an individualized approach developed by Martha Macri. An important resource for language study and research by graduate students is our Native American Language Center, under the direction of Professors Macri, Montejo, and Victor Golla (Humboldt State University). The purpose of the center is to encourage linguistic research on American Indian languages, and to foster the intergenerational transfer of language knowledge in Native American communities. The overall aim of the center is to develop a sustained and productive relationship between American Indian linguistic scholarship and the needs and aspirations of Native American peoples. The center encourages the active participation of scholars and students, both Native and non-Native, in the task of language preservation and revitalization, while also providing the resources and support for the training of a new and engaged generation of research linguists.

The center maintains communication with the Advocates for Indigenous Language Survival, the Master/Apprentice Language Learning Program, and the Native California Network. Members participated in the "Breath of Life Conference" at UC–Berkeley, a meeting for Native Californians studying languages no longer spoken. Components of the center include the Native American Language Center Archives; the materials of the Society for the Study of the Indigenous Languages of the Americas (SSILA); coordination with faculty throughout the UC and CSU systems in providing instruction in Native American languages; and the J. P. Harrington Study Facility, making use of the massive language field notes collected by Harrington in the first half of this century. Research projects currently hosted by the center include: the Maya Hieroglyphic Database Project, funded by the National Endowment for the Humanities and the National Science Foundation, and the Tzeltal Dictionary Project and the Jakaltek Dictionary Project, both funded by the Foundation for the Advancement of Mesoamerican Studies.

Native American studies as a whole, the IRCA, the Gorman, the language center, and the Native American Student Union are all frequent sponsors of conferences, colloquia, exhibits, presentations, and powwows that serve both the public and scholars. A major conference in 1998 took place both in Davis and in Oaxaca, Mexico. Faculty from Native American studies are also frequent presenters in Europe, Canada, Mexico, Guatemala, Venezuela, and elsewhere, as well as throughout the United States. Each year for many years our students have coordinated the annual Culture Days Pow-Wow, which draws participants from all around the United States and Canada and which brings us into close touch with northern California Native families and our alumni.[23]

Students Served and Career Opportunities

The Department of Native American Studies at UC–Davis serves students of a variety of types: (1) those who wish to work for Tribal governments, inter-Tribal agencies, voluntary organizations, and international agencies serving Indian peoples; (2) those who wish to secure a teaching certificate and work as a teacher in Indian country or in schools with multiethnic students (such as virtually all of the schools in California); (3) those who wish to pursue a master's degree in social service areas, such as social welfare and counseling, with emphasis upon serving Indigenous Americans; (4) those who desire an interdisciplinary baccalaureate degree program that allows them to explore intellectual concepts, cultural systems, religious philosophies, and value systems that provide alternatives to the Eurocentric focus of the dominant society; (5) those who seek to understand the original cultures and societies of the Americas as a fundamental aspect of humanistic inquiry in relation to the uniqueness of the American continent; and (6) those who seek to pursue graduate work in relation to Native American or cross-cultural subjects as areas of concentration in a variety of disciplines or fields such as anthropology, history, English, and so forth, or who seek to do graduate work in Native American studies itself.[24]

Graduates are currently employed with Tribal governments, inter-Tribal agencies, state governments, the federal government, education agencies, voluntary or public interest organizations, Indian service agencies, social welfare agencies (i.e., county or local government), and colleges and universities as both staff and faculty. In addition, some are attorneys, art teachers, or directors of Tribal museums and cultural programs; a few are in private business on Indian reservations or elsewhere. Graduates of the program have also gone on to medical school, veterinary medicine, law, and other professional graduate programs.[25]

Career prospects are good because the Native American population is growing rapidly and public agencies do not have enough teachers and other employees who have an Indian background or who have expertise in relation to Indigenous peoples. Throughout Latin America the Indigenous population is the fastest-growing sector, as in Mexico, where a recent presidential commission has publicized that such is the case. Thus the need for persons sensitive to the Indian community will continue to grow rapidly. The A.B. major provides options focusing on Meso-America and South America that will provide opportunities for work in international relations and with international agencies.[26]

Native American studies is a practical major if a student is considering a career in a field such as teaching, law, human services, health, Tribal administration, or interethnic relations, among others. Graduate schools and agencies in these and related areas are often looking for students who are broadly prepared in an interdisciplinary way and who possess knowledge and sensitivity relating to ethnic issues and cultural diversity. Specifically, schools and agencies are increasingly looking for personnel with expertise in relation to Native American peoples since, as noted, Native American peoples constitute a rapidly growing population throughout the entire hemisphere.[27]

Students electing a major in Native American studies may complete one of three plans. Plan I enables students to concentrate chiefly upon the Native experience in North America (north of Mexico). The purpose of Plan II is to encourage interested students to focus upon Meso-America, with some coursework integrating Meso-America with North America and South America. Plan III is intended to encourage students to focus upon South America, with coursework integrating that region with areas to the north.[28]

The department's distinctive features also include: (1) the maintenance of a tradition of close liaison with the Indian community, with Indian educational centers, with the Indian Education section of the California Department of Education, with Title IV centers in school districts, with Indian-controlled community colleges such as D-Q University, with Indian and Chicano programs at CSU–Sacramento and elsewhere, including opportunities for cultural enrichment experiences for Native American studies students in Indian settings; (2) an emphasis upon utilizing theory and basic research to help to solve "real-world" problems in Native American communities; and (3) a program of publications designed to directly help Native communities.[29] These publications consist of general publications of the department, including a newsletter; publications of the Carl N. Gorman Museum; and publications of the IRCA (*Pueblos Originarios*, a bilingual series).[30]

The Graduate Program

The graduate program in Native American studies is designed to allow students to make use of the rich and diverse offerings of the University of California–Davis within a program of studies focusing specifically on the historical, cultural, and contemporary reality of Native American peoples. Students are able to combine a core focus on Native American studies with coursework in related areas that can contribute to the ongoing evolution of American Indian communities, such as work relating to community development, historical heritage and archaeology, or resource management. Other students may choose to focus primarily on courses dealing with Native American history and culture, combining the social sciences and humanities in such a manner as to prepare them for a career of advanced teaching and research in Native American studies.[31]

At the master's level, the course of study is designed to prepare students for practice-oriented work in Tribal administration and management (including governance and education), museums and cultural centers, community development, and public policy. The master's program would also prepare students to teach in any of the Tribal colleges that make up the American Indian Higher Education Consortium (AIHEC), which is a consortium of Native colleges throughout the United States and Canada, in other Native-controlled colleges being planned for Nicaragua, Oaxaca, and elsewhere, as well as other community colleges. The master's program would further prepare students who intend to pursue a Ph.D. in Native American (or American Indian) studies or a related field at another university.

At the Ph.D. level, the course of study is designed to train, strengthen, and enlarge the critical mass of scholars working within the field of Native American studies. Our graduates will be positioned as scholars to contribute to the unlayering of Native critical/creative intelligence in all its complexity. The training will prepare them to take their place as scholars within Native American studies programs and within other departments that are seeking to revitalize their own offerings through the reconfiguration of their disciplinary perspectives.

Obtaining a doctor of philosophy degree with a designated emphasis in Native American studies is also possible at UC–Davis, and it is especially appropriate for future Native Americanists who wish to major in disciplines or subdisciplines such as archaeology, sociocultural anthropology, linguistics, sociology, political science, Latin American literature, comparative literature, North American literature in English, and humanistic psychology, among other fields.[32]

Non-English Language Requirement for the Graduate Student

The graduate program in Native American studies recognizes the importance of Indigenous languages to any in-depth understanding of Native American cultures. Students seeking the Ph.D. degree have two language requirements; for students seeking the master's degree it is recommended that they fulfill one language requirement. Ph.D. students are required to demonstrate competency in two languages other than English that are relevant to research relating to Native Americans. The first language must be a Native American language, and the second may be an additional Native American language or Spanish, Portuguese, French, German, Latin, or any other language approved by the student's adviser.

Students are required to demonstrate knowledge of one (or two) Native American languages in one of the following ways:

1. Demonstrate proficiency in a Native American language. The student has the option of composing a 500-word text, either in writing or by audio recording, in that language. A Native speaker or a qualified linguist may act as a consultant for purposes of judging the language competency. This option is available for students who come to the program as Native language speakers, or who have already completed the language study to achieve a fluency in the language in question.
2. Participate in a language internship program in which at least one quarter is spent off campus doing intensive language study in an Indigenous community or taking classes in an Indigenous language at an outside college or university (such as the Navajo Community College, the University of Oklahoma, etc.).
3. Complete four units of coursework, or independent study giving graduate credit, in which the student examines some aspect of a Native American language relevant to his/her research.[33]

Conclusion

The Department of Native American Studies and the University of California–Davis recently received a gift of $1 million from the Cache Creek–Rumsey Rancheria, of which one-third will be used to fund a permanent chair in California Indian studies. This position will be filled in 2002. This position, along with our post in political and sovereignty issues, filled by Joann Marie Barker, will give us added strength.

We are also looking forward to the arrival of an additional group of Ph.D. students for our doctoral program. We anticipate being able to add other new faculty in the next several years, fleshing out our strengths in areas such as Native languages and cultural-biodiversity issues. We will continue to seek out faculty who are both serious scholars and persons committed to working for the well-being of Indigenous communities, and faculty who bring to their teaching and research a sense of joy, sharing, and collegiality. Our strength has been the high quality of our faculty, and we will seek to maintain that tradition of excellence and vision.

Notes

1. Portions of this chapter are derived from proposals and statements prepared in the course of the development of the Department of Native American Studies at the University of California–Davis. The chapter's authors are all faculty in the department, and all have participated to one degree or another in the preparation of such materials or in their editing and discussion.

2. Adapted from "Proposal for Offering the Doctor of Philosophy [Ph.D.] and Master of Arts [M.A.] Degrees in Native American Studies," draft, February 1992, 1, and final version, April 1992, 1. Also in "The Designated Emphasis in Native American Studies," draft, November 1991, 2, and final version, September 1992, 2.

3. Jack D. Forbes, "Native American and Ethnic Studies," 2, 8, 9; "Proposed Courses in Native American Literature and Native Americans of the Northern Plains," in *Handbook for the Development of Native American Studies,* Jack D. Forbes, Carolyn Johnson et al. eds., (Davis, Calif.: Tecumseh Center–Native American Studies, 1971), 89, 92–93.

4. Forbes, Johnson et al., eds., *Handbook.* See also David Risling, ed., *History of Tecumseh Center, to 1975* (Davis, Calif.: Tecumseh Center–Native American Studies, 1988), and issues of *Coyote,* published by the Tecumseh Center students in the early 1970s and housed in the Jack D. Forbes Collection and the David Risling Jr. Collection in the Special Collections Department, Shields Library, University of California–Davis.

5. Poma's work is available in English as *Letter to a King,* Christopher Dieke, ed. and trans. (New York: Dutton, 1978).

6. Luana Ross, *Inventing the Savage: The Social Construction of Native American Criminality* (Austin: University of Texas Press, 2000).

7. Adapted from Jack D. Forbes, "Thoughts about Native American Studies," in *Native American Studies Association [NASA] Newsletter* 1, no. 1 (May 1990): 1, 7.

8. Adapted from "Proposal for the Establishment of a Native American Organized Research Program," revised April 26, 1991, and prepared by Stefano Varese.

9. Adapted from "Proposal for a Department of Native American Studies," November 1991, 2–3.

10. The first part of this section is largely written by Steven Crum, with the second part by Jack Forbes.

11. Chief Standing Bear, *Land of the Spotted Eagle* (1933).

12. Adapted from Steven J. Crum, "Twenty Years Ago," *NASA Newsletter* 1, no. 1 (May 1990): 1.

13. See Jack D. Forbes, *Native American Higher Education: The Struggle for the Creation of D-Q University, 1961–1970* (Davis, Calif.: D-Q University Press, 1985).

14. David Risling Jr., letter to Officials and Regents of the University of California, June 17, 1969, in Forbes, Johnson et al., eds., *Handbook*, 17–18. See also David Risling Jr., ed., *California Indian Education* (Modesto: Ad Hoc Committee on California Indian Education, 1967). This is the report of the first statewide CIEA conference at North Fork.

15. "Resolution of the Higher Education Committee of the California Indian Education Association," in Forbes, Johnson et al., eds., *Handbook*, 19–20.

16. "Native American Studies at the University of California, Davis: A Status Report," April 1970. For this and other early program documents, see Jack D. Forbes, "A Documentary History of Native American Studies: Proposals and Planning," Forbes Collection, Shield Library (see Melvyl).

17. "Native American Studies at the University of California." See also Jack D. Forbes, "A Documentary History of Some Highlights of Ethnic Studies at UC Davis, 1969–1985" (compiled 1988; housed in Shields Library [see Melvyl]); Jack D. Forbes, "Ethnic Studies, Western and Non-Western at the University of California, Davis, 1969–1988" (Native American Studies, 1988; Shields Library [see Melvyl]); Jack D. Forbes, "Native American Studies," in *The Minority Student on the Campus: Expectations and Possibilities*, Robert A. Altman and Patricia O. Snyder, eds. (Boulder, Colo.: Western Interstate Commission for Higher Education, 1970), 159ff.

18. Ironically, we had anticipated just such problems. See Jack D. Forbes, "Autonomy or Integration: Structural Arrangements for Native American Studies Programs," in Forbes, Johnson et al., eds., *Handbook*, 13–16.

19. Adapted from "Designated Emphasis," November 1991, 2, and September 1992, 2. Also in "Proposal for the Ph.D. and M.A.," February 1992, and final version, April 1992.

20. Jack D. Forbes, memo to Chet McCorkle, December 24, 1969, in Forbes, Johnson et al., eds., *Handbook*, 28–29.

21. Stefano Varese, "The Continental Unity of NAS," *NASA Newsletter* 1, no. 1 (May 1990): 6. Also in "Proposal for a Department," November 1991, 4.

22. From "Proposal for a Department," November 1991, 4. Reprinted in "Proposal for the Ph.D. and M.A.," April 1992; "Information and Requirements for a New Major," April 6, 1993; "Designated Emphasis," September 1992.

23. Adapted from "Proposal for a Graduate Program in Native American Studies for the Doctor of Philosophy and Master of Arts Degrees," April 30, 1998.

24. "Proposal for a Department," November 1991, 4. Also in "Information and Requirements," April 6, 1993.

25. "Proposal for a Department," November 1991, 4. Also in "Information and Requirements," April 6, 1993.

26. "Proposal for a Department," November 1991, 4. Also in "Information and Requirements," April 6, 1993.

27. "Proposal for a Department," November 1991, 5.

28. "Proposal for a Department," November 1991, 5.

29. Adapted from "Information and Requirements," April 6, 1993, and from "Proposal for a Department," November 1991, 5–6.

30. A list of available publications can be found on the department's Web site or can be obtained by mail.

31. From "Proposal for the Ph.D. and M.A.," April 1992.

32. From "Designated Emphasis," September 1992.

33. From "Proposal for a Graduate Program," April 30, 1998.

In Caleb's Footsteps: The Harvard University Native American Program 7

LORIE M. GRAHAM AND PETER R. GOLIA

Figure 7.1.   Harvard University Native
American Program (HUNAP) logo

ARVARD UNIVERSITY'S COMMITMENT to Native American education dates back to the mid-1600s. Benign neglect is a generous description of that commitment over the centuries. So it came as no surprise when we started in September 1995 that the Harvard University Native American Program (HUNAP) was soon to close its doors.

Our assigned task from the administration was clear—raise short-term funds to keep the doors open. Our goal, and the goal of Eileen Egan, the program coordinator, and the students involved in the program at the time, was much broader—put in place a foundational structure that would assist the program in achieving a leadership position in Native American studies in the years to come. Of course, we were not the first to venture down this path. The concept of the American Indian Program (AIP) at Harvard was the brainchild of a first-year doctoral student at the Harvard Graduate School of Education (HGSE), its original mission being the training of American Indian students in the field of education. In 1970, HGSE accepted eleven Native Americans to the master's degree program—the largest number of Indian students to attend Harvard since the mid-1600s, when Harvard made its original commitment to the education of American Indian youth.

> Harvard University Native American Program Mission Statement
> *To bring together Native American students and interested individuals from the Harvard community for the purpose of advancing the well being of indigenous peoples through self-determination, academic achievement, and community service.*
>
> —NATIVE AMERICAN STUDENTS AT HARVARD, 1995

Since that time, many dedicated individuals have given their time and enthusiasm to the survival of the program. It hasn't been easy. Harvard's program, like many Native American programs around the country, has faced a number of significant challenges: issues such as gaining and maintaining institutional support, attracting and retaining Native American students and faculty, and developing a coherent vision that balances all the important components of the program— teaching and research, student services, and community outreach. The purpose of this chapter is to share our experiences in dealing with these and other related issues during our tenure, as well as our thoughts on the future of an American Indian studies program at Harvard University. In addition, we have included information on the current structure and mission of the program.

First and foremost, this is a story about real people whose vision and strength helped keep the original promise of Indian education at Harvard alive and made all that came after possible. Thus, to understand the present, we need to look back 350 years to Harvard's founding purpose.

Step I: Remembering the Past

> *Whereas, through the good hand of God, many devoted persons have been and daily are moved and stirred up to give and bestow sundry gifts, legacies, land, and revenues for the advancement of all good literature, arts and sciences in Harvard College in Cambridge in the County of Middlesex and to the maintenance of the President and Fellows and for all accommodations*

*of buildings and all other necessary provisions that may conduce to the
education of the English and Indian youth of this Country in knowledge
and godliness.*

—THE CHARTER OF THE PRESIDENT AND FELLOWS
OF HARVARD COLLEGE, 1650

Something we learned early on in our tenure is that the history of Native Americans at Harvard is an untold story to most. For instance, many within Harvard itself were unaware that the Charter of 1650, under which the university is still governed, commits Harvard "to the education of the English and Indian youth." This language was written into the charter by Harvard's first president, Henry Dunster, whose ambition it was to make Harvard "the Indian Oxford as well as the New-English Cambridge."

During the mid-1600s, Harvard College faced severe financial hardship. To survive, it solicited charitable funds from England for the future education and religious conversion of Indian students. By far the biggest donor during that time was the Society for the Promoting and Propagating of the Gospel in New England, an organization incorporated by an act of the Long Parliament for the sole purpose of providing funds for the conversion and education of American Indians. The society's funds were used in 1655 to construct Harvard's Indian College, a two-story brick building that was designed to house twenty scholars, and the Indian Library, which contained numerous publications printed in Algonquian and English, including the Rev. John Eliot's "Indian Bible."

The society's mission, as well as Harvard's during those early years, was part of a larger educational philosophy that was predominant in colonial America. Educators, such as the Reverend Eliot, believed that wholesale religious conversion was best achieved through education—that if Indians were educated in "Christian ethics and arts," their souls could be converted. These colonial themes would reverberate throughout nineteenth- and twentieth-century U.S. Indian education policy—from religious indoctrination, to cultural intolerance, to wholesale removal of American Indian children.

It was on this basis that the first two American Indian students, Caleb Cheeshahteaumuck and Joel Iacoomes, were brought to Harvard. Caleb was Wampanoag, and came from the Island of Nope—known today as Martha's Vineyard. He was the son of a sachem and at the age of ten was removed to the mainland to study English at the Daniel Weld Preparatory School in Roxbury, Massachusetts. Two years later, he was transferred to the Elijah Corlet Grammar School in Cambridge, Massachusetts. Joel was also Wampanoag and at the age of eleven joined Caleb on the mainland. At the Corlet School, Joel and Caleb were the top scholars among the English and Indian students. In 1661, after passing a series of entrance exams, both were admitted to Harvard. Caleb was fifteen and Joel sixteen.

Each was considered to be an excellent scholar. Both spoke Algonquian, as well as Latin, Greek, Hebrew, and English. Daniel Gookin states in his book *Historical Collections of the Indians in New England* that the two young men were "good scholars" and "diligent students."[1] Equally important, however, was the self-deprecating system of education these children were expected to endure in the name of Christianity, as poignantly demonstrated in the following passage from an extant letter written by Cheeshahteaumuck to his "most honoured benefactors" in England:

> The ancient philosophers state that this serves as a symbol to show how powerful the force and virtue of education and of refined literature are in the transformation of the barbarians' nature. . . . The lord delegated you to be our patrons, and he endowed you with all wisdom and intimate compassion, so that you may perform the work of bringing blessing to us pagans. . . . We were naked in our souls as well as in our bodies, we were aliens from all humanity, and we were led around in the desert. . . . [M]ost illustrious and most loving men, what kind of thanks . . . should we give to you . . . for our education.[2]

In 1665, Caleb Cheeshahteaumuck became the first American Indian to graduate from Harvard College. A year after graduation he fell ill with tuberculosis and died at the age of twenty in Charlestown, Massachusetts. Joel Iacoomes never made it to graduation. He died in a shipwreck one month before he was to take his degree. Out of the nine students graduating that year—English and Indian—Joel was to take top honors.

Three other Indian students followed Cheeshahteaumuck and Iacoomes during those early years—John Wampus, Eleazar, and Benjamin Larnell. Two died of smallpox before graduation and one left to become a mariner. As for the Indian College, it was torn down in 1698 after falling into disrepair. But the promise of Indian education at Harvard did not end there. The Society for the Promoting and Propagating of the Gospel would only agree to the demolition of the college provided that "in case any Indians should hereinafter be sent to College, they should enjoy their studies rent-free in said building."[3] In addition, Harvard continued to be governed by its original commitment to the education of Indian students. However, this evolving instructive alliance between American Indians and Harvard did not meet with much success. Research to date suggests that there was no identifiable Native American presence at Harvard from 1714 to the establishment of the American Indian Program in 1970.

The American Indian Program, a joint undertaking instituted in 1962 by Harvard University and Radcliffe College, was Harvard's first organized effort to reach out to Native American students. However, it wasn't until 1970, when AIP was established at the Harvard Graduate School of Education, that any substantial progress was made in the recruitment and retention of Native American students. The program's founding was part of the national self-determination movement to provide greater Native control over institutions serving Native peoples. HGSE and the U.S. Office of Economic Opportunity entered into discussions about the feasibility of funding an American Indian studies program at Harvard. These discussions followed on the heels of the 1969 landmark U.S. Senate report "Indian Education: A National Tragedy, a National Challenge." In April 1970 the federal government committed funds to the program for the purpose of preparing Native Americans to fulfill positions of leadership in education.

Eleven Native American students representing eleven different Tribes commenced their studies in the following academic year. In addition to attending classes, the students worked in community agencies, taught courses, recruited new students, and participated in hearings in Washington, D.C., on Indian education. Both the students and AIP itself were quite successful in meeting the program's original mission, enjoying zero attrition, timely completion of degree requirements, and recognition in Native communities.

In 1971, AIP was funded once again by the U.S. Office of Economic Opportunity with additional moneys from the U.S. Office of Education and the Bureau of Indian Affairs. Although Harvard engaged in no direct recruitment during this time, word had spread in Native American communities regarding the success of the program and thirteen new graduate students were admitted the following year. However, an internal evaluation conducted by the director of the program during that same year showed that cost of living, especially housing, was a major problem for these students. Nevertheless, 75 percent of the grades received were As, validating once again that Native Americans could compete on an equal footing in the rigorous Harvard curriculum.

In 1981, when AIP lost federal funding, Native students worked diligently to keep the doors open, paying most of the basic expenses themselves. In 1982 federal funds were restored and the program successfully continued its graduate-level recruitment efforts until 1987, when federal funds were once again discontinued. During the next two years, the program sought alternative sources of financial support from the Ford Foundation and other organizations. Although these funds allowed the program to survive, the loss of federal support had devastating effects on Native enrollment at HGSE, with only two Native students matriculating in the fall of 1989. Inadequate funding also took its toll on the five previous directors of the program, each of whom had worked tirelessly to ensure that Harvard kept its original promise to help educate the Indian youth of this country.

In his 1995 article "Uses of Diversity," President Neil Rudenstine of Harvard states that "the extent of our nation's success in dealing with diversity can be measured only in the full light of our entire history."[4] This statement is equally true for Harvard, an institution steeped in history and a place of many stories. Remembering and making known the story of Caleb Cheeshahteaumuck and his successors have been an important part of securing HUNAP's future within the university. That is why on May 3, 1997, HUNAP staff joined university officials, faculty, Tribal leaders, Elders, alumni, students, and others for the unveiling and dedication of the Native American Commemorative Plaque. The plaque commemorates the history and contributions of Native Americans at Harvard during those early years. An exhibit and lecture series titled *A Circle in Time: Contact, Education, and Change in Native American Massachusetts,* exploring the rich and complicated history of Native American education at Harvard, accompanied the plaque's dedication. It was through the telling and retelling of this story that HUNAP hoped to create a strong foundation from which to build a new interdisciplinary program.

NEAR THIS SPOT FROM 1655 TO 1698 STOOD THE INDIAN
    COLLEGE
HERE AMERICAN INDIAN AND ENGLISH STUDENTS LIVED
    AND STUDIED IN ACCORDANCE WITH THE 1650
    CHARTER OF HARVARD COLLEGE CALLING FOR 'THE
    EDUCATION OF THE ENGLISH AND INDIAN YOUTH OF
    THIS COUNTRY'
THE INDIAN COLLEGE WAS HARVARD'S FIRST BRICK
    BUILDING AND HOUSED THE COLLEGE PRINTING PRESS
    WHERE FROM 1659 TO 1663 WAS PRINTED THE FIRST
    BIBLE IN NORTH AMERICA
THE ALGONQUIAN TRANSLATION BY JOHN ELIOT
OF THE FIRST FIVE AMERICAN INDIANS TO ATTEND
    HARVARD COLLEGE
JOEL IACOOMES ◆ ELEAZAR ◆ BENJAMIN LARNELL DIED
    PRIOR TO GRADUATION
JOHN WAMPUS LEFT AND BECAME A MARINER
CALEB CHEESHAHTEAUMUCK OF THE WAMPANOAG TRIBE
    ◆ CLASS OF 1665
WAS THE FIRST AMERICAN INDIAN TO GRADUATE

This plaque was placed by the Harvard University Native
American Program ◆ 1997

Step 2: Navigating University Crosscurrents and Charting a Course

In 1990 the American Indian Program was reorganized as the Harvard University Native American Program. As the decade began, the program set a new course for the future: expand its focus beyond HGSE to include the entire university while securing a solid funding base. By the mid-1990s there were two important crosscurrents at Harvard that would help shape the program's future.

First, Harvard had instituted a number of interfaculty initiatives that cut across various disciplines, such as children and the environment. While for other universities this may not seem particularly noteworthy, for Harvard, an institution that historically operated as nine autonomous faculties (Business, Education, Law, Arts and Sciences, Medicine, Divinity, Design, Public Health, and Government) rather than a single unified university, it was indeed a substantial undertaking. Another important crosscurrent was the ongoing debate over ethnic studies at Harvard. Unlike other four-year institutions, such as the University of California–Berkeley, Harvard does not have an ethnic studies department beyond Afro-American studies. The 1990s brought a renewed interest among the student body on the study of race and ethnicity within the university, particularly in the area of Asian and Latino studies. Since that time, the Faculty of Arts and Sciences has instituted an Ethnic Studies Committee that is, according to its Web site, participating in "a dialogue on the future of an Ethnic Studies department and opportunities open to undergraduates in the absence of such a department."[5] However, the creation of separate curricular entities continues to be disfavored among the administration. The preferred course of study appears to be cross-disciplinary courses as well as the development of university-wide programs, such as the Center for Latin American Studies and the Center for Jewish Studies. Complementing this debate was the university president's ongoing dialogue on diversity and learning at Harvard.

Both of these crosscurrents helped shape HUNAP's structure and focus, some positively, others negatively. For instance, while the development of a Native American studies department at Harvard was not seen as a viable option, the interfaculty initiatives open the door to the restructuring of HUNAP beyond the Harvard Graduate School of Education to include each of the university's nine faculties. To those working in the field, this interdisciplinary approach to American Indian studies was a logical next step for HUNAP. On an informal level, some of this cross-disciplinary collaboration was already happening at Harvard, particularly among the Native American student body. The university's formal dialogue on diversity and cross-disciplinary studies helped to formalize this approach.

Step 3: Building a Native American Program

Faculty Advisory Board

President Neil Rudenstine has said that the faculty governs the university. Thus for HUNAP to have a place within Harvard, we needed to involve the faculty in the governance of the program. An interdisciplinary faculty advisory board representing the nine faculties at Harvard was the vehicle to accomplish this. The advisory board has been meeting monthly since November 1995 and is a core component of HUNAP. By the end of 1997, it had grown to thirty-two members, including senior faculty, students, university officials, and HUNAP staff. Two faculty cochairs, who serve alternating two-year terms, lead the advisory board, which has been instrumental in:

- teaching interdisciplinary courses
- developing and implementing field-based research projects
- disseminating HUNAP information
- attracting visiting scholars to the university
- recruiting and mentoring students
- raising funds for HUNAP

The internal changes at Harvard required as much time and attention as the external issues. Without support from the central administration, deans, and faculty members, the attempt to rejuvenate HUNAP would have little chance of success. Thus, the primary focus of the faculty advisory board was to restructure HUNAP to complement the movement within the university toward interdisciplinary teaching and research, while remaining true to HUNAP's original mission of educating Native American students and providing community support.

Teaching and Research

The perception of the Harvard University Native American Program among the administration, deans, faculty, and students had been one of a student service program housed within the Harvard Graduate School of Education. For the program to survive and grow, its focus needed to be expanded to meet the mission of the university—teaching and research (see figure 7.2). Through this expansion of focus, The program (1) facilitates and encourages academic teaching and research by university faculty, as well as by graduate and undergraduate students from across the university, and (2) provides linkages between researchers and Native American Nations and organizations in the United States and Canada.

Several innovative interdisciplinary courses of instruction have been developed and taught by university faculty and students in the past several years. The courses

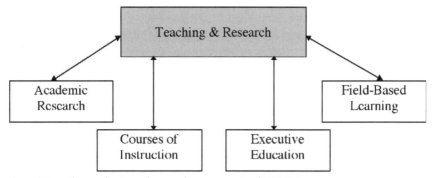

Figure 7.2.   The academic and research components of HUNAP

are designed to encourage multidisciplinary study by interested students from across Harvard. For example, "Native Americans in the Twenty-first Century: Nation Building I" is aimed at upper-level undergraduate and graduate students and focuses on current issues in Indian Country, such as self-governance, economic development, and sovereignty. The course is team-taught by faculty from Arts and Sciences, Government, Law, Business, and Education. "Native Americans in the Twenty-first Century: Nation Building II" provides field-based learning opportunities for students who have completed "Nation Building I," while providing an important research service to Native American communities. The Harvard Project on American Indian Economic Development at the John F. Kennedy School of Government served as a model for this course. Students and faculty take their cue directly from the particular Native American Tribe or organization in defining the issue to be researched, and then utilize Harvard's vast resources to help develop solutions. Both "Nation Building" courses are viewed as "significant pedagogical innovations" in that it they are designed to deepen the understanding of Native American issues in "a forward-looking, positivist approach."[6]

Similar approaches are beginning to take hold at individual faculties such as the Harvard Law School, which is offering a series of new courses and clinical opportunities taught by visiting scholars and taught in conjunction with the University of Arizona. Throughout the university, there are ten courses that focus exclusively on Native American issues and another fifty with Native American content. Complementing these course offerings are a number of independent field-based research projects, from the study of traditional healthcare delivery systems to environmental planning and education. Each of these research efforts focuses on issues identified as important by Native American communities and organizations.

The final component of teaching and research is executive education programs, which are in the planning stages and will be designed to meet the needs of American Indian Nations and colleges. An excellent example is the National Executive

Education Program for Native American Leadership (NEEPNAL) at the Kennedy School of Government, which provides executive education workshops for senior decisionmakers in Indian Country.

Leadership Development

Another important focus of HUNAP is leadership development (see figure 7.3). Recruiting and graduating students in all professions are essential for the development of viable solutions to the economic, health, political, legal, and social challenges facing Native American Nations and communities. Yet according to a Kellogg Foundation study, only 52 percent of Native Americans finish high school, 17 percent finish college, 4 percent graduate from four-year institutions, 2 percent attend graduate school, and less than 1 percent complete graduate school. Faced with these statistics, HUNAP has made a commitment to working with secondary schools, Tribal colleges, and Native American programs across the country to improve the educational success of Native American students.

Educating Native Americans continues to be the focal point of HUNAP. Toward this end, the program administers a university-wide recruitment and retention initiative to encourage Native American leadership across an array of disciplines, which is led by the program's Coordinator of Recruitment and Student Affairs. In the past several years, the coordinator has developed a number of innovative recruitment tools such as *A Guide for Admissions Staff: Recruiting in Indian*

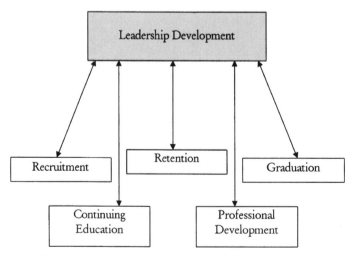

Figure 7.3.   The current and future leadership development components of HUNAP

Country, designed to assist recruiters and admissions staff in the recruitment of Native Americans to Harvard. To help ensure student success upon entering Harvard, a series of events are planned to promote community-building and provide for intellectual and cultural exchange, from monthly talking circles and potlucks to the annual Harvard University Powwow.

The strength and success of the changes implemented by HUNAP can be measured in part by the number of Native American students who enroll and graduate from the nine faculties at the university (see figure 7.4). Preliminary findings indicate that the correlation between program stability and student success is a positive and strong one. The mean Native American student enrollment from 1980–1981 to 1996–1997 is 81. The range is 54, the minimum 57 (1984–1985, 1985–1986), and the maximum 111 (1996–1997). Of note is that enrollments decreased in the mid-1980s when federal funding of Harvard's American Indian Program ceased, and increased in the early 1990s to a high of 104 students in 1993–1994 when a recruitment effort was launched by HUNAP. Native American enrollment decreased slightly during the following two years to 99 students in 1995–1996. This was a period of serious financial difficulty for HUNAP, and the program was scheduled to close its doors in June 1996. However, after an aggressive development campaign and recruitment effort, enrollment reached its highest level to date in 1996–1997 with 111 Native American students enrolled at Harvard University. Equally important is the current Native American student graduation rate of 95 percent.

In addition, HUNAP has made a commitment to developing and implementing programs in pre-professional studies, continuing education, and professional development. Similar to executive education, these programs will be designed to meet the strategic and educational needs of students in Native communities. For instance, HUNAP works closely with a group of medical students and the Four Directions Summer Research Program in bringing young Indian students to campus to conduct research and encourage future interest in science and medicine. HUNAP is uniquely positioned to draw upon the vast resources of the university to design additional leadership programming in the areas of law, business, government, public health, and education.

80/81	81/82	82/83	83/84	84/85	85/86	86/87	87/88	88/8
78	77	76	62	57	57	69	75	85

89/90	90/91	91/92	92/93	93/94	94/95	95/96	96/97
77	78	83	89	104	102	99	111

Figure 7.4. Native American student enrollment, 1980 to 1996

Step 4: Making Connections and Sharing the Vision

Dissemination of information about the Harvard University Native American Program beyond the walls of the university was and remains a key factor to its success. Reaching out brings new ideas, friends, and students to the program, and helps ensure that it continues to meet its stated mission of community service.

To aid in the development and implementation of academic research, courses of instruction, field-based learning, and executive education that are relevant to current issues, HUNAP draws on a network of ties to Nations and Tribes throughout the United States and Canada. For purposes of recruitment and dissemination of information, HUNAP has also been working to develop close relationships with schools and organizations such as:

Alaska Federation of
  Natives Conference
American Indian Higher
  Education Consortium
American Indian Science and
  and Engineering Society
Cambridge Health Alliance
Cornell University
Dartmouth College
Four Directions Summer
  Research Program

Mashantucket Pequot Museum and
  Research Center
Nantucket Resource Center
National Congress of
  American Indians
National Indian Education
  Association
Native American programs
North American Indian Center of
  Boston
Tribal colleges

HUNAP has actively engaged in the creation and presentation of numerous events. Some, such as community gatherings, a spring powwow and alumni weekend, and a special commencement ceremony, take place each year. Following is a partial list of recent events:

1. American Indian Tribal Courts and Self-Governance Conference and Reception with U.S. Attorney General Janet Reno (December 2, 1995), cosponsored with the Harvard Law School and the Native American Law Students Association (NALSA).
2. Forum on the World's Indigenous Peoples Movement (January 18, 1996), cosponsored with the Harvard Law School and the Harvard Graduate School of Education.
3. Forging Forward: Women of Color in the Law Conference and Reception (February 23, 1996), cosponsored with the Harvard Law School.
4. The United Nations Draft Declaration on Indigenous Peoples Rights: U.S. and Tribal Government Perspectives Conference with the U.S.

Departments of State and Interior, and Native American leaders (spring 1996).

5. *How the West Was Lost* film series (monthly, October 1996–May 1997).

6. Meeting with Assistant U.S. Surgeon General and Director of the Indian Health Service Dr. Michael Trujillo to discuss ways to collaborate on future projects (February 27, 1997).

7. *A Circle in Time: Contact, Education, and Change in Native American Massachusetts* exhibit and lecture series, Widener Library Memorial Rotunda (April 3–May 27, 1997).

8. Unveiling and dedication of the Native American Commemorative Plaque, Matthews Hall, southeast corner of Harvard Yard (May 3, 1997).

9. Asset Management Conference for Indian Nations and Tribes (spring 1998), cosponsored with the Harvard Business School.

10. Navajo Nation Supreme Court Visit to Harvard Law School (February 5–6, 1999), cosponsored with the Native American Law Students Association and the Harvard Law School.

As a complement to these events, HUNAP runs an Alumni Speakers Series and Visiting Scholars Program, bringing alumni, educators, Tribal leaders, and Elders to campus to address the Harvard community on a variety of issues and to share their experiences with Native American students.

Electronic data collection and dissemination are indispensable to communicating inside Harvard, outside to Indian Country, and around the world. With the aid of Native American students, the HUNAP Web site (http://hugse1.harvard.edu/~nap/) was created in 1996. It has been updated and expanded recently to include course listings, events schedules, and directory information. In addition, the staff has compiled an alumni and friends database of more than 1,300 names. The database enables HUNAP to keep alumni and friends informed about the program's news and events. The director of development and external relations also maintains databases of foundations and corporations that have authorized grants to programs similar to HUNAP, as well as a listing of national and local sources and contacts.

Most recently, HUNAP has worked to strengthen its ties with local Indian organizations such as the North American Indian Center of Boston (NAICOB). For instance, Harvard students volunteer as "big siblings" to local Native youth. And this past spring, the program joined NAICOB, the Harvard Medical School, and the Cambridge Health Alliance in celebrating the establishment of the Caleb Cheeshahteaumuck Clinic in Sommerville, Massachusetts, the only Indian Health Service facility for the 6,000 American Indians residing in the greater Boston area.

Step 5: Fund-Raising

When we came to Harvard University, the Native American Program was set to close its doors not because of student apathy or faculty disinterest, but because it was running out of operating funds. At its inception, the program drew most of its funds from the federal government. When this source dried up, there was little attempt by the university to make up for it, and the program began to operate on soft money. Without a clear vision of its mission, the program fell into a year-to-year fund-raising cycle. The program staff needed to identify a strategy set within the historical context of Native American education at Harvard and build a foundation for funding from within and outside the university.

First, we needed to convince the university administration and the nine faculties that Harvard University had a moral and financial responsibility to the Native American Program. Without a commitment from the university, it would not be possible to approach donors (alumni, friends, foundations, and corporations). We developed a fund-raising plan with two main components, one internal and one external. Success was dependent on how well we were able to integrate the two.

Organizationally, our original development plan built upon temporary support from the central administration and the nine faculties, as well as support from major foundations and individual donors. The following is a brief overview of some of the development efforts that HUNAP pursued during our tenure:

- The Office of the President and Provost, as well as the nine faculties, contributed substantial current-use funds to HUNAP for a period of three years. These funds were forthcoming only after articulation of a clear vision and substantial relationship building among HUNAP, the faculty advisory board, the central administration, and the various deans.
- A number of special projects, such as outreach on prenatal alcohol use, summer medical research programs for students, and environmental planning and education, were funded by individual donors interested in these particular areas of study.
- With the aid of major individual donors, HUNAP developed a list of fifty new potential donors and solicited contributions from them.
- Alumni and friends contributed funds to HUNAP through the Annual Alumni Gift Campaign. From a database of more than 600 names, alumni were asked to contribute directly to HUNAP's general fund.
- Grant proposals were submitted to several foundations, such as the Educational Foundation of America and the Massachusetts Foundation for the Humanities, for individually targeted projects. However, due to the necessity of raising current-use funds in a very short time frame,

priority was given to finding individual donors rather than foundation or corporate grants.

- HUNAP worked closely with the university's development office to develop a fund-raising advisory board and to identify additional potential donors through the interfaculty initiative.
- A major fund-raising event was planned that had built-in educational components with the potential to raise unrestricted current-use funds.
- HUNAP worked with existing donors to increase its trust fund.

There is no simple answer to why this plan worked for us. Looking back, we learned that by telling the story of Native Americans at Harvard through the centuries and showing where the students wanted to go in the future, we were able to get the attention of the university, alumni, and friends. It was our responsibility to do our homework and have annual reports and financial projections ready for review. In the end, we relied on relationship building. People believed in our cause because we believed in it. We learned to leverage this goodwill into a financial commitment to Native American students and the Native American Program.

From 1995 to 1997, HUNAP raised enough current-use funds to guarantee three more years of stability, while at the same time the program budget more than doubled. The increased budget allowed for an expanded recruitment and leadership initiative, more programming, more events, more research, more outreach, the Native American Commemorative Plaque and its dedication ceremony, and a small but productive staff. With a development plan in place, the goal of long-term financial stability is closer to being achieved.

During 1997, each of the nine faculties contributed substantially to the program's operating budget—a first for the university. That same year, the Office of the President and Provost committed a total of $400,000 to support the program over the next three years. In planning for the long-term, HUNAP also was able to secure trust and scholarship funds from individual donors.

The development task for the future was to raise a current-use endowment for the program. Working closely with the university's development office, HUNAP has kept its fund-raising efforts focused on individual donors. To this end, a fund-raising advisory council made up of previous and potential donors was planned and implemented.

HUNAP and the faculty advisory board have recently developed and implemented a long-range plan for building and endowing the educational efforts of the program, including a case statement that outlines the program's funding objectives. This funding effort is aimed at recruitment, teaching, faculty research, doctoral research, public discourse within the university, and outreach to Native communities. The goal is to reach financial stability within a five-year period through the establishment of an $11 million endowment with an annual projected budget of $450,000.

Lessons Learned

We began our tenure at the Harvard University Native American Program with the idea that somehow this might be easy. Harvard was the richest university on earth. It was steeped in tradition and Native Americans played a prominent role in its early history. The Native American student body was among the country's best and brightest. The program itself had been around for nearly twenty-five years. We had might and right on our side. Or so we thought. The true story of Native American education at Harvard University reads like a Susan Power novel. There were broken promises, failed expectations, heroes and villains. Looking back, it seemed an impossible task.

In the next few paragraphs, we will give our best analysis of what we learned. Yet the truth has a way of blurring as time passes. What appeared to be a crisis in 1995 is not so pressing today. The lessons we learned may have few applications beyond Harvard. Those thoughts aside, we are proud to have been affiliated with what is one of the most dynamic programs in the country, and humbled by the real work that was accomplished centuries before us by Caleb Cheeshahteaumuck and his classmates.

As we discussed in Step 5, fund-raising was our greatest challenge at first. HUNAP existed on soft money; awareness of the history and mission was very low within the university and almost nonexistent outside Cambridge; the perception among the faculties was that we were a student service program; there was no strategic plan. Our training as a lawyer (Graham) and a social scientist (Golia) enabled us to identify the program's problems and devise a plan of action. Our instincts told us to attack, and that is what we did. The moral high ground was ours and we would win. To accomplish our objectives, we needed to know the history of Native Americans at Harvard better than anyone else and be able to communicate it to everyone we met—students, faculty, administration, alumni, foundations, corporations, the media. Through our experiences, we learned that there is no substitute for face-to-face meetings with the people to whom we wanted to tell our story. Whether it was the Native American students scattered across campus, or President Neil Rudenstine at his residence, or a venture capitalist (and possible donor) in Palo Alto, we were prepared and we went.

What we said was well thought out in advance and tailored to the individuals we were to meet. Our message was clear and concise. A HUNAP logo with the turtle and Harvard shield (designed by a Native American student and artist) was created and used everywhere to make the program easily identifiable (see figure

7.1). Included in the materials developed to promote the program were an informational brochure, a press packet, and PowerPoint presentations. Following is a fact sheet we wrote and used many times to communicate information about HUNAP:

Native American Program Facts

- The Charter of 1650, by which Harvard was incorporated, calls for "the education of the English and Indian youth of this country."
- From 1655 to 1698, the "Indian College" stood in Harvard Yard. Here American Indian and English students lived and studied.
- The Indian College was Harvard's first brick building and housed the college printing press.
- From 1659 to 1663, the first Bible in North America was printed at the Indian College in the Algonquian translation by John Eliot.
- Caleb Cheeshahteaumuck of the Wampanoag Tribe, Class of 1665, was the first American Indian to graduate from Harvard.
- In 1970, the American Indian Program (AIP) emerged on campus as part of a national self-determination movement.
- In 1990, AIP became the Harvard University Native American Program (HUNAP).
- Today, there are more than 120 Native American students at Harvard.
- The students represent more than 40 different Tribes and Nations, including Blackfeet, Cherokee, Chippewa, Choctaw, Crow, Hopi, Iroquois, Lakota Sioux, Mohawk, Navajo, Oglala Sioux, Oneida, Rosebud Sioux, and Zuni Pueblo.
- The first annual Harvard University Powwow took place in 1995.
- Three hundred thirty-two years after Caleb Cheeshahteaumuck walked through Harvard Yard to graduation, the Native American Commemorative Plaque was unveiled and dedicated.
- The plaque is carved from a 4-ft. square piece of Buckingham slate by Rhode Island artist John Hegnauer.
- The plaque hangs on the SE corner of Matthews Hall, the approximate location of the Indian College.

Thoughts and Observations

We had a lot to say and were prepared to say it, but the most important lesson we learned was to listen. The plan we devised worked for us because we were willing to listen and learn. Another critical lesson we learned was that as much as we chafed against the idea that somehow we were "selling" people on the program, that is what needed to be done. We were selling the invisible—an idea. Following are some general observations of needs based on our experiences:

- *Need to develop a vision and be faithful to that vision.* For us, part of that vision included the past. We saw HUNAP as a model for the interdisciplinary movement at Harvard and envisioned a greater role for Native American education at the university.
- *Need to acquire strong leadership, as well as stability.* Teamwork is key, since no one person can or should do everything, but someone needs to be at the helm especially when the waters get rough. A key to success for a program is finding and retaining a director long-term. This is partly a money issue, because donors give to the director and they want stability, and partly a political issue, because without stability in leadership it is difficult to gain a university commitment to institutionalize the program.
- *Need to clearly define the role of students.* Often students get stuck "doing the work" and their classes suffer. Students are an important component (they are the future leaders), but they shouldn't be expected to carry the burden beyond sitting on advisory boards, helping to plan classes, providing mentoring to other students, and helping with program activities and conferences.
- *Need to follow through with commitments.* Everyone says they will follow through, but those that actually do will build the necessary trust and confidence of those who may be critical to the success of the program in the years to come.
- *Need to develop feedback loops.* The way information flows in, through, and out of the organization is critical to success. Time needs to be taken to develop feedback loops such as progress reports (for donors and others), talking circles (for students and faculty), staff meetings, and retreats.
- *Need to be able to change paths midcourse if necessary (based on feedback).* In other words, stay flexible while staying true to the vision. Listen and learn.
- *Need to work within and around the university system.* A program cannot exist completely outside of the university system. Our goal was to be an integral part of Harvard. However, at times, in fact many times, we needed to go outside the regular channels to achieve our objectives. This was true of our fund-raising efforts, which began midway through the university's Capital Campaign. Our success in raising funds outside the

system resulted in our invitation to become part of this interfaculty campaign.

- *Need to stay connected.* In other words, remember your ultimate goals. Stay grounded in Native America and communicate with the Nations, Tribes, communities, potential students, and other Native American organizations.

Strengths and Weaknesses

Harvard develops leaders, and it is crucial that Native Americans have a growing and vocal presence within the university. Therefore, the greatest strength of the Harvard University Native American Program is its people—staff, students, the faculty advisory board, alumni, and friends. It is through the efforts of these talented and dedicated individuals that the university receives the following benefits from the program:

- **teaching and research**
  academic research
  courses of instruction
  field-based learning
  executive education
- **leadership development**
  recruitment
  retention
  graduation
  continuing education
  professional development
- **faculty involvement**
  faculty advisory board
  faculty recruitment
  visiting scholars
- **community outreach**
  conferences
  events
  Web site
- **alumni involvement**
  Native American Alumni Association
  alumni speakers series
- **development**
  advisory council
  research grants
  scholarships

- **history**
  fulfillment of the Charter of 1650
- **diversity**

What we gained from our affiliation with the Harvard University Native American Program is a renewed respect for the past and a belief in the future of Native American education at Harvard. The program's fund-raising weakness was and remains a short-term problem. It is unfortunate, but the year-to-year financial concerns do more to undermine the success of Native Americans at Harvard than any other single factor. Until the program becomes a permanent part of the university budget, most of the efforts of the staff, students, and the faculty advisory board will continue to be fund-raising efforts. This is a terrible waste of a valuable resource. However, this problem is solvable and the future holds great promise for HUNAP.

Conclusion

The Harvard University Native American Program is based on a long and rich history that extends back to the founding of Harvard. The program is prepared to carry that heritage into the twenty-first century and beyond. Many innovative changes in programming, research endeavors, faculty involvement, and student recruitment, as well as in alumni and university relations, are under way. Figure 7.5 illustrates the current and future vision for HUNAP.

HUNAP has experienced a time of transition. Program staff and other dedicated individuals made great strides during the 1990s in teaching and research,

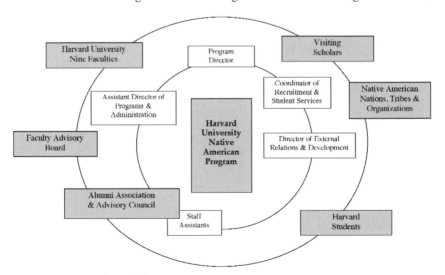

Figure 7.5. Proposed model for HUNAP

leadership development, and fund-raising. But this is only the beginning. To sustain a dynamic, interdisciplinary program that meets the levels of excellence and leadership demanded at Harvard, a commitment to stable, long-term funding from the university administration and others is necessary. Moreover, as in the past, success in the future depends on the continued teamwork of HUNAP staff, members of the faculty advisory board, and students. Working together and remaining true to the vision, we are confident that HUNAP will meet this challenge and continue to grow into the premier program in Native American studies envisioned by President Henry Dunster some 350 years ago. Indeed, we view HUNAP's history and future as Susan Power describes life at Harvard in her short story "First Fruits:"

> I was taught to believe that time is not a linear stream, but a hoop spinning forward like a wheel, where everything is connected, and everything is eternal. In this cosmology, I am here because Caleb came before me, and he was here in anticipation of me. We are bonded together across time.[7]

Notes

This chapter is dedicated to the countless number of students and directors who dedicated their time and enthusiasm to the survival of HUNAP.

1. Daniel Gookin, *Historical Collections of the Indians in New England* (New York: Arno, 1872).

2. The original document is housed in the Royal Society's Archives in London, England, a copy of which is on file at the Harvard University Native American Program. See also Samuel Eliot Morison, *Harvard College in the Seventeenth Century* (Cambridge, Mass.: Harvard University Press, 1936), 355; Wolfgang Hochbruck and Beatrix Dudensing-Reichel, "'Honoratissimi Benefactores': Native American Students and Two Seventeenth-Century Texts in the University Tradition," *Studies in American Indian Literature* (summer/fall 1992): 35.

3. *Colonial Society of Massachusetts*, vol. xv, lxxxiii.

4. Neil Rudenstine, "The Uses of Diversity," *Harvard Magazine* (March–April 1996): 49–62; see also *The President's Report*, 1993–1995, Harvard University.

5. http://www.fas.harvard.edu/cesh/intro/html (last accessed July 2001).

6. *Harvard University Gazette*, December 12, 1993, 3.

7. Susan Power, "First Fruits," *Harvard College News* ix, no. 3 (spring 1997).

A Story of Struggle and Survival: American Indian Studies at the University of Minnesota–Twin Cities   8

PATRICIA C. ALBERS, BRENDA J. CHILD, VIKKI HOWARD, DENNIS JONES, CAROL MILLER, FRANK C. MILLER, AND JEAN M. O'BRIEN

T HE UNIVERSITY OF MINNESOTA–Twin Cities has one of the oldest and continuing programs in American Indian studies with a departmental status. Approved by the Minnesota Board of Regents on June 7, 1969, the Department of American Indian Studies has been dedicated to advancing an awareness and understanding of the histories and contemporary experiences of American Indian peoples, and it has been committed to building knowledges, both theoretical and practical, that bear upon the sovereignty of Tribal Nations in the Americas. Since its inception, the department has worked to maintain high standards of excellence in its classroom and individualized instructional settings, to advance a strong program of faculty scholarship, and to support a commitment of service to the university and the outside communities it serves. And since its beginnings, it has struggled to maintain these missions within an environment where the interests of faculty, administrators, students, and community representatives have sometimes stood at odds. The history of American Indian studies at the University of Minnesota–Twin Cities serves as a backdrop against which the experiences of the past inform our future. We begin this chapter with a brief discussion of the department's history,[1] a prelude against which we critically assess the realities of our present and the possibilities of our future.

The Department of American Indian Studies: Past

American Indian studies at the University of Minnesota was first envisioned in the mid-1960s. As chronicled by Frank C. Miller (1971, 318–324), an ad hoc committee submitted a formal report to the university's higher administration in 1966 that set forth programmatic initiatives in American Indian studies and also recommendations for their implementation. Among other things, the early report established the need to coordinate the university's existing curriculum and create new courses relating to American Indian issues. It argued for programs that assisted American Indian students in practical and academic ways. And it also suggested formal means to establish links with the state's Tribes, and in the process, develop scholarly and community outreach programs that focused on issues of importance to local American Indian constituencies. This report, however, did not generate much support when it was first circulated among university administrators.

Two years later, though, it did draw serious attention when political pressures forced the university administration to respond to the needs of a growing American Indian student population and the interests of the Twin Cities' American Indian community (Miller 1971, 324–328). In the fall of 1968, a newly formed American Indian Student Association under the leadership of C. William Craig began to push the university's administration toward more involvement in Indian affairs. But it wasn't until after African American students occupied the central administration building in January of 1969 that the university actually agreed to press forward in implementing programs that served the needs of students and communities of color.

On March 28, 1969, an ad hoc committee was established consisting of University of Minnesota faculty, American Indian students, and representatives from the local American Indian community (Miller 1971, 328–334). From the outset, the idea of American Indian studies at the University of Minnesota had two goals. One aim was to build a curriculum that would educate the university's general student audience about the complexities of the American Indian experience. Another goal was to develop a curriculum that centered on Native languages, particularly Dakota and Ojibwe. In subsequent months, the committee reached agreement on a proposal that established the specific content and structure of an undergraduate degree in American Indian studies with a strong language emphasis. It also reached consensus on housing the new major in a structure that had a departmental rather than a programmatic status. On May 27, 1969, a proposal submitted to the university's Social Science Divisional Council was approved unanimously, and on June 7 the Minnesota Board of Regents approved the proposal with one dissenting vote.

In the following academic year, preparations were made to institute the major and to fill the three tenure-track faculty positions created for the department (Miller 1971, 335–336). The first hires included Roger Buffalohead as chair, George Morrison, and Timothy Dunnigan. Over the next twenty years, faculty lines in American Indian studies would be filled by other scholars including Russell Thornton, David Beaulieu, Gerald Vizenor, Jacqueline Peterson, and flo wiger. Allan Kilpatrik, Tom King, and Linda Hogan were also associated with American Indian studies, although their appointments were in other departments. After varying lengths of time and for various reasons, all of these faculty left the University of Minnesota. After 1990, when tenure lines in American Indian studies were lost, faculty with tenure homes in other departments, including Brenda Child, Carol Miller, Jean O'Brien, and Frank Miller, played an active role in department teaching and administration. In 1997 the department recaptured its lines and began to recruit new faculty. To date, four positions have been filled by Patricia Albers, David Wilkins, David Martinez, and John Nichols.

From the outset, American Indian studies at the University of Minnesota occupied a structural position equivalent with other disciplines in the university. It was never ghettoized outside the institution's standard line of command for academic programs. It remains situated in the College of Liberal Arts and accountable to an academic dean. As a result, its mission and operations are held to the same standards applied to other departmentally based majors in the university. Although American Indian studies has retained a departmental status since its inception, there were periods in its history when this status was threatened. There is no question that the departmental status conferred on American Indian studies at its founding has been necessary, indeed critical, for its long-term survival at the University of Minnesota, although it has not always been sufficient to secure the program's stability and growth.

Shortly after its inception, the Department of American Indian Studies struggled to maintain a curriculum and place at the academic heart of the university while simultaneously attending to the concerns and interests of American Indian students and the state's American Indian communities. Some of the early enabling documents indicate that while the department had a status equivalent to that of other academic programs within the College of Liberal Arts, the department was unique in its explicit expectation that faculty devote much of their time to student concerns and community outreach.

The University of Minnesota–Twin Cities has one of the largest student populations in the United States, and this also includes a significant and increasing number of students of American Indian ancestry. When American Indian studies was first founded, forty-five American Indian students were enrolled at the university (Miller 1971, 325). Today, this number has increased more than fivefold. Some of today's students are highly motivated and compete well with the best of the student population at the university: some receive top academic awards, some appear on the dean's list, and some even graduate summa cum laude. Many others achieve satisfactory grades, graduate, and move on to successful careers. But there are also many who face difficulties, either because they are ill-prepared academically for a college education or because the university's large and impersonal setting is culturally alienating. Too many of the more at-risk students drop out and never finish their higher education.

Until the American Indian Learning Resource Center was established in 1978,[2] the responsibility to provide extracurricular support for American Indian students fell almost entirely on faculty in American Indian studies, not so much by design but because resources weren't in place to provide American Indian students some of the specialized advising and tutorial assistance they required. American Indian faculty were frequently called upon to meet this need, and since most were located in American Indian studies, students were drawn to the department to provide them resources to survive and succeed at the university. Faculty talents were often stretched beyond the limits of their training and expertise in humanities and social science disciplines. Tensions arose when the department was pressed to provide legitimate support services to students and at the same time meet the performance standards of faculty in other departments who were not expected to assume such responsibilities.

The scholarly pressures placed on faculty sometimes stood at odds with the aspirations of students who expected to succeed in American Indian studies even when they were not prepared academically to do so. This was especially problematic for students who believed they were entitled to succeed in a discipline that ostensibly represented their heritage. Over time, the situation at the University of Minnesota has improved as additional resources have been put in place to address the diverse advising needs of American Indian students, but some of the tensions surrounding a perceived "ownership" of knowledge by virtue of birthright still linger.

Difference and disagreement over who and what an American Indian studies curriculum should address have been evident throughout the department's history. On the one hand, there are those who believe the curriculum should be tailored to the interests of American Indian students. In conjunction with the American Indian Student Association and the American Indian Learning Resource Center, the department is viewed as the curricular arm for a special campus community. From this perspective, the primary mission of American Indian studies entails the creation of courses that preserve and sustain particular cultural knowledges as a means of identity maintenance or as an avenue for retaining students of color in higher education. On the other hand, there is a vision of the department that rests on the belief that American Indian studies is an academic discipline with an identifiable history, a unique subject matter, an integral literature, a distinct epistemology, and a rigorous pedagogy. It is a comparative discipline with theories and methodologies that include but extend beyond local cultural interests. In this view, the department's mission entails building a curriculum that represents the essence of the discipline and that offers courses that inform the widest possible student audience.

In a very deliberate way, the department attempts to serve American Indian student interests by working closely with the Office of Multi-Cultural Affairs, which administers the student cultural association and the resource learning center, presently under the direction of Roxanne Gould. It is committed to developing a curriculum with an emphasis on Dakota and Ojibwe language, culture, and history that attends to the needs of local students. It also acknowledges that many American Indian students at the University of Minnesota come from other parts of the country and that much of its student base is non-Indian. The department has always attracted large numbers of non-Indian students, even before many of its courses filled university-wide diversity requirements. Over the last five years, its class enrollments have skyrocketed and the number of students majoring or minoring in the discipline has reached an all-time high as well. It is the wider sense of our field, as an interdisciplinary and comparative study of the American Indian experience, that sustains most of our student population, and it is this audience who supports the broader range of courses we offer in the humanities and social sciences. Building a department that creatively manages differences between contrasting visions of American Indian studies has never been easy. Nonetheless, the department remains committed, even doggedly determined, to see to it that both visions are expressed in its teaching and scholarly missions.

Another area of tension in the department's history has been its relation to the state's American Indian communities. American Indian studies at the University of Minnesota is situated in an area that contains one of the largest and most educated urban American Indian populations in the United States. The university is also located within a day's reach of more than twenty-five different Tribes in the upper Great Lakes and neighboring Plains regions. The Twin Cities is home to many local as well as national agencies that serve the social, political, economic, artistic, and spiritual interests of American Indians. The University of Minnesota–Twin Cities is also accountable to an American Indian advisory board made up of respected members of the local community who advise the university's president on matters of concern to students and the community. There is also a council of Elders, connected with the American Indian Learning Resource Center, whose counsel is sought on matters pertaining to student advising, cultural activities, and even course development.

From the very outset, American Indian studies faculty have been called upon to provide service that by any conventional definition would be construed as extraordinary. And even though the department established a staff position for an outreach coordinator early on, faculty were still expected to shoulder enormous community responsibilities. Again, one of the original aims of American Indian studies, as proposed in its earliest documents, was the creation of working links between the university and the state's American Indian communities. The historical importance of service to the mission of the Department of American Indian Studies has many origins. One of these is the University of Minnesota's status as a land-grant institution, a position that obligates it to direct much of its teaching and research to the benefit of the general public. Another is the importance of outreach in the American Indian community, where service is seen as an extension of cultural values that place great stock in individuals sharing their knowledges and talents within a wider social nexus.

Back in the 1970s, politics at the university, in the Twin Cities, and in the United States more generally expected, indeed demanded, activism of its young American Indian scholars and a high level of participation in local and national Indian affairs. The nature and degree of involvement varied, but one thing is clear: debates over what kind of community role a department like the University of Minnesota's should sustain created serious internal tensions and rifts among faculty, staff, and students. The ability of young American Indian scholars to succeed in their professions was severely compromised in these highly politicized times. The situation at the University of Minnesota was not particularly unique, although it took on a more intense character here because the Twin Cities is the site of a highly vocal and politicized American Indian community and the home of the American Indian Movement (AIM). Today, even though American Indian studies at the University of Minnesota remains committed to service that builds partnerships with the American Indian community, it is also acutely aware that these ties can be developed only when its faculty meet their scholarly and teaching responsibilities.

Throughout the history of the department, American Indian studies faculty at the University of Minnesota have been besieged by a host of pressures, not the least of which are the university administration's own internal demands. Not only have American Indian and other faculty of color been responsible for performing routine duties necessary to the operation of their own departments, but they are also frequently called upon to fulfill a host of other consulting and committee tasks to ensure "minority" voice and representation in the university at large. The level of demand for service, both internally and externally motivated, has been truly excessive, especially when these faculty are expected to demonstrate the same level of performance and excellence in teaching and research as other faculty in order to make the tenure grade. The story of exceptional service expectations in a job climate that also demands superior teaching and a high level of scholarly output has been repeated at institutions of higher education across the country. And once again, the situation at the University of Minnesota has not been unusual, although the pressures were probably more acute here, and in all likelihood may have contributed to the department's high level of faculty turnover.

By the mid-1980s, most of the tenure lines in American Indian studies were abandoned, either because faculty sought better and less contentious situations elsewhere or because the tenure lines themselves were transferred to other departments under the argument that American Indian studies was not a full-fledged discipline but a focus or concentration whose needs could be adequately addressed by filling faculty lines in older, more established departments. This took place during a difficult period when the future growth and sustainability of ethnic studies departments nationally was being stunted by the forces of academic downsizing. At a critical juncture in their development, just as they were establishing themselves and beginning to make a mark in higher education, their futures were placed in jeopardy. When economic recession forced universities into policies of deep retrenchment, ethnic studies departments were especially vulnerable to the cutbacks. Abandoned tenure lines were not refilled, and new ones were rarely created. At the University of Minnesota, American Indian studies did not escape the effects of some of these horrific budgetary forces. In fact, the department faced the threat of being moved to another campus or demoted to the status of a program and merged with other ethnic studies disciplines under a single department umbrella. Fortunately, neither of these outcomes ever came about.

During the late 1980s, under the leadership of department chairs flo wiger and subsequently Carol Miller, valiant efforts were made to preserve some of the tenure lines linked to American Indian studies at the University of Minnesota. Despite their efforts, the higher administration unilaterally made a decision to put existing tenure lines in other departments for various budgetary and policy reasons that transcended American Indian studies. Two positions with concentrations in American Indian studies were advertised and filled in affiliated departments. These were soon vacated for personal reasons and because of institutional competition for Native scholars, neither of which had anything to do with American Indian studies, the university, or community politics in Minnesota.

A bright spot during this period was the department's receipt of a sizable gift from the McKnight Foundation. Under the sponsorship of the acting dean of the College of Liberal Arts, Craig Swan, an endowment fund was established to support guest lecturers and visiting faculty, both of whom have been critical to the vitality of department teaching and scholarship. Notwithstanding this important endowment, American Indian studies was still not staffed by faculty with in-house tenure lines.

Another source of light was the assistance of the Department of American Studies, whose faculty actively recruited candidates for tenure lines with specialties in American Indian history and literature. In addition, American studies continues to channel some of its own limited resources in ways that not only permit faculty to devote a substantial portion of their teaching load to topics dealing with American Indians, but also allow graduate student teaching assistants to work in courses that carry an American Indian studies designator. Indeed, without the generous and gracious support of American studies over the past fifteen years, American Indian studies would have had difficulty meeting many of its teaching and curriculum responsibilities.

In the early 1990s, the dream of an American Indian studies department at the University of Minnesota, as envisioned by its founders, had clearly floundered. The department had become a shadow of its former self: a phantom structure without tenure lines. Interim chairs from other campus programs now managed the department, and the curriculum was sustained by part-time staff, full-time teaching specialists with one-year renewable contracts, and faculty with tenure homes in other departments. Increasingly, teaching assignments and contracts were covered with soft moneys dependent on generating sufficient student credit hours. The Department of American Indian Studies at the University of Minnesota now looked like many other programs across the country that never achieved a departmental status.

Despite all this, the department continued to survive and rise to the many challenges it faced. On loan from another college within the university, David Born served as an interim chair, and during his tenure the Dakota and Ojibwe language programs were strengthened by appointing Franklin Firesteel and Dennis Jones to instructional positions that carried three-year renewable contracts. A crucial core of affiliated faculty included Jean O'Brien in history and Carol Miller and Brenda Child in American studies. Although funded entirely by their home departments, they taught important courses in American Indian studies and were dedicated to the department's welfare and growth, as was Ronald Libertus, the senior member of the non-tenure-track teaching staff. His outstanding and enthusiastic service to the department over the past sixteen years needs to be singled out and acknowledged here. That the department survived at all through this trying period is testimony to the dedication and commitment of these individuals and a host of educational specialists who have included Pat Amo, the late Jerry Buckanaga, Eric Buffalohead, Yvonne Bushyhead, Jeff Chapman, Robert Danforth, Anita Fine Day, Dan First Scout Rowe, Kim Rossina, Chris Mato Nupa, Winona La Duke, Bill Means, Kim Mammedaty, Carrie Schommer, and Dale Weston. And that the department also flourished under these circumstances provides even stronger evidence of their considerable contributions in making American Indian studies a visible and vibrant field of inquiry for undergraduates at the University of Minnesota.

In 1996 the department and the university president's Twin Cities American Indian Advisory Committee vigorously urged interim dean Robert Holt to make the investments required to rebuild American Indian studies at the University of Minnesota. He had the courage and vision to make a strong commitment to the department, and the incoming dean, Steven Rosenstone, accepted Holt's recommendation that a national search start immediately for a chair whose tenure line would be in American Indian studies. As interim dean, Holt also responded favorably to the department's recommendation that anthropology professor Frank Miller be appointed as an acting chair.

At the same time, the University of Minnesota was also beginning to experience a turnaround in its fortunes. In 1997 the state legislature renewed its commitment to higher education and authorized the infusion of substantial funds for faculty hires, program development, and capital improvements. A new administration took over under the able leadership of President Mark Yudof, who has taken time in his busy schedule to meet personally with various American Indian groups throughout the state. At the cusp of this change, the interim chair, Frank Miller, along with Brenda Child, Carol Miller, and Jean O'Brien, seized the opportunity to urge the new dean of the College of Liberal Arts, Steven Rosenstone, not only to move ahead on the search for a chair in American Indian studies but also to make the commitment for additional faculty lines a reality. While the case was easy to make given the department's large class enrollments and the impressive size of its majors/minors, the dean must be credited with placing the needs of American Indian studies on his list of funding priorities for the college. With his support, a chair and three more faculty lines were authorized for American Indian studies. A staff position for a coordinator of community relations was also established and funded once again.

When the College of Liberal Arts announced its commitment to rebuilding the prominence of the Department of American Indian Studies, it authorized a nationwide search for an internationally known scholar to provide vision and visibility to this historic program. The search for a new chair was successfully completed in the summer of 1997, although the candidate, Patricia Albers, did not assume her position until the fall of 1998. Before her arrival, the department also completed a successful search for its coordinator of community relations, enlisting Vikki Howard, and also succeeded in extending an offer to David Wilkins to fill one of its additional faculty positions. Since then, the department has recruited two other faculty to its ranks, David Martinez and John Nichols. (And Neil McKay joined the staff as a teaching specialist in the Dakota language.)

In October of 1998, American Indian studies held its first faculty and staff retreat at the Grand Casino in Mille Lacs. With the support of an Academic Department Enrichment Program grant from the Bush Foundation, the department began the process of creating some of the vital enabling documents it lacked, including a constitution and a set of standards and procedures for continuation, promotion, and tenure. It laid plans for producing other sorts of materials vital for student majors and department growth. And it also created adjunct positions that formally marked and recognized the active involvement of faculty with tenure homes in other departments, namely, Brenda Child and Carol Miller from American studies, Jean O'Brien from history, and Frank Miller from anthropology. During the past year, Timothy Dunnigan from anthropology, Roxanne Stiuthers from nursing, and David Treuer from English were offered adjunct appointments.

As American Indian studies celebrates the thirtieth year of its existence at the University of Minnesota, and in the process experiences another resurrection of its mission, its faculty, educational specialists, and other staff are confident that the department is now in a position to renew its dreams and move forward with the program of teaching, scholarship, and community outreach envisioned at its founding. Informed by the pitfalls and snares that mark our historical landscape, we move ahead cautiously but with a spirit of optimism.

The Department of American Indian Studies: Present and Future

In its newly created enabling documents, the mission of the Department of American Indian Studies at the University of Minnesota–Twin Cities encompasses the three areas of endeavor—teaching, scholarship, and service—mandated for most departments at research-oriented institutions of higher education throughout the United States.

A major focus of American Indian studies at the University of Minnesota is teaching and undergraduate education, although its faculty are actively involved in research and the training of graduate students from other departments in classroom and individualized instructional settings. Since its inception, the department has offered a baccalaureate major and minor with a wide range of courses at introductory and advanced undergraduate levels. Today, students follow one of two tracks to fulfill requirements in an American Indian studies major. One is based on a selection of courses from the general curriculum with required credits distributed over three areas: policy and government, culture and history, and literature and the fine arts. The second focus is on language. Here students are required to take two years of the Dakota or Ojibwe language, a course in either Dakota or Ojibwe culture and history, and a balanced selection of courses from the three areas listed above.

In both tracks, students must take the introductory course in American Indian studies. Over the years, this class has been developed to meet two needs. It is first and foremost an outreach course that fulfills university diversity requirements. It seeks to disabuse non-Indian students of any false ideas and stereotypes they may have about American Indians and to present them with a more enlightening and critical understanding of the American Indian experience in the present as well as the past. The class also serves as an entry-level course for American Indian studies majors and minors. In recent years, this course has generated some dissatisfaction among faculty as well as students. From the perspective of faculty, the exponential growth of interdisciplinary scholarship in American Indian studies and related disciplines makes it increasingly difficult to provide adequate coverage of the field even at an introductory level. And from the vantage point of American Indian students, as reported in a recent study conducted by the American Indian Urban Higher Education Initiative (Raymond, Buffalohead, and Franzen 1999), the course is redundant insofar as it covers a well-trodden path of knowledge for many of them. In response to these concerns, the department is now considering the possibility of dividing the introductory course into two separate sections: one focused on the humanities (literature and the fine arts), and another on the social sciences (history, society, and political economy). It is also contemplating a third course with a focus on the history and theory of American Indian studies in particular and American Indian intellectual traditions more generally.

Beyond the introductory class, the department offers a wide selection of courses devoted to many different subjects. These courses not only cover the histories and current conditions of American Indians within Tribal settings, but also attend to their experiences in wider regional, national, and global contexts. Course offerings in the department are multidisciplinary. They cover the legal status and sovereignty of Tribal Nations in the Americas, the policies and forces shaping their social, economic, and political conditions, and the unique dimensions of their cultures, languages, literatures, arts, and philosophies. Our courses advance critical interpretations of the historical and current experiences of American Indians, and they emphasize Native perspectives that challenge the conventional and often unsubstantiated assumptions about American Indian peoples.

In the areas of policy, politics, and economy, we have a number of course offerings at an undergraduate level. With David Wilkins's recent arrival, other classes have been added to this curriculum that reflect his considerable expertise in the study of federal and Tribal law. Departmental offerings in history, society, and culture are numerous as well. American Indian history is dealt with in two classes: one covers the period from colonial times to 1830, and another spans the years from 1830 to the present. Local histories and cultures are covered in a course titled "American Indian Communities of the Upper Great Lakes," and in two separate classes devoted to the Ojibwe and Dakota peoples respectively. Plans are also under way to develop additional culture and history courses that deal with other regions of North America. Since we share an office, secretarial staff, and collegial relations with Chicano studies, there is some interest in developing joint courses that focus on the Indigenous Nations of Meso-America and South America. The department also gives courses dealing with education, philosophy, and gender, and its humanities offerings are represented by a wide range of courses in literature, art, music, cinema, and photography. Finally, the department regularly offers upper-division seminars for its advanced-level undergraduates and for graduate students who typically come from the American studies, anthropology, and history departments.

One of the department's oldest and continuing strengths resides in its strong focus on language studies. Indeed, the Department of American Indian Studies at the University of Minnesota is one of the few university departments in the United States to offer intensive training in American Indian languages. Ojibwe and Dakota are the two languages we regularly teach. Our language and culture offerings not only remain the most important and visible part of our curriculum in the eyes of the American Indian community off campus, but also constitute a critical point of synergy and motivation for the university's American Indian student population. Students in the Dakota and Ojibwe language programs host language tables in the community that draw many people from outside the university on a regular basis. The student-run Ojibwe Language Society also puts out a fundraising calendar every year, which gives students concrete experience in applying their language expertise and also in learning business skills. And it annually hosts a "Winter Story Telling" event that draws hundreds of people from the on- and off-campus communities and that gives the language students (Indian and non-Indian) an opportunity to demonstrate their language skills in a public forum.

Even though many of the students who participate in our language programs major in other disciplines from creative writing to history, their shared experience in the Ojibwe and Dakota language programs builds a special sense of partnership, purpose, and place. We believe that this special space is instrumental not only in helping certain American Indian students keep on course and complete their degrees, but also in motivating some of them to continue their educations so they can teach Native languages in a K–12 or higher educational setting.

Our language programs, however, are always vulnerable because of the scarcity of Native speakers with qualifications to teach at the university. The crises we face periodically in staffing the program have led us to the conclusion that we need to train language instructors not only to support our own curriculum, but also to meet the growing demands for Native language instruction in K–12 schools, in Tribal colleges, and in other higher education contexts throughout the region. In cooperation with faculty in anthropology and linguistics, we are in the process of making plans to develop a master's degree that would be tailored to the needs of Native language–speakers who require specialized pedagogical and descriptive linguistic skills to credential them and to enhance their teaching effectiveness. Part of advanced learning in any language is developing a basic competence in the more abstract components of language syntax and grammar—something regularly addressed in the teaching and scholarship associated with other languages on campus. We hope to expand our curriculum in ways that meet this need and that strengthen our beginning and intermediate course offerings in the process.

Overall, the department strives to offer its students a quality education through high standards of instruction in its classrooms and in its individualized instructional settings, which include directed readings, independent research, apprentice-ships, and internships. Our goal is to provide our students not only with a well-rounded body of knowledge about the histories and experiences of American In-dian peoples, but also with the writing, research, and critical thinking skills to apply this knowledge in practical ways. The department also aims to offer ad-vanced-level classes that include the participation of graduate students from affil-iated programs such as American studies, history, anthropology, and political sci-ence. Its faculty regularly enroll graduate students in courses carrying independent reading and research designators, and they often sit on the M.A. and Ph.D. advi-sory committees of these students. In the near future, the department intends to build and formalize a graduate minor in American Indian studies.

American Indian studies at the University of Minnesota is also dedicated to ad-vancing independence and excellence in the research, scholarship, and creative ac-tivity of its faculty. Scholarly discourse in the department is framed comparatively in order to address topics and questions from a variety of different perspectives. Our faculty represent a diverse range of disciplinary backgrounds in the liberal arts, and as such, they engage scholarly projects of different style and substance. Even though the scholarship of our faculty reflects the variety of disciplines in which they were trained, we hold many interests in common. One of these is a mu-tual interest in representations, theories, and practices that shed light on the sov-ereignty and resistance of American Indian peoples locally and in other regions of the Americas. This common intellectual thread brings a positive unity to our pro-gram and its scholarly goals.

Presently, faculty research and writing cover many different subjects. Carol Miller's work (1996, 1999) entails an examination of the literary tradition of American Indian women writers, and the development of a theory based on cul-tural authority rather than the more problematic issues of identity. The recent pub-lication of Brenda Child's award-winning book *Boarding School Seasons: American Indian Families 1900–1940* reflects her long-term interest in the history of American In-dian education, although she is now pursuing research on the history of her own Tribe, the Red Lake Ojibwe. Jean O'Brien's well-received work *Dispossession by De-grees: Indian Land and Identity in Natick, Massachusetts, 1650–1790,* on the resistance and survival of New England Tribes in colonial times, is being followed by a study of how their Tribal presence was persistently silenced in the construction of local his-torical narratives. Patricia Albers's ongoing research and writing (Albers and Breen 1997) continue to focus on questions relating to gender and political economy, and also include work (Albers 1998) on her long-standing interests in the dynamic interplay of tourism and photography in visual representations of American Indi-ans. David Martinez's expertise in philosophy and religious studies adds to de-partmental strengths in these areas. Currently, his research focuses on American

Indian metaphysics, aesthetics, and religious experience. He is also contributing to Penn Publishing's Lands and Legends series. The documentation and preservation of Ojibwe language knowledge are a central focus of Dennis Jones's present studies and publications (1995, 1997) and of John Nichols's work editing *Algonkian and Iroquoian Linguistics*. And last but not least, David Wilkins continues his tradition of pathbreaking research in treaty-making and constitutional law. Following his classic work *American Indian Sovereignty and the U.S. Supreme Court: The Masking of Justice* is the recent publication of his books *Navajo Political Experience* and *Tribes, Treaties, and Constitutional Tribulations*, which he coauthored with Vine Deloria Jr.

Faculty in American Indian studies at the University of Minnesota are expected to develop and maintain a focused and sustained scholarly program and to pursue and share their work in circles with professional mechanisms for peer review. Faculty are further encouraged to involve students in their scholarly work and to communicate the results of their scholarship in classroom and individualized instructional settings. In this context, the department is particularly excited about historian Fred Hoxie's recent initiative to form a working network of faculty and graduate students from institutions of higher education in the upper Midwest to share their research and teaching on American Indians in a variety of collaborative exchanges and meetings.

The department also encourages its faculty to share their knowledges and skills through service to a wider public. Recognizing that higher education in the twenty-first century will require all faculty to be responsive simultaneously to a host of demands on their time and energies (including continued excellence in scholarship, a commitment to more individualized forms of instruction, new competencies in technology, a greater sensitivity to diversity, and an increased level of public service and accountability), the department has decided to attend to these demands through a consensual and systematic plan of action. Given the reality that we will remain a small department with modest resources, we wish to avoid the kinds of rifts and tensions that divide a department and that often make it impossible for young faculty to survive the tenure-track mill. While we uniformly share a sense of responsibility to American Indian constituencies on campus and in the community at large, and while we firmly believe that our success depends on maintaining strong relationships with them, we also recognize that we must cast our web of service wisely and realistically.

The department is in the process of developing its own plans for ways to unite our scholarly, teaching, and service missions. We want to build a structure that generates opportunities for our students to learn through collaborative work experiences that join the interests and strengths of our faculty with the concerns and expertise of community groups. As a department, we strongly believe that a good liberal arts education should not only give students a solid background in the concepts and bodies of information that make up their discipline, but also offer them concrete opportunities to learn the tools for applying this knowledge to "real-world" situations. More specifically, we are working to create situations where student apprenticeships and internships are grounded in experiential settings that deliberately, collectively, and systematically link our faculty and students with local community groups.

We envision educational efforts in American Indian studies as part of a conceptual and physical space dedicated to addressing issues that are of vital concern to American Indian peoples locally and in the United States at large, a site where Tribal Nations, community agencies, and other public institutions establish partnerships with our faculty to carry out education and research projects for which we have expertise and for which we might create opportunities to educate and train our students in a carefully supervised learning environment. What we are envisioning is something more than a conventional service-learning internship where students connect with a community agency on an extended basis as individuals and where faculty are involved very minimally to supervise students' written narratives of their experiences. And it is also something different than a traditional research grant initiated by a single faculty member with funds for graduate and undergraduate assistantships. What we want to sponsor are projects that have very explicit research and pedagogical aims in mind, projects to which faculty are fully committed and that they initiate in collaboration with a community agency around a specific research/practical task. The project would be a group effort, involving a team of faculty, students, and community-based participants working together to accomplish a specific goal. A cohort of students would be trained in the knowledges and skills necessary to carry out the project in one or more specialized courses. Ideally, a project would entail a multiple-year commitment so that later cohorts of students would benefit from the experiences of their student "Elders." After course training, each student would be assigned to complete a specific set of research/practical duties, and they would receive individualized instructional credits of the independent research or practicum variety for their work.

To adequately support and advance the kinds of collaborative research, teaching, and service arrangements we have in mind, we must find ways to create a stable and supervised environment to conduct our research/service and to train our students in practical ways. This can be done in a general way, and one route that has had a proven track record of success is crafted in the model of a center, an agency within the department that negotiates partnerships with the community, organizes faculty and student involvement, and searches for sources of public and private funding to finance projects. Indeed, we would like to name this site, where student, faculty, and community interests come together, the American Indian Sovereignty Center. We recognize that a center of this sort would require the building of a sizable capital endowment to support its infrastructural costs. This is our long-term goal. In the meantime, we are working on the creation of smaller "charter" projects built around the existing strengths of our faculty and staff.

Our first project centers around our commitment to the preservation of Native languages and cultures. Unlike European-language education, which benefits from a wealth of texts, curriculum modules, audiotapes, video materials, and immersion settings for language instruction, language education for Ojibwe and Dakota is hindered by the limited educational materials and support opportunities available in the college setting. Over the years, instructional staff in the Ojibwe and Dakota language programs have been working to change this at the University of Minnesota and at neighboring institutions as well.

In Ojibwe language instruction, Dennis Jones has been involved in the establishment of a bilingual clearinghouse that maintains and updates collections of language and cultural materials for use in pre- and postsecondary educational settings, and he supports a language network as well, where language scholars regionwide are able to pool their knowledges, ideas, and techniques for preserving and teaching the Ojibwe language. He has also been instrumental in holding summer language immersion camps annually in local Ojibwe communities in the United States and Canada. He is also taking steps to develop new and innovative curriculum materials in Ojibwe language education, especially materials that draw upon modern computer-interactive technologies.

In the Dakota language program, Carrie Schommer and Timothy Dunnigan developed a language text for use in beginning and intermediate classes. More recently, the department has worked with Chris Mato Nupa and the Dakota–English Dictionary Project group to support their innovative work on a new dictionary and accompanying database, and with Angela Cavender Wilson on the preschool language immersion project under the sponsorship of the Pezihutazizi Language Preservation and Renewal Program in the Upper Sioux Community, just outside Granite Falls. We were able to offer internship funds for students in the Dakota language program to participate in these projects.

For both languages, Ojibwe and Dakota, we desire to create an environment of instruction, research, and outreach that supports efforts to preserve language knowledges on campus and in local communities. And we intend to do so by building a faculty and teaching staff capable of maintaining a language program with opportunities for a master's-level graduate education.

The department is also aiming to develop charter projects centering around research that assists Tribes in identifying and documenting resources and knowledges for which they have legal, historical, and cultural entitlements. Such work would assist Tribes in their efforts to recover and retain information that not only protects their political and intellectual rights, but also enhances their efforts to strengthen educational curriculums and to build libraries, archives, and information centers that store and preserve various kinds of legal, historical, and cultural knowledge. In our department, we already have faculty with formal training in history, political science, anthropology, and the humanities who have the necessary knowledge, skills, and experience to conduct entitlement research and to train students for this kind of work.

Through the work of our new coordinator of community relations, Vikki Howard, whose position is jointly financed by the College of Liberal Arts, the Office of Multi-Cultural Affairs, and the university's Extension Division, the department also supports other efforts to build partnerships with local Tribes and the Twin Cities' urban communities. We manage an electronic list-serve, originally developed by former acting chair David Born, that distributes news and information of interest to nearly 250 subscribers in the region. The department is also involved in a project of the Woodlands' Wisdom Confederation, which consists of a group of six Tribal colleges in Minnesota, North Dakota, and Wisconsin that have embarked on a historic journey in partnership with the University of Minnesota (under its land-grant status established in 1862) to create nutrition and food science departments at each Tribal college. This unique project, "Woodlands Wisdom," aims to train American Indian health professionals in the struggle to counter the epidemic of diabetes in American Indian communities. Educational Advancement on Reservations with Technology and Heart (EARTH) is another project, representing a consortium of Minnesota Tribal organizations, local educational authorities, and the region's higher education institutions, to address the lack of educational telecommunications and informational infrastructure opportunities on three reservations in Minnesota. Finally, a project initiated in the summer of 1999 on the White Earth reservation involves a summer math and science camp for grades eight through twelve. It establishes a collaboration between the White Earth community and staff from the University of Minnesota, and is funded for three years from resources within the university.

Conclusion

This chapter has represented a longitudinal case study of the Department of American Indian Studies at the University of Minnesota–Twin Cities. It is a study from which much can be learned about some of the dynamics surrounding the formation, struggles, and survival of a department in an ethnic studies discipline at a large, research-oriented university. Among other things we have learned is that the department's present and future rely very directly on the vision and support (or lack thereof) of the university's higher administration. We also have come to recognize our vulnerabilities, especially during periods when university funding is reduced and when resources are no longer available to replace abandoned faculty lines.

It is clear from the history of our experience that we must strengthen the foundation of our department so we stand out of harm's way when university resources are scarce. This means, first and foremost, creating an environment in which faculty are not hard-pressed to meet the excessive and often conflicting demands that interfere with their ability to make the tenure grade and rise professionally in their respective academic fields. Once this happens, everyone associated with the department, from staff and students to Tribal agencies and community groups, will be better served by an organization dedicated to delivering high-quality teaching, scholarship, and service.

Notes

1. We wish to acknowledge Ronald Libertus, Timothy Dunnigan, and Helen Rieger for their helpful information and insights on various facets of the department's history.

2. Justin Huenemann of the American Indian Resource Learning Center shared with us some of his knowledge of the center's history.

References

Albers, Patricia. 1998. "Symbols, Souvenirs and Sentiments: Early Postcard Imagery of Plains Indians." In *Delivering Views*, ed. C. Geary and V. Webb, 84–98. Washington, D.C.: Smithsonian Press.

Albers, Patricia, and Nancy Breen. 1997. "Reaching Gender Parity: The Case of American Indians on or Near Tribal Reservations and Historic Areas." *Race, Class and Gender* 3, no. 2: 75–95.

Child, Brenda. 1998. *Boarding School Seasons: American Indian Families, 1900–1940*. Lincoln: University of Nebraska Press.

Jones, Dennis. 1995. "The Etymology of Anishanaabe." *Oshkaabewis Native Journal* 2, no. 1: 43–48.

———. 1997. "Mewinzha Dash Noongom." *Oshkaabewis Native Journal* 4, no. 1: 31–32.

Miller, Carol. 1996. "Mediation and Authority: The Native American Voices of Mourning Dove and Ella Cara Deloria." In *Multicultural Education, Transformative Knowledge and Action*, ed. James A. Banks, 141–155. New York: Teachers College Press.

———. 1999. "Telling the Indian Urban: Representations in American Indian Fiction." *American Indian Culture and Research Journal* 22, no. 4: 43–65.

Miller, Frank C. 1971. "Involvement in an Urban University." In *The American Indian in Urban Society*, ed. Jack O. Waddell and O. Michael Watson, 313–340. Boston: Little Brown.

O'Brien, Jean M. 1997. *Dispossession by Degrees: Indian Land and Identity in Natick, Massachusetts, 1650–1790*. New York: Oxford University Press.

Raymond, Margaret, W. Roger Buffalohead, and Lenore Franzen. 1999. *Collaborating for Change:*

New Directions for Meeting the Higher Education Needs of Urban American Indians. Final Report for the American Indian Urban Higher Education Initiative.

Wilkins, David. 1996. *American Indian Sovereignty and the U.S. Supreme Court: The Masking of Justice.* Austin: University of Texas Press.

———. 1999. *Navajo Political Experience.* Tsaile, Ariz.: Dine College Press.

Wilkins, David, and Vine Deloria Jr. 1999. *Tribes, Treaties, and Constitutional Tribulations.* Austin: University of Texas Press.

The Department of Indian Studies at the Saskatchewan Indian Federated College 9

BLAIR STONECHILD, WITH WILLIAM ASIKINACK AND DAVID R. MILLER

THE SASKATCHEWAN INDIAN FEDERATED COLLEGE (SIFC) was established in May 1976 as a bold initiative in Indian-controlled postsecondary education. Affiliated with a mainstream public university, the University of Regina in Saskatchewan, Canada, the college has grown from a humble beginning of a dozen students to an institution of over 1,600 students and nearly 1,900 graduates. The Department of Indian Studies, considered to be the academic core of the college, has evolved a broad yet highly articulated curriculum with a strong emphasis on research.

Origins of the College

The SIFC was created as a result of growing political consciousness, in particular a movement that had begun among the Indian peoples of Canada in the early 1970s for "Indian Control of Indian Education." Problems of relevance of education coupled with a high drop-out rate meant that very few Indian students entered universities. For the Federation of Saskatchewan Indian Nations (FSIN), the political organization that represents the seventy-two Indian chiefs and approximately 100,000 First Nations[1] in Saskatchewan (and formerly called the Federation of Saskatchewan Indians),[2] this means control not only over their primary and secondary education, but also over their higher education.

During the 1970s, the Federation of Saskatchewan Indians (FSI) embarked on the creation of a series of institutions at the postsecondary level. In addition to the SIFC, the Saskatchewan Indian Cultural College was established in 1970 to assist with the preservation of culture and development of curriculum. The Saskatchewan Indian Community College was founded in 1974 to offer technical and trades education. First Nation Elders including Smith Atimoyoo, Ernest

Tootoosis, and Jim Kanipitehtew had identified the need for more culturally and socially relevant programs in history, politics, and philosophy at the university level.[3] This would help develop properly trained Indian professionals including teachers, social workers, and administrators. The Saskatchewan Indian Federated College was created under FSI legislation, the Saskatchewan Indian Federated College Act.

First Nation enrollments at the University of Regina up to this time had never exceeded more than about a half dozen students out of a university student body of several thousand. In 1976, newly appointed university president Dr. Lloyd Barber, who had recently completed a term as federally appointed Indian claims commissioner, recognized an opportunity to undertake a new and exciting venture with the Saskatchewan Indian people. At the beginning of his mandate, Barber proposed to the FSIN the "federated college model" of higher education delivery, under which the SIFC would be an entity independently controlled by the Indian people, but would be academically integrated with the university.[4] Federated colleges are intended to allow smaller independent colleges wishing to foster particular environments (usually religious) to exist alongside public universities. The federated college is administratively and financially independent, but is academically integrated with the university.[5]

An Indian Social Work degree program that had commenced at the Saskatchewan Indian Cultural College in Saskatoon in 1974 was also proposed to become part of the new institution.[6] Core funding was provided by the federal Department of Indian Affairs, and the SIFC shared its student tuitions, retaining 40 percent for on-campus students, with the university. A provincial grant reflecting the enrollment of non-Aboriginal students in the SIFC rounded out the funding.[7]

The creation of an Indian-controlled college was regarded by many as a novel experiment, since the institution was being created within a community that had no tradition of university-level education, and that had very few individuals possessing university credentials.[8] For example, no Canadian Indian possessed an earned doctorate in 1976,[9] a testament to the repressive policies of the Department of Indian Affairs, under which Indians who obtained higher education became automatically enfranchised.[10] The SIFC was therefore a novel experiment in institution-building. Under the *Federation Agreement* (see chapter appendix), the institution's proposed program was approved by the academic structures of the university and qualified staff were hired.[11]

The SIFC delivery model remains unique in North America in that it is an Indian-controlled college working in academic partnership with a major public university. It is also unique in that it is funded out of the national Indian Affairs postsecondary fund, the Indian Studies Support Program (ISSP).

The mission of the Saskatchewan Indian Federated College is to enhance the quality of life, and to preserve, protect and interpret the history, language, culture and artistic heritage of First Nations. The College will acquire and expand its base of knowledge and understanding in the best interests of First Nations and for the benefit of society by providing opportunities of quality bi-lingual and bi-cultural education under the mandate and control of the First Nations of Saskatchewan. The SIFC is a First Nations–controlled university-college which provides educational opportunities to both First Nations and non–First Nations students selected from a provincial, national and international base.[12]

The first director of the SIFC, Ida Wasacase, a member of the Ochapowace First Nation and a well-known educator, was directed to establish an institution that was to reflect strong control by First Nations, while fulfilling all of the academic standards and regulations of a university college. She was to report to the SIFC's board of governors, which consisted primarily of Indian chiefs representing ten regions of Saskatchewan, and also included representatives of the University of Saskatchewan, the University of Regina, the Canadian federal government, and Saskatchewan government. Wasacase's particular approach emphasized bicultural education, in which the student would learn about and thus be able to function in both the Indian and the white worlds. For example, while there was to be a department teaching the five Indian languages in Saskatchewan—Cree, Plains Ojibway, Nakota, Dakota, and Dene—there was also a Department of English.

Reaching First Nation students in their own communities was deemed a priority, and a significant amount of teaching activity occurred in the form of off-campus classes as well as in the form of entire degree or certificate programs offered on a onetime basis in First Nation communities. Approximately fifty off-campus classes were offered in various communities across Canada during the 1998–1999 academic year. The SIFC also established campuses in Saskatoon and Prince Albert to meet the needs of significant First Nation urban student populations in those areas,[13] and frequently offers programs on a demand and cost-recovery basis in most of Canada's provinces and territories, including British Columbia, Alberta, Manitoba, Ontario, Quebec, Northwest Territories, and the Yukon.

The SIFC was accepted in 1993 as a full member of the Association of Universities and Colleges of Canada (AUCC), the national accrediting organization. The SIFC was also affiliated from the mid-1980s until the early 1990s with the American Indian Higher Education Consortium (AIHEC), the group representing Indian-controlled colleges in the United States and Canada. This provided an opportunity for the SIFC to explore common goals and interests with similar institutions among Tribes of the Northern Plains.

As of fall 1998 the SIFC has graduated almost 1,900 students, a remarkable advancement from twenty years ago when graduation of a single student was considered to be a great accomplishment.

Development of the Department

In the beginning, the Department of Indian Studies was both influenced and shaped by the first faculty hired. Blair Stonechild, a member of the Muscowpetung First Nation in southern Saskatchewan and then a recent graduate of McGill University, was appointed as the first Indian Studies Lecturer and Developer in December 1976.[14] One of his first tasks would be to further define the direction of the new department. Stonechild recalls, "When I was first approached about working at the College, I was only asked if I wanted to teach an Indian Studies course. Little did I realize to what extent the College would grow."

An ad hoc committee on Indian studies was convened in early 1977 that brought together approximately thirty First Nation individuals from a broad range of perspectives, including Elders, educators, politicians, and community members. From this forum, a few basic points emerged that were transformed into goals and objectives. The committee determined that in addition to academic training, it was essential that the program meet the cultural and social needs of First Nation students. There was a decided sentiment that the SIFC was to resist becoming a stereotypical ivory tower institution often inaccessible and irrelevant to the ordinary Aboriginal person. To accomplish this, the SIFC would not leave development of its curriculum only in the hands of academics, but would also consult with First Nation Elders and community leaders. Cultural and historical perspectives, political aspirations and priorities, including Indian rights and self-determination, were identified with First Nation participation. Moreover, the committee reaffirmed that the SIFC should teach classes whenever possible in Indian communities, and that a general effort should be made to decentralize activities. Such a goal would entail significant financial and logistical challenges.

Indian studies was envisioned as the core of the SIFC's academic programs. It would contain classes crucial to First Nation culture, history, identity, and issues, most of these in support of degree programs in the Faculty of Arts and Fine Arts. Many of the classes also became components of other newly developing degree programs in areas such as Indian teacher education and Indian public and business administration.

The earliest Indian studies statement of objectives had five points:

> 1. First and foremost, the Department of Indian Studies must give priority to the identification and elucidation of Indian thoughts, concepts and aspirations in areas relevant to the Social Sciences.

2. As in other disciplines of the Faculty of Arts, the Department of Indian Studies will endeavor to stimulate independent and critical thinking, and promote intelligent inquiry and free discussion.
3. The Department of Indian Studies views other academic disciplines as having validity in increasing the understanding of Indian matters, but differs from them in that it uses Indian thoughts, concepts and aspirations as the basis for approaching these matters.
4. The Department of Indian Studies will work in close conjunction with the Indian community to clarify and accurately determine Indian thoughts, concepts and aspirations.
5. The Department of Indian Studies will promote Indian thoughts and concepts as a unique and legitimate area of endeavor within the overall academic community.[15]

In the early 1990s, the goals of the department were revised in the following mission statement:

> Indian Studies fosters the intellectual study of indigenous peoples' history and life in Saskatchewan, Canada, North America and comparatively, the world. It strives to counter the marginalization of Indigenous life, history, knowledge and issues; to make post-secondary education more culturally relevant to Indigenous students; to promote Indigenous student retention; and to educate the Canadian public at large.
>
> While Indian Studies is transdisciplinary within the western academic framework, it strives for meaningful balance through traditional teachings offered by Elders and by promoting traditional perspectives, content and pedagogical modes.
>
> On a broader level, Indian Studies faculty endeavor to: develop theoretical approaches, paradigms and methodologies based on traditional Indigenous intellectual traditions; foster and promote Indigenous scholarship; and provide professional service to Indigenous communities through applied research and training.[16]

This approach established unique directions. Courses such as "Indians and the Law" and "Principles of Indian Government" focused on priorities such as promoting the legitimacy of treaty and Aboriginal rights (which had minimal legal standing at the time), and addressed the issue of self-government (at a time when this notion was met with a great deal of skepticism).[17] In the 1970s, these issues were well ahead of Canadian public opinion, and were not yet the subject of extensive research by university scholars.

An important consideration in recruiting faculty during the early development of the SIFC was sensitivity toward and ability to articulate First Nation positions on issues, as well as the ability to relate to First Nation students' needs. Thus minimum possession of an undergraduate degree was sometimes deemed adequate for the beginning instructor. Faculty were expected to be committed to pursuing the unique mission of the SIFC and the initial approach of the department. For example, they were encouraged to integrate opinions and oral history of Elders in as many aspects of the curriculum as possible—a practice little heard of on university campuses at the time. All SIFC faculty appointments required the concurrence of the University of Regina president and the appropriate faculty dean.[18]

While this approach to institution-building was unorthodox, few could dispute the results; the department expanded rapidly from a few core courses to three-and four-year degree programs, honors programs, and eventually to a special-case master of arts program. The Indian studies degree has evolved into a highly specialized social science area within the SIFC's larger curriculum. One of the reasons for this direction is the existence of other departments with their own entire degree programs in areas such as Indian languages, literatures and linguistics, Indian fine arts, Indian social work, Indian education, Indian administration, Indian communication arts, and science.

Overall enrollments in the college rose from 12 in 1976 to almost 1,700 by 1998, making the SIFC among the fastest-growing university institutions in Canada.[19] The college operates primarily in three major centers, the Regina operation on the University of Regina campus, the Saskatoon campus, where the social-work program began and a wing of Indian studies now exists, and the northern campus in Prince Albert, out of which the SIFC's Department of Extensions operates. SIFC enrollments today constitute nearly 15 percent of the University of Regina's 12,000-member student body.

At critical points in the history of the SIFC, individual Indian studies faculty members have assumed various administrative positions including president, dean, and executive director, which has taxed the department's teaching and research resources. Teaching duties no longer include obligatory off-campus instruction as was the case during the early phase of the college. With the development of a separate Department of Extensions, Indian studies became an increasingly important service department providing classes required for select degrees such as social work and human justice offered at the University of Regina.

Other challenges included ensuring that courses were supported by adequate research and documentation, and that the teaching resources needed to support a rapidly growing program were found.[20] An issue that is still the subject of periodic debate is defining the unique nature and approach of Indian studies, while continuing to incorporate a broad interdisciplinary approach. The establishment of the Indian Studies Research Centre in 1984 assisted faculty and students with research efforts, especially in gray areas such as collecting unpublished documents.[21] Areas of recent research utilizing the research center include select land claims, band histories, economic development, government policy development, and international issues. Plans to develop an archive in the new college facility will permit the processing of collections currently in college storage. A de facto archives program has been initiated by the SIFC library, even though the college does not currently employ a full-time archivist. Finally, the 50,000-item collection in the SIFC library complements the University of Regina's collection of over 2 million items.

The Indian studies course offerings and degree structures underwent a major review and transformation in 1992 when the University of Regina converted its academic programs and course formats from the four-credit-hour–course full-time equivalent to a three-credit-hour, five-course full-time equivalent system. For the department, this opportunity entailed evaluation and reformulation of individual classes and the entire Indian studies degree structures. The self-directed review by the faculty of the department resulted in the addition of cultural heritage classes, the creation of systems courses in areas such as religion, economics, and politics, and the creation of methods courses in areas such as oral history and community-based research. Consequently, the fifty courses constitute one of the most articulated Native studies programs available.

Courses within the department required toward a four-year bachelor's degree are Indian Studies 100, 101, 225, 228, 229, and 301. In addition, all majors are required to take at least one cultural heritage course, one systems course, and one methods course, as well as six other Indian Studies courses at or above the 200 level, including a minimum of one at the 300 and one at the 400 level. Honors students also take Indian Studies 380, 490, and 491 as required classes. This ensures a firm grounding in research methods, and the ability to produce a high-quality honors paper. The honors student also must take a minimum of eight additional courses at the 200, 300, and 400 levels. Within the degree structures of the University of Regina, students take a distribution requirement of subjects to complete their degree, including classes in a second language, logic, mathematics, natural science, humanities, and fine arts.[22]

At the introductory level, Indian Studies 100 is a critical thinking–skills class, which is paired with the Indian Studies 101 thematic essays class. Besides focusing more on individual topics, the second class assists students in acquiring the experience with written expression necessary for success in the university environment. The department has produced the introductory textbook *Survival of a People* (1986), a reader, as well as *The First Ones: Readings in Indian/Native Studies* (1992),[23] and has offered a satellite distance-education introductory course on the

Saskatchewan Communications Network (SCN) in collaboration with the University of Saskatchewan.

Apart from teaching, faculty conduct a broad range of research and have produced a variety of published works. For example, the historical work *Loyal till Death: Indians and the Northwest Rebellion* by Blair Stonechild and Bill Waiser won a Saskatchewan Book Award and was a finalist in the nonfiction category in the 1997 Governor-General's Award, Canada's premier literary competition.[24]

As of spring 1998 the Department of Indian Studies has approximately 1,300 student course enrollments annually. Over 200 individuals are taking Indian studies as a subject major or minor. A significant number of the SIFC's graduates, about half of whom are female single parents, began as mature students in the University Entrance Program (UEP). Altogether, there are approximately 300 recipients of a bachelor's degree in Indian studies among the 1,900 graduates of the college.[25]

Indian studies offers a special-case master of arts program in collaboration with the University of Regina's Faculty of Graduate Studies and Research. Two students have graduated and four students are currently writing theses; an intake of new students is anticipated for the 1999–2000 academic year. As more graduate students complete the program, the department intends to develop a regular M.A. program once six degrees have been completed.

Administrative Contexts

The Department of Indian Studies coordinates its activities within two major administrative systems, one internal to the SIFC, and the other related to the University of Regina, mainly through the Faculty of Arts. The SIFC has its own academic structures of deans and departments, which tend to focus on collegewide issues of administrative concern. In terms of academic approval processes, the department originates curriculum or policy within the department, then channels it to the SIFC Academic Council, a representative college forum, for discussion and approval. Proposals are then forwarded to the university's Faculty of Arts Program Development Committee, then to the Faculty of Arts itself, and finally to the university's Faculty Executive of Council before going to the university senate for final approval. Working relationships between the SIFC and the University of Regina have generally been good, and the process, though cumbersome, produces thorough results. The university does not interfere in the SIFC's operations because of the principle of administrative autonomy. On the other hand, SIFC faculty, who are members of respective university faculties, have representation on some, but not all, university committees. Consequently, all faculty of the SIFC are recognized as faculty of the university.[26]

Another unique aspect of the department's organization is its dual presence in Saskatchewan's two major cities—Regina and Saskatoon. While the department is based at the University of Regina campus, Indian studies courses began to be offered as a component of the Indian social-work program based in Saskatoon. Demand from the city's First Nation population led to gradual expansion until all of the classes required for the Indian studies degree could be obtained. Classes offered at the Saskatoon campus are considered to be on campus for administrative purposes. Numerous individual Indian studies off-campus classes are offered through the SIFC's Department of Extensions in First Nation communities across western Canada, particularly in British Columbia, Alberta, and Manitoba.[27]

SIFC faculty currently have the benefit of a collective agreement that was negotiated as a result of the need for mutually agreed-upon processes of faculty appointment, promotion, and dismissal. In 1993 an SIFC bargaining unit under the University of Regina Faculty Association (URFA), and by extension under the Canadian Association of University Teachers (CAUT), was established. Acceptance of the faculty union was politically controversial for the Federation of Saskatchewan Indian Nations. The agreement is unique in including processes not in the agreement between the university and its faculty association, such as the Tawaw Committee, which utilizes traditional methods of conflict resolution. The agreement also provides assurances of academic freedom.[28]

Indian studies has undertaken novel initiatives such as developing courses on international Indigenous issues. This endeavor began in conjunction with the World Assembly of First Nations in 1982, and helped lead to the eventual creation of the Centre for International Indigenous Studies and Development at the SIFC, which provided training to Indigenous peoples from across the world, with particular concentration in the Caribbean and Central and South America. Funding for the center is provided mainly by grants from the Canadian International Development Agency of the Canadian federal government.

Under center director Del Anaquod, professor of Indian studies and former president of the SIFC, the department is currently working with the National Autonomous University of Chiapas (UNACH) to develop what will become the first Indigenous studies bachelor's degree in Mexico.[29] Other groups and institutions with which the center is active include Chirapaq in Peru, the Central Institute of Nationalities in Beijing, People's Republic of China, and the United Nations University for Peace in Costa Rica. The center's major long-term goal is support toward the establishment of an International Indigenous University, a role that the SIFC is interested in fulfilling.

Conclusion

SIFC's presence within the larger academic environment at the University of Regina adds breadth to students' learning and experiences, as does contact with the several hundred non-Aboriginal students who constitute close to half the numbers in many Indian studies classes. The impact of exposure to differing perspectives, often for the first time, broadens students' horizons and creates a climate of mutual understanding and respect.

Funding of the SIFC and therefore the Department of Indian Studies comes primarily from federal Indian Affairs, and is supplemented by other sources such as tuitions and grants. This has allowed the department to grow to eleven full-time faculty, fifteen to twenty sessional lecturers, and a seminar leader and two support-staff positions.

In the 1980s, in an effort to economize instructional resources, the department mounted large introductory classes of as many as 175 students. However, during the 1992 curriculum review process, the difficulties associated with large classroom instruction were recognized and the department consciously decided that introductory classes should be no larger than fifty students in Indian Studies 100 and thirty students in Indian Studies 101. This has improved student retention and success.

In a difficult decision, the *Saskatchewan Indian Federated College Journal*, started in 1984, was discontinued after volume 5-1 (1989) when it became clear that institutional support for a high-quality journal could not be maintained.

The Canadian Indigenous/Native Studies Association (CINSA), pioneered and hosted until recently by the SIFC, provided an important national reference group for Indian/Native studies instructors and researchers. Its official publication is the *Canadian Journal of Native Studies*. The association adds enhanced credibility by virtue of its participation in the Learneds Societies, and its membership in lobbying bodies such as the Social Sciences Federation. Activities of the association had been in hiatus for a few years; however, a meeting of interested scholars in Saskatoon in May 1998 has led to CINSA's renewal. A national Steering Committee is overseeing a new membership drive and organization of annual conferences.[30]

Construction of a unique new facility for the SIFC commenced in 2001 with projected occupancy in 2003. The building, designed by architect Douglas Cardinal, incorporates the circle and four directions in its design, and its site on the east side of the University of Regina campus is to be designated as an Indian reserve. The building will include areas for an expanded library, an archive, and a research center. Approximately $15 million in funds have been provided by federal and provincial grants, $6 million has been raised from corporations and individuals, and a further $3 million remains to be raised.[31] On a related note, the SIFC's board of directors has also agreed to eventually rename the institution to reflect its status as a First Nation university.

Overriding issues still facing the SIFC include the need to obtain clarification of its status as a national First Nation institution in harmony with its current national funding. The federal government ought to ensure that the SIFC is able to maintain a quality program by funding it at a level equitable to other Canadian universities.[32]

The specter of arbitrary government cutbacks to First Nation higher education could jeopardize the institution's long-term potential. Many First Nation peoples are financially able to attend universities only by virtue of the grants provided by the Department of Indian and Northern Affairs. The extent of that funding has been capped since 1987, and should it ever be curtailed, it could have crippling impacts on Indian enrollments at the SIFC.[33]

Despite the obstacles faced over the past twenty-three years, the future for Indian studies appears promising in terms of demographics, which indicate strong growth in the numbers of Aboriginal students. In Saskatchewan, for example, a recent study indicates that the Aboriginal population of the province will grow from 134,000 in 1995 (13 percent of the population) to 434,000 in 2045 (32 percent of the population).[34] Similar Aboriginal growth patterns are also expected in neighboring regions in Manitoba and northern Ontario.

Graduates of the SIFC's Department of Indian Studies are finding roles in preparing for tomorrow's world through careers and work they have chosen in such areas as medicine, law, Tribal leadership, administration, policy analysis, teaching, and research.[35]

Appendix: Federation Agreement of the Saskatchewan Indian Federated College and the University of Regina

I. AIM

The aim of federation is to associate with the University of Regina and to integrate with it in matters academic, post-secondary institutions within the Province, which are legally and financially independent of the University, for the purposes of (a) assisting the University in its task of presenting, reflecting upon and scrutinizing as broad a spectrum as possible of values and viewpoints, and (b) providing students with an opportunity to become associated, within the context of the University, with a smaller college environment.

2. DEFINITION

A college federated with the University of Regina is a post-secondary institution, legally and financially independent, but academically integrated with the University. This means:

    i. The college employs its own administrative, academic, and support staff and constructs and maintains its own buildings which must be on or adjacent to the University.

    ii. By agreement, the college offers classes in mutually agreed upon disciplines, which are part of degree programs of the University. Its students take other classes needed for degrees from other university professors.

   iii. The academic standards of the college are governed by Senate By-Laws.

   iv. The college selects and appoints its own professors, provided the University approves their academic qualifications.

    v. The President, Dean and faculty of the college are voting members of the Faculty of Arts or Faculty of Science or such other Faculties as are approved in the federation agreement, and the University Council. The President is a member of Senate.

3. GENERAL TERMS

The Saskatchewan Indian Federated College (Federation of Saskatchewan Indians), hereafter referred to as the College, shall be recognized as a federated college under the following terms and conditions:

    i. Initially, a Bachelor of Arts Degree, with a major in Indian Studies, will be granted by the University to those students of the College who satisfy the admission requirements of the University as well as the curriculum requirements for the Degree in Indian Studies.

   ii. There shall be established, within the Saskatchewan Indian Federated College, a Department of Indian Studies with academic program duties and responsibilities similar to departments within the Faculty of Arts.

   iii. Where the general terms of federation provide for interaction and agreement on academic program matters between the Saskatchewan Indian Federated College Department Head and a University of Regina Department Head, such liaison and agreement shall be between the Saskatchewan Indian Federated College Department of Indian Studies and the Dean of the appropriate Faculty.

   iv. While non-Indians will be encouraged to select where appropriate, classes in Indian Studies as electives for Degrees other than the Indian Studies Degree, students of Indian and Inuit ancestry will normally receive priority for admission.

    v. The Bachelor of Arts program in Indian Studies will be open to all students, but priority will normally be given to students of Indian or Inuit ancestry.

vi. The College may, from time to time, approach and enter into agreement with other Faculties of the University of Regina, and will seek approval from Council and Senate for such agreements.

vii. Initially the Saskatchewan Indian Federated College will not have its own building on or adjacent to the campus and, therefore of necessity accommodation for administrative and academic functions of the Saskatchewan Indian Federated College will be provided from existing university space.

viii. The division of tuition fee revenue between the College and the University of Regina will be by mutual agreement and subject to annual review. The fees of the College shall not differ materially from that of the University.

ix. The members of the College teaching staff, teaching university classes, must possess qualifications sufficiently high to be recognized as members of the appropriate Faculties and shall be so recognized.

x. Academic appointments to and promotions within the College shall be made by the President of the College, but, prior to making such appointments or promotions, the President of the College shall secure the approval of the President of the University.

xi. The officers and faculty of the College are entitled to voting membership in the following academic bodies:
- The Senate: The President.
- The Council: The President, Dean, Professors, Associate Professors, Assistant Professors, full-time Lecturers, Special Lecturers and Instructors.
- The Faculty of Arts: The President, Dean, Professors, Associate Professors, Assistant Professors, full-time Lecturers, Special Lecturers and Instructors teaching classes offered by Departments of the Faculty and recognized for Bachelor's degrees.
- The Faculty of Science: The President, Dean, Professors, Associate Professors, full-time Lecturers, Special Lecturers and Instructors teaching classes offered by the Departments of the Faculty and recognized for Bachelor's degrees.
- Other Faculties when provided for by agreement: The President, Dean, Professors, Associate Professors, Assistant Professors, full-time Lecturers, Special Lecturers and

Instructors teaching classes offered by the Faculty and recognized for Bachelor's degrees.

xii. Students enrolled in the college who have satisfied the University requirements for admission shall be admitted to such university classes as they are qualified to enter and continue therein on the same terms as other University students, provided the fees required for such classes have been paid to the college. Students enrolled in the University ordinarily, with the permission of the college, may take classes in the college recognized for the Bachelor's degrees in the Faculty of Arts, the Faculty of Science, or such other Faculties as may be agreed, provided that the fees required for such classes have been paid to the University. These conditions will apply provided the same tuition fee is required by both the college and the University.

xiii. All students enrolled in a professional school or faculty must pay to the University the full tuition fee required for each year of the professional course, though the University may grant credit for any class or classes taken in the College and accepted by the Faculty for the corresponding class required in a professional course.

xiv. The University will recognize instruction given by the College in subjects as may from time to time be agreed upon by the Council of the University: Provided that the instruction is given by competent teachers and that the work done in each class is equivalent in extent and standards to those given in the University; this equivalence is to be determined by the Academic Head of the College and the appropriate unit of a Faculty of the University of Regina working out in cooperation the extent of the classes, the standard and all the particulars pertaining to the subjects, including the examinations, to their mutual satisfaction or in cases of difficulties to the satisfaction of the President of the University.

xv. The University will confer the appropriate Bachelor's degrees on such students of the College as have satisfied the requirements prescribed by the University.

Notes

1. The term *First Nation* has come into common usage among Indians in Canada to denote an individual band of Indians. As such, it does not denote a Tribal Nation.

2. The renaming to FSIN occurred after the signing of a political convention in the mid-1980s.

3. According to the John R. McLeod papers (held by Professor Neal McLeod, Saskatchewan Indian Federated College), Smith Atimoyoo, Ernest Tootoosis, and Jim Kanipitehtew were the Elders most closely involved in this process.

4. Dr. Barber had been a vice president at the University of Saskatchewan when a proposal by the Federation of Saskatchewan Indians for an Indian-controlled college was made to that university in 1975. The University of Regina became independent from the University of Saskatchewan in 1974. Aboriginal academic D'Arcy McNickle had spent three years in the Department of Anthropology at Regina in the early 1970s, but was not directly involved in the formation of the SIFC. Dr. Bob Thomas spent several months at Regina in 1975 assisting with planning for the college.

5. For a history of early development of federated colleges in Saskatchewan, see A. de Valk, "Independent University or Federated College?" *Saskatchewan History* 30 (1977).

6. The Saskatchewan Indian Cultural College was founded in 1970 in Saskatoon to preserve and teach Indian culture and languages. Its name has since been changed to the Saskatchewan Indian Cultural Centre. The Saskatchewan Indian Community College has been renamed the Saskatchewan Indian Institute of Technology.

7. The university was to receive 40 percent of tuitions for on-campus students in consideration for the usage of university classrooms and other facilities, but was to retain 100 percent of tuitions for off-campus registrants.

8. During this period, the Federation of Saskatchewan Indians was politically strong and was taking a leading role in implementing what it believed to be institutions of higher education appropriate for self-determination.

9. Department of Indian and Northern Affairs, "The Indian and Inuit Graduate Register," Ottawa, 1976.

10. For example, section 86(1) of the Indian Act of 1876 stated: "Any Indian who may be admitted to the degree of Doctor of Medicine, or any other degree by any University of Learning, . . . shall ipso facto become and be enfranchised under this Act."

11. Instructor approval consisted of a recommendation to the university president, who in turn approved the appointment with concurrence of the relevant faculty dean.

12. SIFC, *Academic Calendar, 1998–2000,* 1.

13. The urban Aboriginal population in Saskatoon would be comparable to that of Regina at approximately 20,000. The high proportion of Aboriginal people in and around Prince Albert led Indian chiefs of the area to request the establishment of a northern campus. In 1996 there were 610 students enrolled at the Regina campus, 402 students enrolled at the Saskatoon campus, and 229 off-campus students.

14. Stonechild had been involved recently with the establishment of Manitou Community College at La Macaza, Quebec, prior to coming to the SIFC.

15. SIFC, *General Calendar Information,* 1986.

16. Department of Indian Studies information brochure, 1997.

17. Since treaties were never ratified by Canada's Parliament, they were legally mere promises. This changed when treaty and Aboriginal rights were recognized in the Canadian constitution in 1982.

18. For a listing of and information about departmental faculty and courses, see the SIFC current Web site: www.sifc.edu.

19. Sharon Carrier, Dean of Students, was the first Indian studies graduate of the SIFC.

20. At one early university curriculum meeting, a professor questioned the phrase "extinguishing Indian rights"—Were we trying to put out a fire? he wondered. It took reference to a book on Old English to determine that the word usage was correct. The course quickly passed without further questions.

21. Early funding for development of the research center came from a major grant from the Native Economic Development Program (NEDP), which provided funds for the development of curriculum in Aboriginal economics and administration.

22. University of Regina, *General Calendar, 1998–1999*, 79.

23. In a 1995 review in *Ethnohistory*, Duane Champagne calls *The First Ones* "a pioneering, useful work and teaching aid."

24. For listings of faculty publications, please consult "Indian Studies" on the SIFC Web site: www.sifc.edu.

25. Department of Indian Studies, "Statistics."

26. An example of a committee with no SIFC representation would be the Faculty of Arts Executive Committee.

27. The development of the northern campus was largely due to pressure from the Prince Albert Tribal Council for increased programming in northern Saskatchewan.

28. URFA, *Collective Agreement.*

29. International Indigenous Studies and Education Program: A Collaborative Project between the Saskatchewan Indian Federated College and the Universidad Autonomous de Chiapas, Chiapas State, Mexico, 1998.

30. Information about the history, activities, and membership of CINSA can be found on the SIFC Web site: www.sifc.edu/inst/history.htm. The association is now operating out of the Department of First Nations Studies at Malaspina University College in Nanaimo, British Columbia, and a new Web site is being planned.

31. SIFC, "Facility Proposal," May 1993. Information on the building project and fundraising can be found on the SIFC Web site: www.sifc.edu. Amounts are in Canadian dollars.

32. The SIFC's level of funding is approximately 80 percent of the national average.

33. Darlene Lanceley, "The Post-Secondary Assistance Program for Indian Education," in Terry Wotherspoon, *Hitting the Books* (Toronto: Garamound Press, 1991), 215.

34. FSIN, *Saskatchewan and Aboriginal Peoples*, 60.

35. David Miller, "Indian Studies Alumni Make Diverse Contributions," *SIFC Magazine* (1998–1999): 50.

Bibliography

Barnhardt, R. "Higher Education in the Fourth World." *Canadian Journal of Native Education* 18, no. 2 (1991): 199–231.

Department of Indian Studies, Indians, and the Northwest Rebellion. *Survival of a People.* Regina: SIFC Press, 1986.

Douglas Cardinal Architects. *Master Plan—Saskatchewan Indian Federated College.* Ottawa: Douglas Cardinal Architects, 1993.

Federation of Saskatchewan Indian Nations. "An Act Respecting the Saskatchewan Indian Federated College." May 26, 1994.

————. *Saskatchewan and Aboriginal Peoples in the Twenty-first Century: Social, Economic and Political Challenges.* Regina: Printwest, 1997.

Hampton, E., and S. Wolfson. "Education for Self-Determination." In *Aboriginal Self-Government in Canada—Current Trends and Issues,* ed. J. Hylton. Saskatoon: Purich, 1994.

Miller, D., C. Beal, J. Dempsey, W. Heber, eds. *The First Ones: Readings in Indian/Native Studies.* Regina: SIFC Press, 1992.

Royal Commission on Aboriginal Peoples. Report of the Royal Commission on Aboriginal Peoples. Chap. 5, "Education." Ottawa: Royal Commission on Aboriginal Peoples, 1995.

SIFC. *Academic Calendar, 1998–2000,* Regina.

————. Department of Indian Studies. "Course/Instructor Enrollment Statistics, 1994–98."

————. Office of Institutional Research. "The Saskatchewan Indian Federated College at Twenty Years." Unpublished document, 1995.

————. *SIFC Magazine.* 1998–1999 edition.

Smith, S. "Report of the Commission on Canadian University Education." Report to the Association of Universities and Colleges of Canada, 1991.

Stonechild, B., and B. Waiser. *Loyal till Death.* Calgary: Fifth House, 1997.

Stonechild, B., and D. McCaskill. "The Development of Indian/Native Studies in Canada." In *Education, Research Information Systems and the North,* ed. P. Adams. Ottawa: Association of Canadian Universities for Northern Studies, 1987.

University of Regina. Senate. "Revised Terms for the Federation Agreement of the Saskatchewan Indian Federated College and the University of Regina." May 26, 1977.

URFA. *Saskatchewan Indian Federated College 1995–1999 Collective Agreement.*

O'ezhichigeyaang (This Thing We Do): **10**
American Indian Studies at the University of Minnesota–Duluth

ROBERT E. POWLESS

SINCE THE 1960S, WHEN ethnic studies programs were developing across the country, such programs and departments have been coming and going with surprising rapidity. In the early 1970s at the University of Minnesota–Duluth (UMD), a small group of American Indian Vietnam veterans became students. They immediately became concerned about the lack of American Indian faculty, staff, and courses in the institution. These men sought support from individuals in the local urban Indian community and on the Fond Du Lac Ojibwe Reservation about thirty miles away. This group of Indians, who saw the value of culturally relevant education for Indian people, wanted a variety of courses that would demonstrate the body of knowledge available in Indian history and culture, to Indian and non-Indian alike. They also saw the need to teach an American Indian language (in this case, Ojibwe) to help preserve the language in the area (Minnesota, Wisconsin, and Michigan).

Robert E. Powless, an Oneida, was hired in April 1972 and developed and taught the first course in the program, "American Indians in the 20th Century." We determined that this course would be relevant, would have broad appeal, and would require presentation of a volume of introductory material to make the twentieth-century American Indian history more understandable for the students. The first class attracted 104 students. By the fall of 1972, a minor in American Indian studies had been developed. The American Indian studies program remained unchanged until the fall of 1988, when it became a bona fide department in the College of Liberal Arts.

Dr. Powless had left for a period of time, including a five-year stint as an independent college president in Wisconsin, and staff in UMD American Indian studies, although certainly skilled teachers and administrators, tended not to have the intrinsic academic credentials necessary to give the department the needed credibility in the College of Liberal Arts. He was asked to return in 1988 to work toward stabilizing the teaching faculty situation and toward establishing a major in American Indian studies. In the fall of the 1993–1994 school year, the process of moving the proposal for the American Indian studies major through to the University of Minnesota Board of Regents began. On October 13, 1994, the major was approved by the regents. On January 12, 1995, our department received approval for the major, to become effective in the spring of 1995, from the office of the vice chancellor for academic administration at UMD.

We are encouraged on our campus of about 7,200 students (about 100 of whom are American Indian) to have graduated to date over a dozen majors, with twenty-four majors and a like number of minors on the books. The majors are equally Indian and non-Indian, with the great majority having double majors.

Our department is one of eleven in the College of Liberal Arts, which is one of five colleges/schools within the University of Minnesota–Duluth. Our department head reports directly to the dean of liberal arts. We currently have three full-time, tenure-track lines (two filled by tenured professors), one 80 percent (.8 full-time equivalency) "instructor" position (Ojibwe language specialist), and three part-time positions. We receive faculty salaries, a supplies and equipment budget, and some faculty research/travel funds.

We have been successful in receiving funds via the chancellor's diversity initiatives, which have enabled us to sponsor some extra-classroom activities, such as the Ombi Mazini-Kamigiziwin, "exciting art event," that featured American Indian student artists from our campus alongside some of the well-known American Indian artists from Minnesota and Wisconsin. Our weeklong Ojibwe Language Immersion Camp in the summer is partially funded by a private foundation in St. Paul, Minnesota. The College of Liberal Arts has also been very helpful over the years in assisting us, by funding regular field trips in two of our classes, "Chippewa History and Culture" and "Indians in the Fur Trade."

We have worked especially hard over the years in developing a curriculum that we consider to be the basis (along with good teaching) for a strong ethnic studies department. The following course examples should give the flavor of what we are attempting to do (see also chapter appendix).

"American Indians in the 20th Century" was the first American Indian studies course taught in the spring quarter of 1972. It is the prerequisite for virtually all of the upper-division courses and is taught every quarter (two sections in the fall quarter). Some time is spent providing students with the necessary background to better understand why the twentieth century impacted Indians as it did. The course reflects Dr. Powless's bias against "Introduction to American Indian Studies" courses in preference to a more direct approach. The course attempts to provide a balance in regard to the number of Tribes discussed, as well as a balance among local, regional, and national history. Texts include *A Short History of Indians of the U.S.* by Edward H. Spicer (Malabar, Fla.: Krieger, 1983), and *Women in American Indian Society* by Rayna Green (New York: Chelsea House, 1992).

"Indian–White Relations" is a key course and is a prerequisite for a number of more advanced, upper-division courses. It is designed to provide more opportunity for discussion and is therefore held to an enrollment of twenty-five to thirty students. Selected topics from "American Indians in the 20th Century" are enlarged upon and new topics added at the discretion of the professors.

"American Indian Prose, Poetry, and Oratory" is our introduction to the "arts." Dr. James Robinson, who was first to teach the course, found an outstanding text, *American Indian Literature* by Alan R. Velie (Norman: University of Oklahoma Press, 1991). This course is designed as a precursor to two other courses: "American Indian Novel" and "American Indians and the Media."

"Chippewa History and Culture" is of particular importance in our region. Because we have access to key sites of Anishinaabe/Ojibwe history and culture, we take a field trip to the Madeline Island/Red Cliff area in Wisconsin.

"Survey of American Indian Arts" is another course that enables us to incorporate much regional and local American Indian material. We endeavor, however, to provide art history that will span the hemisphere. Dr. Marilyn Russell-Bogle, a Leech Lake Ojibwe, adds to the course her own expertise as a well-known artist. She also teaches a painting course in the School of Fine Arts at UMD, and is a full-time member of our UMD library staff.

"Fur Trade in Canada and U.S." has been a popular course and is highlighted by a field trip to Old Fort William, Thunder Bay, Ontario. The course enables us to show the effect of the trade on Minnesota Indians and to discuss the Métis (Mixed Blood) people. As one Minnesota student recently remarked, "Why didn't we learn about this in high school?"

When UMD moves to the semester system in the fall of 1999, the course "Current American Indian Legal Issues" will be blended into our other two law courses: "Tribal Law and Government" and "Introduction to Federal Indian Law." These courses had been taught (one each quarter) in the evening by attorney Jim Robinson, who, although not an Indian, is nevertheless an expert on Indian law. With the hiring of Mark J. Gonzalez, J.D., we have started to also include the courses in the regular two-year rotation during the day. Professor Gonzalez is also working on a second minor in American Indian studies in the area of legal issues. We will most likely add this to the curriculum after the switch to semesters.

Last but not least, among our regular courses are two in "Beginning Chippewa," two in "Intermediate Chippewa," one in "Advanced Chippewa," and an "Independent Study of the Chippewa Language." These courses are currently taught by David Niib Aubid, who is arguably the best Ojibwe language teacher in

Minnesota. He has taken the double-vowel system to a new level in his constant striving to improve the pedagogy of the Ojibwe language. We have had some problems rotating all of these language courses into the two-year rotation. We believe that the change to semesters will actually put us in a better position to do this. Aubid's abilities have also enabled us to conduct a successful Ojibwe Language Immersion Program for one week each summer.

"Projects in American Indian Studies" has been the most popular of the independent-study courses. It is aimed at sophomores and juniors. Students are encouraged to do some interviewing and on-site study in addition to library research.

For three years we have been offering the course "Legal Aspects of Federal Indian Policy for Human Services" under a 5000-level "Special Topics" rubric (allowing the inclusion of graduate students). It is taught by Dr. John Red Horse, who also has an M.S.W. The course exemplifies our attempts to cooperate with other departments and colleges, as it is a "strongly recommended" course in the M.S.W. graduate program. This course will be added to the regular curriculum under the semester system.

A particularly successful segment of the curriculum has been the internship component required for the major. We have had excellent cooperation from a variety of Indian and non-Indian agencies in the region. Our interns have received outstanding ratings from their site supervisors, and two have been hired after graduation by the agencies at which they interned. Internship is seen not only as a way to gain valuable "hands-on" experience, but also as a way to give back to the Indian community. Another working relationship that has been developed is a transfer agreement with the two-year Tribally controlled community college at the Fond Du Lac Ojibwe Reservation.

Our most recent external review (May 1998) found no significant flaws in our department. The reviewers did help us, however, by strongly recommending more secretarial help for the department, a recommendation the administration was quick to address. So, to list strengths and weaknesses is not an easy task, especially regarding the latter.

WEAKNESSES:

1. Because women have played, and do play, such an important role in the culture, it would be desirable to have a full-time, tenure-track female faculty member as we did previously (prior to a retirement). We now have an all-male department, with the exception of two American Indian women who teach part-time.
2. Although all of us have some background in the humanities/arts/ literature area, we would benefit from having a faculty member who is a specialist in this field.

3. We need to increase our outreach efforts with local reservations. Our Ojibwe language component should be an ideal way of working with both children and adults in these communities.

STRENGTHS:

1. Our faculty has good rapport with students, both Indian and non-Indian. This has been developed without sacrificing any course rigor.
2. The department has a good reputation within the College of Liberal Arts and with the university at large. We are known for rigor and organization in our classes, and for scholarship that is both meaningful and practical.
3. We have, over the years, been able to steer around, through, or over the vicissitudes of Indian politics. When we have run afoul of an individual or small group, we have been able to work out a compromise or at least reach a conciliation. All Indians reading this, especially reservation Indians, know that this is no mean feat.

When looking more broadly at American Indian studies across Minnesota, the Midwest, and the United States, there are a number of factors and facets that must be pondered. Our particular position at UMD is a solid one, and our expected growth as a department will likely include the addition of an M.A. program in American Indian studies within five years. Other institutions in the state seem to believe that their Indian studies departments and programs will grow and prosper as well. Regionally and nationally, however, the outlook would seem less optimistic, especially as budgetary demands force more colleges and universities to hire more adjunct and temporary faculty.

Here are five critical points to consider as we look to the future of American Indian studies in the twenty-first century:

1. We must continue to fight the stereotype of ethnic studies as a place where students sit in a circle and condemn white people. Unfortunately this idea still exists, along with the fallacy that courses in these areas are all "mickey mouse" types.
2. We must continue to attract the best and brightest to the teaching ranks. A Ph.D. does not simply appear. Rather, he or she must be nurtured almost from birth. Our American Indian families and Tribes must identify students with academic potential early and ensure that they receive the best education possible. As simple a thing as reading regularly to a small child can have a profound effect on that child's learning ability.
3. We should be constantly looking for funding opportunities to enable us to pursue as many facets of our discipline as possible, but we should be

leaning on our parent institutions to make certain that we are funded just as any other discipline on campus is. This means, of course, that we must be good stewards of all funds provided.

4. We should be constantly refining as well as expanding the body of knowledge in our discipline. Since technology has become omnipresent, we should at least be conversant with it. At the University of Minnesota–Duluth we have been experimenting with interactive television in teaching the Ojibwe language on another of the University of Minnesota campuses.

5. We should be interacting more with each other to enhance what each of us is doing. A conference in which a faculty member, a staff member, and a student from each American Indian studies department or program across the country would come together, would enable some good discussion and sharing to take place.

As I said in an article written many years ago: "As Indians, we should realize that, though many negative things have happened to us, we must try, if we are to continue to survive as a people, to think positively most of the time—and Indian always."

Appendix: American Indian Studies Major—Semesters

Lower Division: (21 credits required)   Credits

A. *Chippewa Language Emphasis Option*

	Credits
AmIn 1103–1104 (Beg. Chippewa) & 2203–2204 (Interm.) (3 cr. each)	12
AmIn 2105 Survey of American Indian Arts	3
AmIn 1106 American Indian Prose, Poetry, and Oratory	3
AmIn 1120 American Indians in the 20th Century	3
	21

Or

B. *Social Studies Emphasis Option*

	Credits
AmIn 1103 Beginning Chippewa	3
AmIn 2105 Survey of American Indian Arts	3
AmIn 1106 American Indian Prose, Poetry, and Oratory	3
AmIn 2115 Chippewa History and Culture	3
AmIn 1120 American Indians in the 20th Century	3
Anth 1604 Cultural Anthropology	4
AmIn 3300 Projects in American Indian Studies	2
	21

<u>Upper Division</u>: (Choices)

A. General

Select seven (7) credits from the following:

AmIn 3106 Indian–White Relations	3
AmIn 3300 Projects in American Indian Studies	1–2
AmIn 3410 Fur Trade in Canada & U.S.	3
AmIn 2520 Tribal Law and Government	3
AmIn 4970 Tribal Economic Development & Management	3
AmIn 3333 Introduction to Federal Indian Law	3
AmIn 3750 American Indian Psychology	3
AmIn 5905 Legal Aspects of Federal Indian Policy for Human Services	3
AmIn 5910 Topics in American Indian Studies	3
AmIn 4990 Directed Research	1–3
Educ 5381 Teaching the American Indian Pupil	3
AmIn 3905 Special Topics	3
	7

And

B. Specific

1. 3 credits from AmIn 3260(3), 3301(3), 4302(2–3), 4630(3)
2. 3 credits from Anth 3614, 4621; Geog 3112;
SW 5235, 5267, 5275, 5280; WS 3101

6

C. Internship: AmIn 3997

Eight (8) American Indian Studies credits which must be taken during the junior year or first semester of senior year.

8
Grand Total = 42 credits

(Please note that Comp 3XXX is required of all students for graduation. When fulfilling this we would prefer that you took Comp 3160—Advanced Writing: Social Sciences.)

Standing in the Gap: American Indian Studies 11
at the University of North Carolina–Pembroke

STANLEY KNICK AND LINDA E. OXENDINE

T HE DEPARTMENT OF AMERICAN Indian Studies grew up among the ashes.
When someone proposed in the early 1970s that the historic Old Main
Building be torn down to make way for a new building, many people in
the local Native American community were outraged. Their beloved Old Main,
the first brick structure of the old Indian Normal School, had been a central part
of their lives since 1923.

Even before the proposal to destroy Old Main, the seeds of an American Indian studies department had already been germinating. For as long as anyone here
could remember, the Native Americans of Robeson County had been asserting
their Indian identity. In virtually every decade since the 1860s they had expressed
their Native heritage at local, state, and national levels.[1] In addition, the heighten-
ing cross-cultural consciousness that accompanied the civil rights movement in the
1960s, and the associated development of ethnic studies departments at colleges
and universities across the country, augmented the growing desire for an American Indian studies department here in the land of the Lumbee. The Old Main
Building was exactly the right location for it.

All kinds of activities had been held inside Old Main's walls—the administration of the college, the teaching of classes, public gatherings, and film presentations. Old Main had become a tangible symbol of opportunities in higher
education for Lumbees. For much of Old Main's history, local Native Americans had not even been allowed to attend the state's other institutions of higher
learning.

Lumbee people weren't about to let Old Main go without a struggle. Marches
were organized. Songs were sung. Poems were written. Politicians were called and
visited. Support was enlisted. The voice of the Save Old Main Movement was
heard all over North Carolina and throughout the United States.

Leo Vocu of the National Congress of American Indians and Louis Bruce of the Bureau of Indian Affairs both visited the community and spoke in favor of the preservation of Old Main. In their book *One Hundred Million Acres,* Kirke Kickingbird and Karen Ducheneaux equated the Lumbee struggle to save Old Main with the national struggle by people of many Tribes and Nations to hold on to traditional lands. Kickingbird and Ducheneaux observed that the state's attempt to close Old Main created "a direct confrontation with the Lumbee community, which regarded the building as the only visible evidence of their once extensive tribal lands. . . . Rallies were held to 'save Old Main' and the state surrendered."[2]

Virtually in the middle of the debate about the best course of action to take, Old Main mysteriously burned in 1973. With only a shell of walls remaining, it would have been easy for the people to quit. But something else remained, something unseen—the spirit of Old Main. Ruth Locklear Revels wrote in her poem *I Am Old Main:*[3]

> The walls that hold so many secrets, fears, memories, hopes,
> dreams and knowledge of those great men and women who were, are
> and will be the
> cornerstone of our community. . . .
> Destroy me, and I tell you, you destroy the very heart of the Lumbee
> people.

That spirit was kept alive by the Save Old Main Committee and others, and among the ashes arose a remodeled Old Main. Eventually it would become home to an academic Department of American Indian Studies, and to the Native American Resource Center.

To understand the history of the Department of American Indian Studies at the University of North Carolina–Pembroke, it is important to know a little about the history of the local Indian population, the Lumbee. The modern Lumbee are an amalgamation of various Eastern Siouan people (including Lumbee, Cheraw, Waccamaw, and Saponi), with apparently smaller additional contributions from Iroquoian (Tuscarora) and Coastal Algonkian (Hatteras) sources.[4] The archaeological record in the vicinity of Pembroke indicates that Native American peoples have consistently lived along the banks of the Lumbee River from Paleo-Indian times (ca. 12,000–8000 B.C.) through Archaic times (ca. 8000–2000 B.C.) and throughout Woodland times (ca. 2000 B.C.–A.D. 1750).[5] Native peoples were living here when the first permanent white settlers arrived in the mid-1700s, and some of the descendants of those Native peoples can now trace their genealogy back to that same period. Their history lives on in the oral, kinship, and other cultural traditions handed down from their Elders. Approximately 40,000 Lumbee people live in Robeson County today.

The beginning of the university itself goes back to the 1880s. Two men of the area—Hamilton McMillan, a white politician from nearby Red Springs, and W. L. Moore, a local Indian minister—shared a vision about the education of Indians residing in Robeson County. These men became key players in the establishment of the Croatan Indian Normal School, which has evolved into the University of North Carolina–Pembroke.

McMillan believed that the Indians of Robeson County were the descendants of a merger of Coastal Algonkian Indians of Croatoan Island with the survivors of John White's (late sixteenth century) Lost Colony at Roanoke Island. Also a state legislator, McMillan introduced legislation in 1885 that would legally designate the Indians of Robeson County as *Croatan* (a word McMillan apparently derived from the place-name *Croatoan*). At the same time, the bill sought to establish a separate school system for the Indians. An Indian School Committee was created with the power to hire teachers of their own choosing for the schools. However, while the Indian community seemed appreciative of this effort, there is no evidence that any schools were started as an immediate result of the new law.

There had been no public schools open to local Indians since 1835. Thus in the 1880s the illiteracy rate was extremely high. Few Lumbee people were qualified to teach in the Indian schools. With this realization, Moore and a number of Lumbee leaders concluded that what was needed for their people to make educational progress was a central institution offering studies from the elementary level to the teacher training (or Normal School) level—an institution that could train Indian people to serve as teachers for their own children in their own communities. With the assistance of McMillan in the state legislature, a bill was passed in 1887 establishing what McMillan labeled as the Croatan Indian Normal School.

This 1887 act put the school under the direction of an all-Indian board of trustees. It provided that students had to be Indians from Robeson County and at least fifteen years old. Students also had to agree to teach Indian people for a given period. The legislature appropriated $500 for the school, but the money could only be used to pay teachers. No funds were allocated for the purchase of land or the construction of a building. In fact, the act stipulated that unless the Indians provided a building, the law would be repealed in the next session of the North Carolina General Assembly. Thus it was left to the Lumbee people to provide both the land and building for their school.

Initially, most Indians were suspicious of the Normal School, finding it difficult to believe that after so long the government would do something positive about their educational needs. Understanding this sentiment in the Indian community, Moore called a meeting to discuss the Normal School, but few attended. Nevertheless, with a great deal of energy and faith Moore aroused enough interest to purchase an acre of land for $8 and to get the Tribal community to donate about $1,000 in labor and materials for a new building. Moore was so committed to this effort that he contributed $200 of his own money to get the school started. He became the first teacher of the school so that the requirements of the 1887 act would be met before the deadline of the next legislative session. In 1889 the state increased the annual allocation for the school to $1,000.

Although the school was called a Normal School, there was no advanced study beyond the elementary level for almost two decades. Finally in 1905, D. F. Lowry received the first certificate for completing a course of scientific study, and is considered the first graduate of the Indian Normal School (the Lowry Building is named in his honor). In 1909 the present site at Pembroke was purchased and $3,000 appropriated for a new building. In 1911 the school's name was changed to Indian Normal School of Robeson County to reflect the state's designation of the local Indian people away from the unsatisfactory (and externally imposed) "Croatan" in favor of the more widely acceptable "Indians of Robeson County."

This generic designation, however, did not satisfy some local Indian leaders. Two years later, and through the efforts of a relatively small group of people, the Indians of Robeson County were legally designated by the state as "Cherokee Indians of Robeson County" and the school's name was changed again (to Cherokee Indian Normal School). This change was made because of the notion held by a few people that *Cherokee* was somehow a better name, although the change was made without substantive evidence of any historical connection between the Indian peoples of this region and the Cherokee of western North Carolina. Nevertheless, the local community was called by this name until 1953, when they petitioned the state legislature to change their name to the more historically appropriate *Lumbee*, the ancient name of the river along which the people lived and still live today.[6]

Despite many obstacles, the school continued to grow. In 1914 the first two students finished high school studies, and by 1939 the high school was separated from the Normal School and the fourth year of a college program was added. In 1940 the school graduated its first class with a four-year college degree, with Charles W. Maynor (who still lives in the area) being the first college graduate of this institution. Commensurate with its newly acquired collegiate status, in 1941 the school's name was changed to Pembroke State College for Indians, and later shortened to Pembroke State College.

From the founding of the institution until 1945, enrollment was limited to Indians of Robeson County. In 1945 the school was opened to any Indian group recognized by the federal government. From 1940 to 1953 it was the only state-supported four-year college for Indians in the United States. In 1953 admission was opened to whites with the condition that their numbers not exceed 40 percent of the total enrollment. (Ironically, the first white graduate was named Christian White!)

In 1954, when the U.S. Supreme Court outlawed segregation, Pembroke State was opened to all students regardless of racial designation. In 1969, after receiving university status and becoming one of the sixteen regional campuses of the University of North Carolina, Pembroke State College became Pembroke State University.[7] In 1996, Pembroke State University was renamed the University of North Carolina at Pembroke as a way to better reflect this relationship.

More than a century has passed since that small Indian school began with fifteen students. Today the University of North Carolina–Pembroke has over 3,000 students, fifty-five major programs, forty-one minor programs, nine graduate programs, and twenty-two academic buildings. The University of North Carolina–Pembroke is the only school in the University of North Carolina system that offers an American Indian studies major, and is one of only two institutions east of the Mississippi River that confers an undergraduate degree in American Indian studies (the other is Dartmouth). Today the University of North Carolina–Pembroke continues to grow and progress in curricular offerings as well as physical facilities.

Back in the 1970s, one of the people who was involved in the saving of Old Main was Dr. Adolph L. Dial, then professor of history at the university. Dial realized that something more than just the preservation of the building was needed to augment recognition of, and pride in, the school's origins as an educational institution for Native Americans. He knew that with the celebration of heritage comes the acknowledgment that such a legacy of the past would also be the challenge of the future.

Professor Dial had been teaching American Indian history courses for some time, but he knew that for true justice to be done to such a complex topic as the study of Native America, it would be necessary to develop and offer more than a few courses. From the department's formalization in 1972, a multidisciplinary approach was taken. Department professors were incorporated from philosophy and religion (Robert Gustafson), from art (Ralph Steeds), from history (David Eliades), and from communicative arts (Robert Reising).

The Old Main Commission, founded in 1973 in response to the plan to destroy the landmark, and led by local community members, provided the perfect complement. Professor Dial's vision was shared by the commission, and together they worked to establish a museum focusing on Native America as an enhancement to the nascent academic department of American Indian studies. But it would be eleven more years before the department would grow sufficiently to offer a baccalaureate degree.

Dial's vision of the department was that it should seek to appreciate Native America from as many angles as possible—history and culture to be sure, but also prehistory, literature, art, philosophy, and so on—seeing Native Americans not only as the central figures in ancient America, but also as active participants in present-day and future America. He and others foresaw a museum and an academic department of American Indian studies that would literally stand in the gap between the proud Native American heritage of the university and the bright future that lay ahead as the school negotiated the mainstream of North Carolina's university system.

The next major step in the collective vision of Dial and the Old Main Commission was the opening of the Native American Resource Center in 1979. What began as a collection focusing on the local Native American community gradually expanded to include art and artifacts from other areas of Native America. Exhibits were developed to help the public glimpse the world of the Eastern Woodlands, the Southwest, and the Plains. From north of the Arctic Circle to south of the equator, exhibit items came to tell the story of diverse Native American cultures.

As time went by, the Native American Resource Center developed into a multifaceted museum and research institute of the university. The center's mission is to educate the general public about the prehistory, history, culture, art, and contemporary issues of American Indians, with special emphasis on the Robeson County Native American community; to conduct scholarly research; to collect and preserve the material culture of Native America when appropriate; to encourage Native American artists; to support and enhance the Department of American Indian Studies; and to cooperate on a wide range of projects with local, regional, national, and international agencies concerned with Native America.

The center approaches its complex mission in several ways. The educational aspect of its mission begins with the presentation of exhibits and tours to the general public and to public school students. Approximately 12,000 people visit the center every year, from every state in the United States and from many foreign countries. The center has displayed traveling exhibits from the Smithsonian, Duke University Museum of Art, Partners of the Americas in Bolivia, United Tribes of North Carolina, and numerous individual Native American artists.

Special educational programs are presented by the Native American Resource Center throughout the year. Some of these programs include Indian Heritage Week activities, and lectures for public and private groups locally and around the state. The center's public education column about American Indians appears each week in a local newspaper. The center also publishes a quarterly newsletter (SPIRIT!), which brings information to a mailing list of more than 2,000 families and agencies. The center has produced two volumes about the archaeology of this area in addition to a reader about Native Americans and a recent monograph about the Lumbee.[8] The center's Web site carries information all over the world (www.uncp.edu/nativemuseum/).

In addition, various courses included in the American Indian studies curriculum are offered in the Native American Resource Center.

Since its inception in 1972, the Department of American Indian Studies has experienced a slow but steady growth. From the beginning, the program has had departmental status under the aegis of the Office of Academic Affairs, but it was not until 1984 that approval was received for a degree program. The first B.A. in American Indian studies was conferred in 1986. In addition to a major, American Indian studies offers a minor and an academic concentration (similar to a second major, designed especially for students majoring in education).

The mission of the Department of American Indian Studies reflects both the unique heritage of the University of North Carolina–Pembroke and the commitment of the university to instill in its students an appreciation for diverse cultures. As part of this mission, it is the goal of the department to provide a comprehensive program with an academic and public orientation focusing on the history and culture of American Indian Tribal groups. The department's objectives are to educate students about the rich diversity of American Indian history and culture, to promote research and scholarship concerning American Indian issues, and to prepare students for professional or scholarly careers in the field. These objectives are implemented through a variety of courses. As the following list illustrates, the courses are designed to provide the student with a multidisciplinary and integrated approach to the study of American Indian Tribal groups from prehistory to the present (some courses are cross-listed with other academic departments):

- AIS 105, Introduction to Cultural Anthropology—a survey of the various processes and conditions involved in cultural growth and change, including the relationships among technology, religion, art, literature, language, and personality development; emphasis is placed on human ecology and contacts between cultures.
- AIS 201, American Indian Cultures—an introductory survey of American Indian cultural traditions through the study of film, art, oral and written literature, music, and religion.
- AIS 210, History of the American Indian—a survey of North American Indian history from arrival in the Western Hemisphere to the present, with emphasis on inter-Tribal and Euro-American relationships, prominent persons, political and economic developments, and adaptation to European culture.
- AIS 213, American Indian Religious Traditions—an introduction to the contributions that American Indian religious traditions make to the general study of religion; a survey of the religious traditions and practices of American Indians.

- AIS 220, American Indian Literature—an introduction to American Indian literature through texts written, collected, or edited by American Indians.
- AIS 239, American Indian Education—a study of Indian education policy and practice in the United States, focusing on traditional Tribal methods as well as on contemporary federal, state, and Tribal programs.
- AIS 302, Workshop in American Indian Studies—a workshop designed especially for elementary and secondary school teachers; emphasis is given to aspects of Indian history, textbooks and their treatment of American Indians, contemporary Indian problems, American Indian writers, and Indian cultures and the changing lifestyles of Indian peoples.
- AIS 324, Indians of Latin America—a study of the history, culture, and contemporary achievements of the Indians residing south of the Rio Grande.
- AIS 325, Indians of the Southeast—a thorough examination of the history, culture, interaction, and present condition of the major Tribes of the southeastern United States.
- AIS 360, History and Culture of the Lumbee—a study of the Lumbee, the largest Tribal group east of the Mississippi River; while the focus is primarily historical, all facets of Lumbee culture are treated, including the economic, political, and religious structure of the people as well as artistic and literary accomplishments.
- AIS 395, Archaeology in North Carolina—an approach to the study of archaeology as a way to learn about human beings; emphasis is placed on prehistoric Indian cultures of North Carolina, especially those of Robeson County, homeland of the Lumbee; topics include application of archaeology to present-day issues, recovery and care of archaeological materials, stages of Indian prehistory, and theoretical, practical, and ethical issues faced by archaeologists working at Native American sites.
- AIS 401, Special Topics in American Indian Studies—an investigation into selected topics through the reading of significant books, discussions, and supplementary reports; topics have included Indian Women, Indian Wars, and Indians in Film.
- AIS 402, Federal Policy and the American Indian—a study of federal Indian Policy from the colonial period to the present.
- AIS 404, Field Methods in Archaeology—a study of field methods and techniques in archaeology, including site reconnaissance, systematic sampling of surface and subsurface materials, excavation, and record-keeping. (This course does not involve human remains or funerary materials.)

- AIS 405, Contemporary Issues of American Indians—a seminar examining principal issues of concern to American Indians today; both national and local in scope, topics include politics, economics, treaty relationships with federal and state governments, education, alcohol and substance abuse, the environment, cultural identity and survival, relations with non-Indians, religious freedom, land and water rights, Tribal sovereignty, and other issues as they arise.
- AIS 427, North American Indian Art History—a survey of the range of artistic expression of the North American Indians from prehistory to the present, including painting, sculpture, types of habitation, crafts, and ceremonial arts.
- AIS 450, Seminar in Native American Literature—a study of selected American Indian literature topics.
- AIS 460, American Indian Health—an examination of nutritional, cultural, demographic, and socioeconomic aspects of the health of American Indians from prehistory to the present, evaluated with a view toward lessons for modern Indian health practitioners; topics include effects of European contact on Indian health, modern health problems in Indian communities, and traditional medical practices.
- AIS 499, Independent Study—a course involving directed reading and research for advanced students under the guidance of an instructor in a specific area of American Indian studies.

In addition to the general education courses required for all students at the university, students who receive the baccalaureate degree in American Indian studies are required to complete AIS 210, 213, 220, 360, 395, 405, and 427. They must also take two courses from among AIS 302, 324, 325, 401, 450, and 460, as well as three more elective courses in the department. Students who minor in American Indian studies are required to take AIS 210 plus six additional courses from the department's offerings. The academic concentration in American Indian studies (designed for education majors) consists of any eight courses from the department's offerings.

There are several reasons why the American Indian studies program at the University of North Carolina–Pembroke is unique. First, it is one of only two programs east of the Mississippi to offer a degree in the field. Second, rather than having a specific Tribal focus, American Indian studies courses allow students to study the history and culture of many Tribal communities. Third, the curriculum is broad-based; to obtain a degree in American Indian studies a student must take courses including American Indian history, art, literature, prehistory, religion, and contemporary issues. Fourth, the University of North Carolina–Pembroke is located in the middle of the Lumbee community—a situation that provides students and faculty direct access to Tribal resources that otherwise would not be available.

American Indian studies also has the commitment of the university administration to the growth and strength of the department. In the early years, when enrollment numbers did not particularly warrant such a specialized program, the University of North Carolina–Pembroke recognized the importance of maintaining and supporting the growth and development of American Indian studies.

Along with the strengths, however, come many challenges. There is a need for the department to move beyond its dependence on particular faculty (who may come and go) to a dependence on permanent positions. Because of the interdisciplinary nature of the program, other departments must see and support the importance of including American Indian studies as an integral part of their curriculum. More funds are needed for faculty development in areas of research, publication, and travel to conferences and seminars. There is also a need for more extended outreach through promotion of both the department and the major.

With the present number of faculty positions, there is little room for program expansion. If new areas are to be developed, resources must be made available for additional faculty positions. Despite these limitations, however, the Department of American Indian Studies continues its commitment to ensuring a quality academic program that enhances the knowledge and skills of students during their time at the University of North Carolina–Pembroke, and that prepares them for professional and scholarly careers after graduation.

In the fall of 1995, American Indian studies began a new initiative by offering a select number of American Indian studies courses to other University of North Carolina campuses through distance learning. The expansion of the curriculum into this electronic medium was a new challenge for American Indian studies. The decision to take American Indian studies on the information highway was seen as a means not only to maximize resources but also to strengthen the University of North Carolina–Pembroke program in a number of areas. Distance learning was viewed as a vehicle for program promotion and recruitment of new students into American Indian studies; as a way to expand program curriculum by receiving courses from other campuses; and as a means for providing students from other institutions the opportunity to participate in courses to which they otherwise would not have access. For example, the course titled "History and Culture of the Lumbee" is not offered on any other campus in the University of North Carolina system.

In 1997 the Department of American Indian Studies and the Native American Resource Center launched the Adolph Dial Lecture Series in American Indian Studies. This is an annual event funded by an endowment established by the late

Adolph L. Dial, the founder and first chairperson of the Department of American Indian Studies. The focus of the lecture series is to bring noted scholars in the area of American Indian studies to the University of North Carolina–Pembroke campus as a means of broadening the experience of our majors and that of all students at the university.

Although the University of North Carolina–Pembroke is the only college or university in North Carolina offering a degree in American Indian studies, there are a number of other institutions that teach at least one course in American Indian studies through other disciplines (e.g., anthropology, history, literature, etc.). Given the limited resources available in the state for American Indian studies, in terms of both programs and individual courses, several faculty and staff members from North Carolina higher education institutions have formed the Carolina's Consortium on American Indian Studies. The consortium is a way to provide information, share resources, and establish a network among researchers and scholars interested in the field. The consortium meets two or three times a year on different campuses throughout the state. The Department of American Indian Studies at the University of North Carolina–Pembroke plans to continue active participation in this consortium.

Through the many aspects of their complementary missions, the Department of American Indian Studies and the Native American Resource Center celebrate the beauty, wisdom, and diversity of Native America. They keep alive that spirit of Old Main that would not disappear even in the ashes of burned memories, hopes, and dreams. They search for a better understanding of the traditional ways and contemporary issues of America's original inhabitants. They stand in the gap between Native past and Native future, connecting in a vigorous continuum the best traditions and aspirations of the Native American community with those of academia.

Notes

1. G. Sider, *Lumbee Indian Histories: Race, Ethnicity and Indian Identity in the Southern United States* (New York: Cambridge University Press, 1993); W. Evans, *To Die Game* (Baton Rouge: Louisiana State University Press, 1971); O. McPherson, "Indians of North Carolina," 63rd U.S. Congress, document 677 (Washington, D.C.: U.S. Government Printing Office, 1915); H. McMillan, *Sir Walter Raleigh's Lost Colony* (Wilson, N.C.: Advance Press, 1888).

2. K. Kickingbird and K. Ducheneaux, *One Hundred Million Acres* (New York: Macmillan, 1973), 12.

3. Poem in the permanent collection of the Native American Resource Center, UNC Pembroke.

4. A. Dial and D. Eliades, *The Only Land I Know* (San Francisco: Indian Historian Press, 1975); J. Pierce, C. Hunt-Locklear, W. White, and J. Campisi, *Lumbee Federal Recognition Petition* (Pembroke: Lumbee River Legal Services, 1987).

5. S. Knick, *Robeson Trails Archaeological Survey: Reconnaissance in Robeson County*, Native American Resource Center Publication Series (Pembroke: UNC Pembroke Printing Office, 1988); S. Knick, *Along the Trail: A Reader about Native Americans*, Native American Resource Center Publication Series (Pembroke: UNC Pembroke Printing Office, 1992); S. Knick, *Robeson Crossroads Archaeological Survey: Phase II Testing in Robeson County*, Native American Resource Center Publication Series (Pembroke: UNC Pembroke Printing Office, 1993).

6. McMillan, *Lost Colony*; McPherson, "Indians of North Carolina."

7. D. Eliades and L. Oxendine, *Pembroke State University: A Centennial History* (Columbus, Ga.: Brentwood University Press, 1987).

8. S. Knick, *The Lumbee in Context: Toward an Understanding*, Native American Resource Center Publication Series (Pembroke: UNC Pembroke Printing Office, 2000).

One University, Two Universes: Alaska Natives and the University of Alaska–Anchorage 12

MICHAEL L. JENNINGS AND JENNIFER ROBIN COLLIER

IN MANY WAYS, the historical experience of Alaska Natives in Euro-American education is familiar to all Native American peoples. Originating in missionary, federal, and economic projects that saw assimilation as an alternative to extermination, achievements in the Euro-American system have been coupled with destruction in Native cultures. In this light, some Native scholars have strongly argued that the education of Native Americans has been an agent of cultural genocide well into the twentieth century.

Despite this history, the Alaska Native studies program at the University of Alaska–Anchorage (UAA), again like many Native American studies programs in the United States, exists only as a result of hard-won, grassroots initiatives for higher education that emerged from Alaska Native communities themselves. This demand for higher education has been one important component of a larger Native agenda mobilized in the past three decades. In the wake of the Alaska Native Claims Settlement Act (ANCSA) in 1971, it was clear that new sets of skills were required to sustain Native lands and communities in the face of Euro-American encroachment. This challenge required new leaders, who—in conjunction with traditional Native leaders and Elders, local communities, and students—have been the driving force behind a powerful, statewide movement for Native education. They see Western skills as tools that forms of leadership can use to work within, as well as in opposition to, Western institutions. Meanwhile, of course, a sense of entitlement to appropriate services from the state came with citizenship and subjugation under federal authority.

The goal of this movement has not been one of mere inclusion within Western educational institutions, or of access to opportunity structures in non-Native society. Rather, Alaska Natives demand culturally appropriate education, in terms of both curriculum and delivery, that is defined by the needs and interests of their communities. This distinction has been central to the inherent and ongoing conflict between Alaska Natives and the University of Alaska. Opposing worldviews, and different understandings of the function of education in society, have been at the root of failed programs, inappropriate structural responses, and power struggles within the university system. Western educational institutions have traditionally been at odds with Native survival. Alaska Native leaders believe that to truly serve the university's Native constituency, the university will have to make both institutional and philosophical changes that it has been reluctant or unwilling to undertake.

Today, two primary structures exist within UAA as a result of Native struggle. They are Native Student Services (NSS) and the Alaska Native studies minor. The story of their inception, and an appropriate evaluation of their current success and status, require a specific historical approach. Social science research typically evaluates Native societies along a continuum that positions continuity as authenticity on one end, as opposed to assimilation (documented "scientifically" as "empirical" change in cultural forms or social institutions) on the other. An understanding of Native demands for higher education in Alaska cannot emerge from such a simplistic paradigm, for continuity and change have never been such contradictory concepts to Native peoples. Its static concept of authenticity erases the feats of institutional and cultural innovation and creativity produced by Alaska Native cultures and worldviews, as well as Native understandings of the persistence and continuity of their spirituality and worldviews. The following discussion will instead be framed by Native concerns of sovereignty and subsistence in their fullest cultural, economic, and political contexts. The central questions that emerge are: When did educational agendas begin to be formulated from within Native communities, as opposed to being merely imposed upon them? How did Natives come to identify participation in institutions of Euro-American education as central to their survival—not as assimilated individuals, but as self-determining communities? Given that Euro-American and Native initiatives for education arise from opposite sides of historical experience, as well as from within conflicting philosophies and worldviews, can Native American studies and Native services within Euro-American institutions actually be successful in promoting Native values and goals? When do degrees of cultural continuity and cultural change in Native communities reflect moments of colonization and assimilation, and when are they assertions of Native sovereignty and innovation?

Land and Education

While the historical pattern of conflict between Indigenous and colonial peoples in the United States has been rooted in control of Native land and resources, the relationship between land and education—in terms of both political economy and worldview—has been insufficiently addressed in the education literature.[1] Ideologically and structurally, Euro-American educational achievement is oriented toward the facilitation of an individual's economic and social mobility upward in the social hierarchy.[2] The expectation has been that every successive generation will be increasingly successful, increasingly assimilated, decreasingly reliant on ethnic "enclaves," and decreasingly thwarted by cultural "barriers."

The concept of education as mobility has a literal spatial as well as economic dimension. Educational delivery and curriculum content are approached from the capitalist and colonial point of view in that the goal of Western education has been economic development. Development, in turn, advances an urban/rural dichotomy akin to the center-periphery relations discussed in world systems theory. Providing both educational resources and the accoutrements of material wealth, cities are centers of political and social power, while rural areas are sites of resource extraction and agricultural production for sustenance of the urban majority. As economic and cultural policy with respect to Native Americans, education was meant to "civilize" Indigenous peoples and to instill in them a Western ethic of "hard work." In addition to christianizing them in missionary schools, the effort toward "civilization" and "work" has meant settling them on small, individual tracts of land where they can become self-sufficient farmers, or otherwise moving them into the cash economy, thereby freeing up large tracts of land for the influx of European immigrants to America.

The relationship between land and education should not be relegated to a historical process, and Alaska provides a particularly pronounced example of its ongoing importance in contemporary institutions of higher education. Alaska Natives—traditionally with large land bases, subsistence economies, and non-individualized ownership—have been of great interest to the assimilationist agendas of Western education. They have been subjected to a system that is structurally opposed to their existence as Tribes—as sovereign political entities, and as cultures with spiritual and economic relationships with the land. This is true both historically and presently.

Prior to ANCSA, the course of Native education in Alaska resembled that in the lower forty-eight states. The colonial experience began with the arrival of Russian explorers in 1741, who surmised after forty years of occupation and Native holocaust that this state of war ultimately detracted from the harvest of furs. Thus colonial methods changed their strategy. The charter of the Russian American Company, toward the same goal of opening land and resources to colonial exploitation, provided funding for schools in which Russian Orthodox missionaries worked to acculturate Native peoples through education and conversion. When Alaska was sold to the United States in 1867, a similar strategy was pursued by the Seattle-based Alaska Commercial Company, and the provision of education for both Natives and non-Natives remained in the domain of commercial and religious ventures. The transition from military to educational apparatuses is paradigmatic. Throughout North America, the interchangeability of a standing army and missionary education as instruments for executing the policies and interests of the U.S. government reflects the prevailing belief in the power of Western education as a means of acquiring Native lands without the need for payment or mutual treaties.[3]

There were two major developments in Alaskan education in the next half century. The first came in 1884 when the United States extended standard federal policy in Indian Country with the first Organic Act for Alaska. Despite the resulting shift in administrative control over education from economic to federal political bodies, however, there was direct continuity in the ideology, personnel, and curriculum. Land, together with the educational budget, was divided among religious denominations, and mission schools, developed in areas of economic interest to the United States, remained the focus of educational provision.

The second major development was the racial segregation of education. The 1905 Nelson Act established compulsory-attendance public schools in Alaska. It enabled incorporated towns to manage their own schools, and unincorporated communities having a school population of at least twenty "white children and children of mixed blood who lead a civilized life" could petition for the establishment of a school district. Meanwhile, schools for "Eskimos and Indians in Alaska" were to remain under the control of the Department of the Interior—responsible also for the transformation of subsistence economies to cash economies.[4] Then the second Organic Act (1912), which granted control of the white school system to the new Territorial Legislature, codified the two racially segregated school systems, and they would remain in place until Alaska became a state in 1959.[5] Alternatively, many Alaska Natives were removed to Bureau of Indian Affairs (BIA) schools in the lower forty-eight states.

In the meantime, a state university system for whites had been formed by a special act of the Alaska Territorial Legislature in 1917. Regarding Indigenous peoples, Lester Henderson, former commissioner of education in Alaska, stated at the time that "in relation to higher education, account need be taken of representatives of the white race only. . . . The aboriginal population, while [numerically] equal to the white in many sections and larger in other sections, is not a consideration when the establishment of higher education institutions of learning is contemplated."[6]

Traditional lands were increasingly leased, withdrawn, and sold, in unilateral actions of the state and federal government. Alaska Natives were not being pacified by education; rather, they began to mobilize against assimilation and the destruction of their land base. New forms of leadership and political struggle were forged "in the fire" of direct threats to survival. This leadership would develop the Native agenda for higher education. In considering this contemporary agenda, it is essential to bear in mind this overriding reason for the Native turn to Western politics: resolution of the land claims. In regional associations galvanized by local threats to continued use and occupancy of traditional Native lands, Alaska Natives began to acquire a level of sophistication in various Western contexts. Travel, and for some future leaders the boarding school experience itself, provided access and exposure to policymakers at the state and national levels, and placed Native leaders in positions to further the Native cause in the terms that were most intelligible to the non-Native community.[7]

By 1962 there were five regional organizations: the Tlingit Haida Central Council (founded as the Alaska Native Brotherhood in 1912), Tanana Chiefs Conference (Dena Nena Henash, 1962), the Inupiat Patiot (Peoples' Heritage, 1961), the Fairbanks Native Association (1960), and the Association of Village Council Presidents (1962). Among the issues that engendered the Inupiat Patiot, for example, was the infamous Project Chariot (1958). In this case, the Bureau of Land Management licensed the Atomic Energy Commission to use 1,600 square miles in the Arctic Circle for a nuclear test that would explode two 1-megaton and two 200-kiloton nuclear bombs.[8] Project Chariot is also the first case in which the University of Alaska, inherently prodevelopment, took a very public stand in opposition to Native interests.

The Alaska Federation of Natives (AFN) was formed in 1966 as a strategic vehicle for making Native interests in land claims audible to the federal government. Similarly, land claims were the main issue behind the development of a block of rural Native legislators known as the Bush Caucus. The achievement of a land freeze pending the settlement of Native land claims, in addition to demonstrating the ability of Alaska Natives to influence state and local elections, sent a clear message to non-Native political and development interests that the Native leadership was independent, increasingly strong, and growing in their ability to influence the actions of government in order to advance the interests of Native communities.[9]

For the most part, this first generation of Native leaders had no higher education or formal training in the Western contexts. Rather, their education consisted of direct experiences on boards of directors, in the state legislature, and through the creation and operation of various nonprofit corporations. When the land-claim settlement was reached, it was up to each region and Native corporation to interpret, implement, and enforce ANCSA. Each would need new skills and educational opportunities to be able to do so, for the need to work with and within Western institutions was now codified as a future way of life. Not only

AFN and the Bush Caucus, but also Native communities, Elders, and traditional leaders, realized that the education of succeeding generations in new social arenas was critical for the survival of Native lands, cultures, and peoples. A statement by one Elder reflects the common view that the younger generation be allowed to serve as "cultural brokers," representing their people's interests to the Western world: "[B]ecause you will be working with your own people's money, their birth right and their settlement and because in many cases, many of the Native people do not know what decisions to make because of a lack of [Western] education, this will be the greatest responsibility of leadership."[10]

It was clear that battles for Native survival would be fought in Western political arenas, not Native ones. Because traditional Native authority structures would not be recognized as legitimate by the dominant society, the burden fell on Alaska Natives to acquire new sets of cultural and technical skills. A new leadership was needed to use the foreign, authoritative structures and concepts of the larger society as a means to promote and protect Native values and interests. Thus, while contemporary Native organizations often appear to mirror Western organizational arrangements and public behaviors, their similar structures belie a fundamentally different set of goals. Similarly, they approach higher education with distinctly Native agendas. The effort and vision required in overcoming regional and ethnic divisions, in entering and mastering unknown political arenas, and in articulating values and pursuing programs in radically foreign terms, cannot be overstated. Alaska Natives were forced to accomplish these acts of translation, cross-cultural understanding, political savvy, creativity, and structural innovation very quickly when the stakes were high.

The Alaska Native Agenda for Rural Education

> So right off the bat, we had a list of things we needed to do. The most important of which . . . we had lost our aboriginal rights to subsist off the land . . . we had used about three quarters of Alaska to subsist and they had given us one tenth—that wasn't enough. We couldn't continue our lifestyle like that.[11]

Upon the passage of ANCSA, AFN underwent a restructuring from which it reemerged in October of 1972. The primary difference was a shift of decision-making power and negotiating authority from statewide to regional, or even sub-regional, levels.[12] While AFN would continue to represent common Native interests and coordinate political resources on the statewide level, a new organizational structure was required to diffuse authority to each distinct and autonomous region where initiatives would be developed locally. Demands for education followed this overall paradigm: Alaska Natives desired local control, local delivery, and content appropriate to the needs of local communities in the post–ANCSA period.

In poignant contrast, the organizational flexibility of AFN in the face of social change stands as a persistent failure on the part of the University of Alaska to undergo any substantive reexamination of its structure or of the content of its mission—and this despite the fact that its own constituency was rapidly changing. Alaska Natives would soon become the fastest-growing group of university students. Sam Kito, a Native member of the University of Alaska Board of Regents, noted that "you need a system that can make the transition because they can shift their programs very fast and that's what we need. We need to be able to have more programs on a community basis, that allow a person to get enough education to function in the environment that they choose, which may be Nome, Kotzebue, Barrow, Bethel, or wherever it is."[13] The university did not initiate change, but would *submit* to it—and then only reluctantly. Native leaders, and not the university itself, "are really the driving force for change in the [university] institution. External pressures make the institution change, not internal."[14] This was true on both structural and substantive, curricular levels.

An AFN assessment of university services found that, with the exception of a few largely ineffective programs, the University of Alaska's rural involvement was by the early 1970s confined to the fifteen sites of the Cooperative Extension Service, and targeted non-Native populations. These locations were sites either of non-Native economic activity or of national defense–related significance. Between 1895 and 1950 only 24 Alaska Native individuals had attained college degrees, and from 1950 to 1965, just 101.[15] With funds from the Kellogg Foundation, AFN participated in the creation of the Policy Council of the Alaska Native Human Resource Development Program (ANHRDP) to determine exactly what types of programs were important to Alaska Natives and how they might be structured to maximize Native involvement. While the study's findings were of no surprise to the Native community, they seemed to leave the university at a loss. An overwhelming interest documented in vocational skills development, as opposed to more academic, degree-oriented programs, reflected the training needed for cultural survival under the terms of ANCSA. The most frequently requested areas of study were natural resource management and financial management, and needs were expressed in terms of an overriding theme of local control over the delivery of education.[16]

According to Kito, "it has been the Native leadership's position that college services should be as close to the village as possible."[17] A primary approach of the leadership was to place bush or rural community colleges in Native communities, and these were to be established on an individual, case-by-case basis. Two underlying assumptions, revealing the role of education within a larger Native strategy

post–ANCSA, were that: (1) immediate material benefits would accrue to the villages in which the institutions were located, in the form of local employment in
construction and related activities at least; and (2) long-term benefits would appear in the form of educational programs relevant to developing the economies of
villages within these regions.[18] One position paper of AFN's Committee on
Higher Native Education (COHNE, 1992) stated that "the development of educational programs that prepare people to live in the bush and the city must be
one of the highest institutional priorities of the University."[19]

AFN also created the Alaska Student Higher Education Services (ASHES) to
provide orientations, counseling, and tutoring; develop relevant curricula; and
promote institutional change. Field counselors became the conduits through
which information flowed to and from the villages. This system reflected the new
organization of AFN: information and control were generated at local levels,
which field counselors voiced at the statewide level.

Increasingly strong in the legislative arena, the Bush Caucus also made some
hard-won gains toward localizing control, with an agenda framed by the creation
of rural community colleges. In a particularly savvy maneuver, Representative
George Holman of rural Bethel was able to hold hostage the state of Alaska's
budget during the 1972 legislature in an attempt to force the university to address
the needs of his rural constituents. Refusing to report the budget out of the
House Finance Committee for nearly a month, he succeeding in obtaining au-
thorization and funding for the establishment of a community college for
Bethel.[20] Whereas prior to 1972 all community colleges in the Alaska system were
located in urban, primarily white communities, between 1972 and 1976 three rural community colleges were established by legislative actions in Bethel, Nome,
and Kotzebue.

Local control of community college curricula was also contested. The two
Native legislators for the village of Kotzebue believed that the University of
Alaska was failing to meet the educational needs of the region by refusing to offer locally requested courses at Chukchi Community College. They proposed that
Chukchi be removed from the university system and placed under the control of
the Northwest Arctic School Board. Needless to say, the university resisted. The
primary concern of the university's president, Jay Barton, was the maintenance of
the central University of Alaska administration as the locus of control over higher
education[21]—and he was unwilling to providing locally appropriate programs or
delivery within the system. Intensive negotiations brought a final compromise that
included the establishment of a university-supported vocational/technical school
in Kotzebue under the management of the Northwest Arctic School District; an
increase in the university's system of satellite communications; and the creation of
the Rural Alaska Honors Institute for Alaska Native Youth at the Fairbanks cam-

pus, including an increase in tutorial and social support programs for Native students at Fairbanks.[22]

Lessons from such experiences led the Native leadership to force the university to create a senior policy–level, or vice presidential, position within the statewide administration.[23] The Division of Rural Educational Affairs (REA) was inaugurated at the end of 1975, but this event immediately replicated the lines of division between the university and Alaska Natives. It also brought into the university a leader who would be central to the existence today of Alaska Native services and studies at the University of Alaska–Anchorage.

Elaine Abraham, a Tlingit Indian from Yakutat, Alaska, born of the Raven moiety, of the Copper River Clan from the Owl House, and the daughter of the Brown Bear, was appointed as the vice president of REA and began her duties in January of 1976. Abraham had graduated in 1952, at the top of her class from the Sage Memorial School of Nursing in Arizona, and worked for two years on the Navajo Reservation before returning to Alaska to work in the urban and rural hospitals in Juneau, Anchorage, Bethel, and Mt. Edgecumbe. Her concern for the health of Native villagers led her in the early 1960s to organize the Southeast Health Aide Program, as well as the first Native Board of Health in Yakutat, the Southeast Native Board of Health, and the Statewide Native Board of Health. After eighteen years of nursing, Abraham continued her education at Sheldon Jackson Junior College, where upon her graduation she was hired as the associate dean of students, then as the director of special services, and finally as the vice president for institutional development. During this time, she developed the Tlingit and Haida Language Teachers Training Program, helped write the Alaska Legislation for Bilingual Education, and assisted with the creation of the Alaska Native Language Center at the University of Alaska–Fairbanks. Abraham had been very active in the revitalization of Tlingit language, dance, and religion—she has a particular interest in the Raven Dancers, a Native group who are traditional from their dress to the spirituality and education embodied in their presentations. She was and remains deeply committed to the Native worldview. In 1973 she received the American Indian Achievement Award, and in 1974 the title of Distinguished Alaskan from the Alaska state legislature.

Elaine Abraham does not have a Ph.D., and the University of Alaska did not appoint her willingly. Having failed to secure its own choices for the post (all men and mostly non-Native), and under pressure from the U.S. Department of Health, Education, and Welfare, which was investigating a complaint filed by AFN that there had been improprieties in the recruitment, the university installed Abraham in REA.

From philosophical conflicts to logistical inadequacies, troubles with REA preceded Abraham's arrival. There were problems with office space: indeed, there was none.[24] There was legislative support for REA, yet no institutional support from the university in the areas of budget, fiscal management, staffing, or facilities. The duties of the REA vice president were expanded to include oversight of the Alaska Native Language Center, ten of the Cooperative Extension Service sites, and the four rural community colleges, the geographical distribution of which necessitated extensive travel. Acting on the Native desire for the local boards to be effective policy boards, Abraham considered her office to be a mouthpiece through which regional concerns and needs were communicated to and leveraged with the university, thus fostering control on a local level. This required familiarity with local operations, staff, and community leadership in order to establish a working relationship with each of the communities being served. University of Alaska president Donald Hiatt's concern that Abraham performed too much work outside the central office represented a difference of philosophy: for Hiatt, the REA vice president was an office through which the university's administration of the affairs of such geographically disparate programs could be centralized.

The conflict eventually came to a head at the end of 1976, when Abraham was removed from her post (she later filed a successful outcome of the lawsuit against the university over her removal). The vice presidency of REA was downgraded to vice chancellor and later to dean, and REA was disbanded and subsumed in the Division of Community Colleges and Rural Education and Extension Services (CCREE). A reactive, structural attempt to reconsolidate administrative control, CCREE was charged with the administration of all community colleges, extension centers, and rural education.[25] Reduced to a unit within an urban division, rural education was required to compete for limited resources at the division level rather than from the statewide policy position so coveted by the Native leadership. Authority over community colleges was assigned to the nearest four-year campus. Thus by 1985 the university had set in motion a plan that would complete a circle. Just as all rural education had once been controlled from Fairbanks, the plan called for the return of control over all rural programs to the Fairbanks campus.

This experiment in rural education failed because the university sought to extend itself into the bush rather than allowing the bush into the university. It tried to take into the bush conventional courses and conventional teachers who could not relate to the villagers, and offered standard programs of study rather than those that met the immediate needs of the local peoples.[26] Mitch Demientief, a member of the ANHRDP policy council and president of the Tanana Chiefs Conference, wrote in 1974 that "the University is bound by a bad case of institutional racism. . . . As with all things in the bush, the people of rural Alaska will have to develop their own post secondary educational systems."[27] In the same year, Louis Jacquot, director of the ANHRDP policy council, wrote that "most re-

gional leaders, time and time again, very strongly indicate that the higher educational institutions in this state were not listening to them and they had strong
doubts if they ever would."[28]

Alaska Native Education in Urban Anchorage

While the content of student needs might be different in urban settings, the Native educational agenda remains philosophically consistent. The principles of
community involvement in curriculum content and delivery, local control, and administrative decentralization were likewise pursued in urban Anchorage, and
Alaska Natives likewise faced similar conflicts with the university.

Following her brief assignment as the first and last vice president of REA in
1976, Elaine Abraham joined the staff of the urban Anchorage Community College (ACC), which merged in 1987 with the University of Alaska–Anchorage. At
that point, there were no services for Alaska Native or American Indian students
on the Anchorage campus. Research *on* Alaska Natives in anthropology and other
departments was still largely irrelevant to the curriculum content that Native peoples themselves sought, and was sometimes simply racist. Other services desired by
Alaska Natives are specific to the fact that many students come to UAA from rural villages or other small, isolated communities, which tends to compound their
difficulties in adjusting to an urban, university environment. Attempted university
services for Native students had been marginally successful programs that, being
designed by university administrators, did not articulate with the needs and aspirations of Native students and communities. Thus Abraham and a few Native students, with the support of the Native Anchorage community and statewide organizations, initiated Native Student Services. The program provided peer
advising, tutoring, course selection advice, assessment, and assistance with financial aid, housing, transportation, and other needs.

In founding NSS and nurturing it as director or staff member for seventeen
years, Abraham used an approach that reflected her goals as vice president of REA
in 1976, as well as the political strategies of the Native leadership in the
post–ANCSA period. In NSS, she sought to create an organization whose agenda
would be fashioned by grassroots initiatives and integrated into the community.
Embedded in this approach is the assumption that the most important knowledge
to be gained regarding the content and delivery of services in any locale exists
amongst the people being served, their surrounding community, and their larger
social networks. The role of an administrator, then, is to gather local knowledge
and advocate for its perspectives on an institutional level. This person must translate such knowledge into functioning programs, and translate it into terms the
larger institution can understand, while maintaining the upward flow of expertise

and priorities from constituents in the community to the delivery system. This is opposed to the dominant university system, in which knowledge and structure flow from a privileged class of administrators and educators to the students and community being served.

To create a knowledge base for program development, Abraham in 1983 initiated the first sophisticated survey of Native students. The resulting report included a number of recommendations for improving services for Native students, which NSS implemented or advocated. Abraham established the position of Native Student Coordinator as a conduit for continuous student input into NSS, became adviser to the Native Student Organization (NSO), formed in 1981, and provided NSO with NSS meeting space, the use of facilities and office equipment, and some staff support. NSO has been a vocal advocate for NSS and other Native issues on campus, and has served as a leadership training ground for many students. "Eventually," said Mary Reeve, a Yup'ik from Dillingham who returned to school at the age of thirty-four and served as the secretary, and later the president, of NSO, "through the mentoring and support that I got from Native Student Services, I became the first indigenous woman on the [University of Alaska] Board of Regents."[29]

Like most Alaska Natives, Elaine Abraham is the product of an extended family, and she has fostered a family atmosphere at NSS. Because making Native students feel at home helps retain them, Abraham encouraged students to participate in the NSS program as members of a family, and they became involved in nurturing the well-being and scholastic success of other students as well as themselves. She organized potluck luncheons for students featuring traditional Native foods and often including prayers led by Native Elders; brought in Anchorage community members to discuss topics of importance to Alaska Natives; and encouraged the participation of the faculty in Native-sponsored events to promote their greater understanding of Native issues. Many Native students and graduates referred to Abraham as their mother and grandmother. They point out that NSS provided them with a familial sense of belonging, and they say that this feeling is what kept them struggling toward a degree as they dealt with personal and academic problems. In bringing Alaska Natives into the university system, Abraham sought to bring with them the full context of Native needs, cultures, politics, and community relations.

Struggles for Autonomy

During the 1980s and early 1990s, Native Student Services struggled for survival in the face of two opposing statewide trends. The first was a rapid increase in the Alaska Native student population, accompanied by a corresponding increase in the need for appropriate services. The second was continuing administrative centralization in the university system following the replacement of REA by CCREE in 1976.

Between 1987 and 1991 the number of Alaska Native students at UAA increased by 51.9 percent to 667, and the number of American Indian students rose by 45.9 percent to 178. While Alaska Natives and American Indians formed the largest and fastest-growing group of non-Caucasian students at UAA, the growth rate of all minorities as a group during this period totaled 35.7 percent, compared to 19.9 percent for Caucasian students. By the fall of 1991, non-Caucasian students represented 19 percent of the total UAA student population in terms of credit hour production.

In response, UAA in 1990 created a new administrative unit, Minority Student Services (MSS). Native Student Services was placed under the umbrella of MSS— an administrative melding of Native and minority services that would quickly prove deleterious to Native Student Services. Certainly, minority and Native students often work in solidarity with each other, and recognize some commonalities of need within the university system. Native and other non-Caucasian students frequently created political alliances, and continue to do so. Nevertheless, because various groups are forced to vie with each other for limited funding allocated to "minorities" as a general category, this administrative structure fostered an atmosphere of competition within MSS, and downgraded the status of NSS. From the university's point of view, subsuming the previously independent Native programs under the control of MSS made sense for two reasons. First, the university considered the combination of Native student programs and other non-Caucasian student programs to be a logical grouping for budgetary allocations, insofar as these allocations assume that programs within any category are similar enough and interchangeable enough that they should be funded only relative to each other rather than justified as independently funded entities. Second, the strategy is an outgrowth of administrative structures that prioritize rationalization and centralization. Distinctions between allocation units represent intended divisions of labor, the assumption being that administrative independence for any individual program within a unit would constitute a superfluous replication of services. In the resulting hierarchy, control over various programs is centralized under single administrative heads, again asserting an interchangeability of—in this case—programs within the unit "minority services." It is also important to note that this administrative structure of "minority" programs is congruent with evaluation standards for most sources of funding, including both state and federal governments, and many private foundations. Funding, recognition, and awards are granted to "multicultural" or "diversity" initiatives as a whole, and this contributes to an incentive system in which any single component of minority services is interchangeable, and thus competitive, with any other.

The "walk-through" orientation program is one example of the suffering of both minority and Native programs under this administrative confluence. In December of 1990, NSS walked Native students through the class registration process, as it had done every semester since Elaine Abraham's survey reported that many Native students found registration very difficult. A number of non-Native minority students joined the Native students in the walk-through and demanded the same services, creating an upset among registration personnel and the administration. In response, Vice Chancellor Larry Kingry forbade continuation of the registration walk-through, pitting Native and minority students against each other as groups competing for "special services." The administrative and philosophical structure of MSS did not allow a response that recognized the needs emerging from a rapidly changing student population, and no new programming funds had been allocated when MSS was expanded. It was clear to Abraham and Native student leaders that organizational independence for NSS was necessary to maintain its hard-won identity and the meager resources.

During this struggle, as in other periods of conflict with the university, Native students at UAA were sustained and encouraged by the counsel of Native Elders, who serve as traditional role models for perseverance in the face of seemingly insurmountable barriers. Abraham and the Native students also focused their energies on building bridges from NSS to the Anchorage Native community and between NSS and other units within UAA, working jointly with a variety of academic units, programs, and organizations to develop and implement their curricular initiatives and support services.

This close alliance with the Native community did more than sustain the students in the system: it transformed the system, and should be credited with the existence of all programs and services for Native students now at UAA. The Alaska Native studies program was one success of a cooperative, grassroots movement that began in the spring of 1990 and included students at UAA; Native Student Services; Minority Student services; the dean of the UAA College of Arts and Sciences (CAS); numerous CAS faculty members; a task force made up of Anchorage Native educators from outside UAA; the Coalition on Higher Native Education (COHNE); and the Alaska Federation of Natives. UAA chancellor Donald Behrend and his administration reacted defensively, rather than providing leadership, when pressured by this cooperative effort.

A critical catalyst of these grassroots initiatives was a visit to the Anchorage campus by a national advisory committee formed by the American Association of State Colleges and Universities. The team met with UAA administrators, faculty, and students, and held public forums to assess the status of multicultural education at the institution. Its report issued a strong and definitive statement:

> We believe there is a larger issue of insensitivity in Student Services which results in institutional racism more pernicious that the most blatant of individual racism. It is our conviction that if this institutional racism is not immediately addressed, the entire multicultural effort is moot. . . . In particular, [the administration] must address the concerns of Alaska Natives and the larger community.[30]

This finding contains a number of important assertions. Declaring structural racism within UAA, and acknowledging the unity between Alaska Native education and the agenda of the larger Native community, it clearly reiterates the fundamental conflicts between the university and Alaska Native peoples. The committee went on to make recommendations in three areas—programs, students, and community—and assigned an implementation time frame to each.

Grassroots efforts were now fueled with the strong, public recommendations of an outside committee. In June of 1992, Michael Jennings was contracted by UAA to develop a working plan for an Indigenous Studies Center, including a curriculum based on input from the advisory committee and information garnered from other Native American study groups across the United States and Canada. Quickly, however, these initiatives were threatened by persistent administrative moves toward centralization, in direct opposition to the recommendations of the advisory committee. To illustrate the university's subsequent disregard for the committee's report, some of these recommendations, alongside a progress report issued by the UAA student newspaper (in brackets below), are worth quoting at length. The report demanded that the university provide:

> hard funding for programs that deal with minority students, especially Alaska Natives. . . . Without this institutional commitment, programs cannot be viewed as serious. ["No significant new programs of this type have been funded."]
>
> a strategic plan for a multicultural environment within the University that involves the community in its development. ["(N)o plan has been developed."]
>
> programs in which the University and the community are co-equals, such as research, education, and community planning . . . a process of faculty development . . . that encourages faculty to look at attitudes, values, and assumptions in relation to multicultural students and Alaska Natives in particular. ["No major outreach has been done to involve Native leaders from the community."]
>
> a report discussing a comprehensive program of multiculturalism with specific reference to Alaska Native Studies and language studies . . .

shall lay the framework for a comprehensive approach to curriculum development. ["Such a report was drafted by Michael Jennings calling for the creation of an indigenous peoples Center. The Chancellor rejected his report."]

administration and faculty need to look at ways in which they can develop close articulation, cooperation, and working relations with the Anchorage schools. ["No new efforts have been made to establish such a link."][31]

Again, at the expense of the strength or independence of any particular program, the UAA response was an insulated effort seeking an administrative "solution" to the perceived problems, rather than an open effort to address the issues raised by the report. Even the director of MSS raised an immediate objection to NSS independence in a memorandum to the chancellor, and countered the development of an Indigenous Studies Center with a proposal for an Alaska Center for the Study of Race and Ethnicity that would combine Indigenous studies with three other multicultural programs. Further, the director of MSS proposed that the Native Student Center (currently housed in NSS offices) be combined with the Multicultural Center. In September of 1992, the Chancellor reversed an earlier decision to renew Jennings's contract that would have enabled him to complete a plan for the proposed Indigenous Studies Center.

A number of public protests ensued. Chanting "Save our services, Native Student Services," Native students, UAA faculty members, and others who supported services for Native students marched across the UAA campus in a protest that represented several generations of Alaska Natives, some dressed in traditional regalia. Another march to demonstrate solidarity among ethnic groups on campus sent a crucial message to all who would listen: strong, political support among minority groups coexisted with a mutual recognition of their need for independence in terms of services and curriculum. Students testified to the board of regents on behalf of establishing an Indigenous Studies Center at UAA. The Alaska Federation of Natives passed three resolutions demanding that: (1) a senior-level policy position for Alaska Native and American Indian higher education be established at UAA; (2) an Indigenous Studies Center be a top priority, with NSS housed within it; and (3) more space be allocated to meet the needs of a growing Alaska Native student body. AFN president Emil Notti further requested information regarding the efforts by statewide university administration to oversee and advocate student retention and graduation; policies and actions regarding the hiring of Alaska Native staff, faculty, and administration; and the development of Alaska Native studies and language programs, degrees, and majors.

In the face of this overwhelming pressure, Chancellor Behrend finally announced support for the independence of NSS, and agreed to discuss the need to strengthen the organizational status of NSS and the need for courses in Alaska Native studies. Of particular importance to the students were language courses. Still, the students found that when they addressed language instruction, the chancellor rustled papers impatiently, and responded that there are twenty Alaska Native dialects—did the students expect twenty dialects to be taught?[32]

Chancellor Behrend then announced a UAA–wide "Diversity Initiative," to be coordinated from his office. He appointed a Campus Diversity Core Team consisting of twenty administrators, four faculty members, and one student. Regarding this core team, the student newspaper *The Northern Light* reported:

> The administration admits it has implemented few of a year-old study's recommendations regarding multiculturalism at UAA. . . . Instead, the administration has recently formed its own in-house task force. . . . [I]n fact, the only student member of the new Campus Diversity Core Team, Stephen Parham, said a copy of the multicultural study was not included in the packet of materials provided to members by the administration. . . . [C]ritics argue that the new group is just another smoke screen and will accomplish very little in the way of implementing any changes.

The article further quoted political science professor David Maas:

> I think it's a charade. It's overloaded with administrators. In effect very little will change in regard to the different groups it serves. . . . (The committee is) a top-down group that is bound to fail. . . . [Y]ou cannot expect anything visionary from an administration that lacks vision. . . . It is a top-down effort to obtain a Ford Foundation grant through the Western Interstate Commission on Higher Education [WICHE], which has funds from the foundation for multiculturalization of universities. During its first meeting in late November, the core team looked at all UAA systems and discussed unity. Native students are considered usable as qualifications for UAA to obtain WICHE's Ford Foundation funds.[33]

Given the direction of the Campus Diversity Core Team, members of COHNE naturally questioned whether plans for the Indigenous Studies Center would go ahead. As a result, some NSS supporters turned to the possibility of starting a Tribal college as an alternative home for the Indigenous Studies Center. Then came the long-awaited approval of a minor in Alaska Native studies.

Although Alaska Natives and their supporters welcomed the minor as an important programmatic addition, institutional support was limited to the minimal funds that the dean was able to scrape together from a budget under severe pressure from the university administration as well as from cuts in the state legislature.

Elaine Abraham accepted a position as part-time coordinator for a new Alaska Native studies minor a few months after announcing her retirement from the directorship of NSS. She resigned at a time when the status of NSS was a potent and strategic issue: defense of its independence was a major priority for its grassroots constituency. It was precisely this grassroots support that was a thorn in the side of centralized administrative efforts to consolidate "multicultural" programs and win grant money for its diversity efforts. This issue was resolved by the administration, and in particular by the administrator negatively singled out in the advisory committee report, by the appointment of an outsider without knowledge of local grassroots or NSS history. No Native leaders or students were consulted—not Abraham, the Native students, COHNE, AFN, or any other Native leaders or community organizations. When queried, the affirmative action office responded that the chancellor had selected an NSS director for *direct* appointment from among qualified nominees. The affirmative action director further explained that direct appointments were made as an "expedient business necessity," and that the affirmative action office reviewed and approved the process. The chancellor, claimed the director, had discussed the appointment with his Alaska Native/American Indian advisory committee—a committee that did not exist at the time of the hire, but that was created over a month later. COHNE, in an informal poll of its members, failed to find anyone who had been consulted or who knew of *any* Native leader who had been consulted about the selection.

The new NSS director was lukewarm in her reception of the Native Student Organization and it appeared to the Alaska Native students and community that she was implementing the university's model of consolidated control over Native programs. NSO president Mitch Inga pointed out that "Native students have done all this, but now they are being pushed out of the picture. . . . [W]e get one step, then take two steps back."[34] Having created NSS in collaboration with students, and having based her leadership on their expressed needs and priorities, Abraham stated that "NSS was built on students. That was always there from 17 years back. As Native people, we operate in an extended family, and what NSS does is retain students. Making them feel at home retains them. That's why an Alaska Native Student Coordinator was always hired; a student knows better than staff what student needs are. It's distressing because there was no separation before."[35]

Other factors made retention of Alaska Native students difficult. In a state with a 15 percent Native population, there currently was not a single Native in a tenure-track position in the university. The student newspaper reported that, of 369 instructors, UAA personnel records identified only four permanent faculty members as Alaska Natives or American Indians, none of whom could be named.[36] In 1997 the assistant vice chancellor for campus diversity attended a COHNE meeting. He brought the message that eventually six groups of faculty members, each representing a particular subject area, would be formed to recommend changes needed at UAA in relation to the chancellor's "Diversity Initiative," and that their recommendations would be implemented by the Campus Diversity Core Team. When Abraham was asked by COHNE to contact the vice chancellor to recommend members for the six groups, she pointed out that there were no Native American tenured faculty at UAA to serve on such committees. When the vice chancellor responded that UAA staff members could serve on the six groups, Abraham pointed out that there were too few Native professional staff members at UAA to serve on six committees (at the time there were three such individuals). This exchange emphasizes the clear flaw in administrative committees that are limited to university faculty and employees and emphasizes that the university administration fails to recognize the validity and importance of Native community leadership and involvement. As is the case with most such proposals, the diversity initiative at UAA died a quiet death after publicity dissipated enough to be ignored by the university.

Alaska Native Studies

Meanwhile, when the minor in Alaska Native studies (AKNS) was established in the College of Arts and Sciences, Wayne Miller, dean of the college, decided to house the program in the political science department. This department had long been supportive of Abraham's efforts, and provided both protection for AKNS from departments seeking to absorb the program merely to add to their student count, and competent administrative support for Abraham. AKNS initially consisted of two new courses focused on Alaska Native cultures and traditions: a lower-division course on Native perspectives, and an upper-division course titled "Cultural Knowledge of Native Elders." All existing courses offered by colleges and departments that were appropriate to the minor were included in the program. Finally, provision was made for the teaching of nine major Indigenous languages of Alaska, including but not limited to: Tlingit, Haida, Tsimshian, Athabascan, Yup'ik, Siberian Yup'ik, Inupiaq, Alutiiq, and Aleut.

In considering the curriculum for AKNS, it is again critical to keep in mind the reasons Alaska Natives seek higher education in the first place—to acquire new skills required in managing Native villages and corporations as well as in managing Western institutions, and to acquire more in-depth knowledge regarding

Native rural and urban political and social life and Native/non-Native relations. The minor is described as

> an introduction to Alaskan Native ways of knowing and seeing the world; an experiential and theoretical exploration of Alaskan Native cultures; and a series of critical perspectives on traditional and contemporary Native experiences and politics in a pluralistic society. Students may select one of two programs to complete the requirements for the minor: a policy focus and/or a language focus. Both of these options emphasize the dynamic nature of Alaska Native cultures and the conflict between traditional Native values and those of the dominant Euro-American society. The Alaska Native Studies minor is highly recommended for people living and working in Alaska's rural and urban areas.[37]

As Elaine Abraham's work at NSS demonstrates, the incorporation of Native culture, events, social life, and values into student life is critical to meaningful learning and student retention. However, Native peoples generally do not view the university setting as an appropriate place for cultural learning per se: Native cultural and spiritual life is generated and sustained through family, extended family, and Tribal relations. Thus, the AKNS minor was not created to teach art, dance, tradition, and ritual: these are the providence of Native communities and Elders. When these topics are presented in the classroom, instructors arrange for Native Elders to lead sessions and control the presentation of the material. It would be inappropriate for the academy and professional academics to control or deliver this knowledge.

Abraham continued to face resistance from the university in the years she spent getting the fledgling program off the ground. AKNS was pushed out of its offices by a relocating nursing program, and assigned to a small office in what can best be described as a former broom closet in the same building. This separated the program from the political science department, and from the administrative support needed to supervise student workers and volunteers upon whom Abraham had to rely because of the small budget. Adjuncts, who taught the bulk of the classes offered through the program, found it nearly impossible to use the offices to prepare lectures, syllabi, and related materials. Abraham was not accepted as a member of the "club" by many faculty and administrators, and it was especially difficult for her to work cooperatively with a large percentage of the full-time faculty at UAA to promote AKNS classes to degree-granting departments and schools.

The isolation of the program also resulted in missed communications from the administration and an inability to complete the paperwork requirements of the university that determine whether classes appear in the course schedule each semester. As a result, enrollments in most of the AKNS classes offered during the first three years of the program were very low. A systemwide revenue decline increased administrative demands for increased enrollments, and increased the program's focus on revenues and numbers rather than student retention and performance. A "program review" of all academic departments and programs was soon undertaken in 1994 to determine candidates for elimination. This was proven to be an unnecessary exercise, but was particularly stressful for Abraham. She was forced to spend much of her time defending a program that was effectively two years old, with low enrollments and thus high costs per student, which prevented her from focusing on the more substantive tasks of developing the program and attending to students.

Finally, when Wayne Miller resigned as dean of arts and sciences to accept a position with an eastern university, Abraham decided to retire for good from the university at the end of the 1995–1996 academic year. The combination of active resistance to AKNS by the UAA administration, passive resistance by academics and the majority of administrators, the undisguised attempts to usurp Abraham's position of authority and remove Native Student Services from her sphere of influence, and the continued practice of the university of essentially ignoring the contributions made to UAA by Alaska Native corporations, other Native organizations, and individuals became an increasingly heavy burden upon Abraham.

Noteworthy are the continual honors awarded to Abraham: in 1984 she was recognized as the Cook Inlet Native Association Educator of the Year; in 1996 she was the National Congress of American Indians Educator of the Year; in 1997 she won the Meritorious Service Award from UAA; and in 1998 she won a Women of Achievement honor from the Young Women's Christian Association. In 1997, over objections from the administration, Abraham was also given a Meritorious Service Award from UAA.

Political science professor David Maas was assigned to the position of acting director of AKNS for the 1996–1997 academic year, and a search committee was appointed to seek out and hire a permanent director to replace Elaine Abraham. For reasons known only to the chair of the committee, the search took almost an entire year, during which the program essentially languished as fiscal and clerical support from the chancellor's office awaited the new director. Michael Jennings, then assistant professor of education at the University of Alaska–Fairbanks, accepted the directorship of AKNS for the 1997–1998 and 1998–1999 academic years, and the offices were moved to their current, and much more spacious, location.

The following three years have seen consistent and continued growth in AKNS in those measures deemed important by the administration: student credit hours and enrollment. For example, enrollments in the fall of 1999 were up 1,033 percent over the fall of 1997 in lower-division classes, and were up a more modest

44.4 percent in upper-division classes.[38] However, these increases have not allevi-
ated the problem of financial support to the program, which remains at minimal
levels. The contract to be offered to Jennings's successor, the search for whom began in late October of 1999 has resulted in the hiring of a Lakota, Dr. Jeannie
Eder, who assumed the directorship in the spring of 2001. Dr. Eder received an
increased salary, but the department received neither faculty lines nor any increase
to the operating budget. In other words, even this stunning success on the university's own terms has not translated into real financial, administrative, and philosophical support for AKNS.

Conclusion

There are at least three lessons of importance to Indigenous education efforts to
be learned from this discussion. First, policy within the institutional framework
of the larger society does not necessarily lead to effective control, or even influence, over the educational programs delivered at the local level. Knowledge of policymaking processes, impressive experience within the legislative system, and political status enabled Native leaders to force the university system to place
community colleges in rural villages. This affected neither the content of the programs delivered by the professionals within the university system nor the maintenance of even nominal local control over the physical plant within the villages. Put
differently, rather than leading to innovative approaches in Alaska Native education, participation at this level effectively helped to stifle it.

Second, as long as the centralized authority does not provide innovative approaches to educational delivery, participation that leads to effective control of
educational programs is necessary. In this case, participation is necessarily based
on local resources, not upon the generosity of the dominant political system. Included in these resources are the value systems and the cultural experiences that
help to define Native needs, those that the non-Native institutions find so difficult to address in an innovative manner. Money, as well as expertise and individual energies, is among the other resources upon which local control is dependent;
obviously, genuine local control, and thus innovation, are unlikely without them.

Finally, and perhaps most importantly, innovation in education and local control of the educational process do not imply anarchy or chaos for either the educational system or the society as a whole. An innovative approach can lead to effective provision of postsecondary educational programs designed to meet Native
or Indigenous peoples' needs in the context of modernization. Rather than leading to the destabilization of society, local control and innovation provide the
means for groups to integrate themselves, to the extent that this is possible and
desirable, and thus to stabilize that society.

These are important lessons, especially when the sweeping changes taking place globally in the last decade of the twentieth century are considered. The extent to which minority populations, whether Indigenous or not, have received just and equitable treatment from the central authorities of modernizing countries is of increasing concern in this context. In the same vein, knowledge of the extent to which industrialized countries achieved their status at the expense of Native American and First Nation peoples, and the extent to which vestiges of those relationships remain, is of increasing concern in the world today. The question is, whether the tendencies toward centralization and concentration of authority (to provide services such as education) will lead to continued suppression of justice and equity for Indigenous peoples, or whether, instead, the tendencies can be overcome so that participation, equal opportunity, and justice prevail.[39]

In most cases, the problem is that central authorities have usually been extremely slow to recognize these lessons, and to apply innovative approaches. The difficulty for Native/First Nation/Indigenous peoples then becomes one of determining the resources available and how they can be utilized to accomplish local control and appropriate curricula. As Willy Hensley, former Representative from Kotzebue and an original member of the Bush Caucus, states, "the knowledge must be usable within our world view. This has, and continues to be, a real sore point between the university and the Native communities, and I don't think the University will be able to address Native needs until there are more Natives in the system."[40] This statement reveals the dilemma faced by Natives with respect to their position in the university: the system cannot be responsive to Native needs until more Natives are in that system, yet in this context such access and entrance requires a rejection of those Native needs and the values they reflect. This problem is experienced by Indigenous peoples everywhere. As long as the dominant society remains uninterested or uninvolved with territory controlled by Indigenous peoples, the pace and extent to which change occurs are controlled locally; however, when the dominant society becomes interested and involved in a territory, it intrudes and changes both the territory and its peoples. Furthermore, such changes ignore the knowledge of and expertise in local conditions acquired by Indigenous peoples over hundreds of years, resulting in negative rather than positive impacts on the Indigenous population. This point is perhaps best made in the observation of a Native Elder concerning the changes in construction methods that had occurred in his village as a consequence of development and modernity:

> Before the missionaries came . . . we lived underground in sod houses and laid our dead out on the tundra. Now we live aboveground and bury the dead, and I haven't been warm since.[41]

Notes

1. The field of comparative education has addressed some of these issues in international and Third World development contexts, and this work is usefully reviewed in Robert R. Arnove and Carlos Alberto Torres, eds., *Comparative Education: The Dialectic of the Global and the Local* (Lanham, Md.: Rowman & Littlefield, 1999).

2. David Tyack, *One Best System* (Cambridge: Harvard University Press, 1974). See also David Tyack and E. Hansot, *Managers of Virtue* (New York: Basic Books, 1982); David Tyack and H. Kantor, eds., *Work, Youth, and Schooling* (Palo Alto, Calif.: Stanford University Press, 1982); Peter Scott, *Strategies for Postsecondary Education* (New York: Wiley, 1975).

3. Francis Paul Prucha, *The Great Father: The United States Government and the American Indian*, abridged ed. (Lincoln: University of Nebraska Press, 1984, 1986).

4. Angie Debo, *A History of the Indians of the United States* (Norman: University of Oklahoma Press, 1988), 356.

5. Frank Darnell, *Alaska's Dual Federal–State School System: A History and Descriptive Analysis* (unpublished Ed.D. dissertation, Wayne State University, 1970), 49. Not until 1975 did a truly single system of education emerge.

6. Lester Henderson, *Should Alaska Establish Junior Colleges?* (unpublished master's thesis, Stanford University, 1930), 23.

7. Robert R. Nathan Associates, *Federal Programs and Alaska Natives: Introduction and Summary* (prepared for the U.S. Department of the Interior) (Washington, D.C.: U.S. Government Printing Office, 1975). Opposing interpretations, suggesting that the training of Alaska Native leadership made the processes intelligible to otherwise culturally deprived minorities, are made in Gerald McBeath, *North Slope Borough Government and Policymaking* (Anchorage: Alaska Institute of Social and Economic Research, 1981); Thomas A. Morehouse, Gerald McBeath, and Linda Leask, *Alaska's Urban and Rural Governments* (Lanham, Md.: University Press of America, 1984).

8. The smaller bombs were each ten times more powerful than the bomb dropped on Hiroshima.

9. Robert D. Arnold, *Alaska Native Land Claims* (Anchorage: Alaska Native Foundation, 1978).

10. John Sackett, "Editorial," *Tundra Times*, January 16, 1972, 1.

11. John Schafer, interview with Michael Jennings, October 9, 1990, Anchorage, Alaska.

12. This statement is supported by an analysis of Alaska Native organizations that Michael Jennings undertook in conjunction with his Ford Foundation Leadership Development Grant. Report on file with the Ford Foundation, New York, 1973.

13. Sam Kito, interview with Michael Jennings, October 28, 1990.

14. Kito, interview with Jennings.

15. John I. Erichman, *Who's Who in Alaska: 1895–1965* (Juneau: Bureau of Indian Affairs, 1967).

16. "Higher and Adult Education Needs in Rural Alaska: A Report by the Alaska Native Foundation to the Policy Council of the Alaska Native Human Resource Development Program" (Fairbanks: University of Alaska–Fairbanks, 1974).

17. Schafer, interview with Jennings.

18. Willy Hensley, interviews with Michael Jennings, October 11, 1990, Anchorage, Alaska; John Sackett, interview with Michael Jennings, October 10, 1990, Anchorage, Alaska.

19. Lisa Rude, Alaska Federation of Natives Report on Education (Anchorage, Alaska: AFN Archives, 1972).

20. George Holman, interview with Michael Jennings, September 25, 1990, Bettles, Alaska.

21. Michael Jennings was Special Assistant to President Barton from 1980 to 1985. This interpretation comes from discussions with President Barton over the course of several months during 1981 and 1982.

22. Michael Jennings's personal files. Jennings was part of the university's negotiating team and was instrumental in bringing the Native leadership to the negotiating table.

23. Alaska Native Foundation memo from Erik Ekvall, Director of ANHRDP, to Roger Lang, President of Alaska Native Foundation, and Emil Notti, President of Alaska Native Foundation, February 20, 1975 (Anchorage: Alaska Native Foundation Archives).

24. University of Alaska, internal memo to Howard Cutler, Chancellor, UAF, from the Fairbanks Campus Space Committee—subject: "Office Space for Central Staff of REA (VP Ramos)," November 28, 1976 (Fairbanks: University of Alaska Archives).

25. President's files, report from Mike Metty to Jay Barton: "Rural Educational Delivery," December 12, 1982 (Fairbanks: University of Alaska Archives).

26. "Center for Northern Educational Research Holds Meeting in Anchorage," *Tundra Times,* January 15, 1975.

27. Letter from Mitch Demientief to the ANHRDP policy council, June 6, 1974, (Anchorage: Alaska Native Foundation Archives), 2.

28. Louis Jacquot, director of ANHRD, memo to the Policy Council ANHRD, August 6, 1974, (Anchorage: Alaska Native Foundation Archives), 3.

29. Mary Reeve, Alaska Natives Commission Hearing, October 12, 1992.

30. Arnold L. Mitchem, George Ayers, and Ed Beekham, American Association of Colleges and Universities National Advisory Committee Report to Donald Behrend, Chancellor (Anchorage: University of Alaska–Anchorage, 1992), 6.

31. From the committee report and Ryan Olson, *The Northern Light,* March 23, 1993, 2.

32. Michael Jennings's personal notes. This conversation took place in the chancellor's conference room, among representatives of the advisory committee, Michael Jennings (consultant), and the chancellor.

33. Lynn Louise La Barge, "Native Issues Addressed," *The Northern Light,* April 10, 1992, I.

34. La Barge, "Native Issues Addressed," I.

35. La Barge, "Native Issues Addressed," I.

36. La Barge, "Native Issues Addressed," I.

37. "Alaska Native Studies," brochure for the Alaska Native studies program, 1998.

38. University of Alaska Anchorage, Office of Institutional Research, "UAA Student Credit Hours (SCH), Enrollment, and Sections by Campus/School/Department and Course Level, Fall Semester Opening, 1997–1999."

39. Gabriel A. Almond and G. Bingham Powell Jr., *Comparative Politics: System, Process, and Policy,* 2nd ed. (Boston: Little, Brown, 1978).

40. Hensley, interviews with Jennings.

41. Norman A. Chance, *The Inupiat and Arctic Alaska: An Ethnography of Development* (Fort Worth, Tex.: Holt, Rinehart and Winston, 1990), 208–219. See also Joseph Jorgensen, *Oil Age Eskimos* (Berkeley: University of California Press, 1990).

Index

About the Authors

Patricia C. Albers received her Ph.D. in anthropology from the University of Wisconsin–Madison. She is professor and chair of the department of American Indian studies at the University of Minnesota. She has published many articles on American Indian history and culture that focus on the subjects of gender, political economy, intertribal relations, and visual representation.

William Asikinack (Anishinabe of Walpole Island, Ontario) has been involved in education for, by, and about First Nations people at all levels, from kindergarten to the postsecondary level. He has been active in many of the developmental stages of Indian or First Nations education in Canada, especially in the province of Ontario. He started teaching at the university level in the late 1960s in Ontario and joined the faculty of the Saskatchewan Indian Federated College in 1983.

Colin G. Calloway is chair of Native American studies and professor of history and Native American studies at Dartmouth College. He has taught at the University of Wyoming and served as assistant director at the D'Arcy McNickle Center for the History of the American Indian at the Newberry Library in Chicago. His books include *First Peoples: A Documentary Survey of American Indian History* (1999); *New Worlds for All: Indians, Europeans, and the Remaking of Early America* (1997); *The American Revolution in Indian Country* (1995); *The Western Abenakis of Vermont* (1990), and *Crown and Calumet: British–Indian Relations 1783–1815* (1987). He is currently writing a history of the American West before Lewis and Clark.

Duane Champagne is professor of sociology and director of the American Indian Studies Center at UCLA. He is a member of the Turtle Mountain Band of Chippewa from North Dakota. Professor Champagne has been director of the

UCLA American Indian Studies Center since 1991 and editor of the *American Indian Culture and Research Journal* since 1986. He has authored and edited more than seventy publications, including *Native America: Portraits of the Peoples, The Native North American Almanac,* and *Social Order and Political Change: Constitutional Governments among the Cherokee, Choctaw, Chickasaw and Creek.* Champagne's research focuses primarily on issues of social and cultural change in both historical and contemporary Native American communities. He has written about a variety of Indian communities including Cherokee, Tlingit, Iroquois, Delaware, Choctaw, Northern Cheyenne, Creek, and California Indians.

Brenda J. Child is an associate professor of American studies at the University of Minnesota. She is the author of *Boarding School Seasons: American Indian Families, 1900–1940* and a member of the Red Lake Band of the Chippewa Tribe.

Jennifer Robin Collier is a graduate student in geography at the University of Cambridge.

Steven James Crum (member of the Shoshone-Paiute Tribes of the Duck Valley Indian Reservation, Owyhee, Nevada) is associate professor of Native American studies at the University of California, Davis. He received his Ph.D. in history from the University of Utah in 1983 and is the author of *The Road on Which We Came: A History of the Western Shoshone* (1994).

Jack D. Forbes is professor emeritus and former chair of Native American studies at the University of California, Davis, where he has served since 1969. He is of Powhatan-Renape, Delaware-Lenape, and other background. He received his Ph.D. from the University of Southern California in 1959. In 1960–1961, he developed proposals for Native American studies programs and for an indigenous university; in 1971, the D-Q University came into being as a result of that proposal. Forbes is the author of numerous books, monographs, and articles, including *Red Blood: A Novel* (1997); *Columbus and Other Cannibals* (1992); *Only Approved Indians* (1995); *Apache, Navaho and Spaniard* (1960, 1994); and *Africans and Native Americans* (1993). Other books in print include *Native Americans of California and Nevada, Native American Higher Education: The Struggle for the Creation of D-Q University,* and *Proposition 209: Racist Trick or Radical Equalizer.* He is also a poet, a writer of fiction, and an international guest lecturer. He was the recipient of the Before Columbus Foundation's American Book Award for Lifetime Achievement in 1997.

Mary Jo Tippeconnic Fox (enrolled member of the Comanche Nation of Oklahoma) currently holds the position of associate director of American Indian studies, ambassador to the Indian Nations, and associate to the president for American Indian affairs at the University of Arizona. She earned her Ph.D. from the University of Arizona in 1982 and has more than twenty-five years of teaching and administrative experience. Her research interests are American Indian women's issues and American Indian higher education, including American Indian studies.

Peter R. Golia is special assistant to the Nation representative for the Oneida Indian Nation. Dr. Golia has a bachelor's degree in economics and a master's degree in journalism from New York University. He holds a Ph.D. in human ecology/mass media from Michigan State University and did postdoctoral work at the Harvard University Graduate School of Education. Before coming to the Oneida Nation, he developed marketing and communications strategies for high-tech start-ups and not-for-profit organizations in Boston, New York, and San Francisco. He is the former director of corporate relations for New York University, and he served as the director of external relations and development for the Harvard University Native American Program. As a journalist, he worked in television news and documentaries at PBS and Turner Broadcasting. He has also been an adjunct faculty member at Michigan State, Central Michigan, and the State University of New York's Institute of Technology, where he taught courses on mass media and developmental psychology.

Lorie M. Graham is a professor of law at Suffolk University Law School in Boston, Massachusetts, where she teaches courses on American Indian law, indigenous peoples' rights, and human rights. She is the former director of the Harvard University Native American Program and current member of the program's faculty advisory board, and she has been a visiting scholar at Harvard Law School and University of Massachusetts–Amherst. She has served as legal consultant to several indigenous nations and organizations and facilitated several conferences and seminars on a range of issues. Her most recent publications include *Reparations and the Indian Child Welfare Act, Self-determination for Indigenous Peoples after Kosovo: Translating Self-determination "Into Practice" and "Into Peace,"* and *The Past Never Vanishes: A Contextual Critique of the Existing Indian Family Doctrine.*

Inés Hernández-Ávila (Nez Perce/Chicana) is associate professor of Native American studies at the University of California, Davis. She teaches Native American literature, religion, and performance classes and is an accomplished poet. She is the editor of the forthcoming volume *Reading Native American Women: Critical/Creative Representations.*

Vikki Howard (Leech Lake Ojibwe Nation, Minnesota) has served K–12 Indian education programs in the Twin Cities area for nearly fifteen years before moving

into higher education. She currently serves as the community relations coordinator for the department of American Indian studies, University of
Minnesota–Twin Cities campus. She is a graduate student in the College of Education and Human Development with the Leadership Academy, and she is the
mother of one awesome beautiful six-year-old daughter.

Michael L. Jennings is an associate professor of philosophy and humanities at
the University of Alaska Fairbanks and president of the statewide faculty union
(United Academics). He has held faculty posts in political science, education,
and Native studies, serving as director of the Alaska Native studies department
at the University of Alaska, Anchorage. He has also served as special assistant to
the statewide president of the University of Alaska system, special assistant
to the president of the Tanana Valley Community College, and deputy director
of the Fairbanks Native Association. He has also worked for the Alaska Federation of Natives and with United States Senator Mike Gravel and Alaska Gover-
nor William Egan.

Dennis Jones (Ojibwe) is a language instructor in the American Indian studies department at the University of Minnesota–Twin Cities in Minneapolis.

Clara Sue Kidwell is currently director of the Native American studies program
and professor of history at the University of Oklahoma in Norman. Her tribal
affiliations are Choctaw and Chippewa. She was born in Tahlequah, Oklahoma,
and raised in Muskogee, Oklahoma. She received a B.A. in letters (1962) and an
M.A. and Ph.D. in history of science (1970) from the University of Oklahoma.
Before joining the faculty there in 1995, she served for two years as assistant director of cultural resources at the National Museum of the American Indian,
Smithsonian Institution. She has also taught at the University of California at
Berkeley, Dartmouth College, the University of Minnesota, Haskell Indian Junior College (Lawrence, Kansas), and the Kansas City Art Institute. She has
taught courses on American Indian history, philosophy, and medicine. Her publications include "Systems of Knowledge" in *America in 1492*, edited by Alvin
Josephy (1991); "Indian Women as Cultural Mediators" in *Ethnohistory* (volume
39, 1992); "Choctaw Women and Cultural Persistence in Mississippi" in *Nego-
tiators of Change: Historical Perspectives on Native American Women*, edited by Nancy
Shoemaker (1995); and *Choctaws and Missionaries in Mississippi, 1818–1918*
(1995).

Stanley Knick received a Ph.D. in anthropology at Indiana University. He is director of the Native American Resource Center and research associate professor

in the American Indian studies department at the University of North Carolina at Pembroke. He teaches courses in archaeology, Native American health, contemporary issues of Native Americans, and cultural anthropology. His interests include archaeology in southeastern North Carolina, art and culture of Native Americans, Native American health, and global traditional cultures. He was born in Virginia and raised in Texas, and he is a veteran of the United States Army, an Episcopalian, and an honorary member of the Lumbee Tribe. Among his publications are *Along the Trail: A Reader about Native Americans* (1996) and *The Lumbee in Context: Toward an Understanding* (2000).

George Longfish (Seneca/Tuscarora) is professor of Native American studies and former director of the Carl N. Gorman Museum at the University of California, Davis. In 1994, he received his B.A. and M.F.A. from the School of the Art Institute of Chicago. Longfish is nationally and internationally known for his use of color and personal iconography in works on canvas and sculptural masks. His work has appeared in more than 250 exhibitions during the past twenty years. Currently, his work has been seen in the traveling exhibition "Indigena: Contemporary Native Perspectives," sponsored by the Canadian Museum of Civilization in Hull, Quebec, and in "Keepers of the Western Door" at the Castelloni Museum in Buffalo, New York. His latest exhibition was "Humor and Rage" in Barcelona, Spain, in 2001. George Longfish is coauthor with David Penny of *Native American Art.*

Shelly Lowe (member of the Navajo Nation) is a doctoral student in higher education at the University of Arizona. She grew up in Ganado, Arizona, a small town on the Navajo Reservation. She has taught summer courses in American Indian studies at the University of Arizona, where she received her master's degree. Her research emphasis is on American Indian higher education.

Martha J. Macri is chair and associate professor of the department of Native American studies and anthropology. She is a linguistic anthropologist specializing in Native American languages and Mesoamerican scripts.

Don McCaskill is professor in the Native studies department at Trent University, Canada. He is coeditor of *In the Words of Elders: Aboriginal Cultures in Transition.*

Carol Miller is a professor in the departments of American Indian studies and American studies at the University of Minnesota. She is a member of the Cherokee Nation of Oklahoma and is currently working on a book about contemporary fiction by American Indian women writers.

David R. Miller served as the department head of Indian studies at Saskatchewan Indian Federated College from 1989 to 1994, where he continues to teach courses for advanced students and honors and graduate students. His current research includes land claims processes in Canada and comparative policy issues between Canada and the United States.

Frank C. Miller, professor of anthropology at the University of Minnesota, was chair of the faculty-student-community committee that established the department of American Indian studies there in 1969, and he served as acting chair of the department from 1996 to 1998. He has published many works about cultural change in Mexico and among the Ojibwe people in Minnesota.

John Milloy (Scot) was born in New York City and raised in Scotland, France, and Canada. He completed his B.A. at St. Patrick's College, Ottawa, an M.A. at Carleton University, and his doctorate in the imperial and commonwealth history department at Oxford. His original doctoral thesis was on the evolution of British imperial policy for the First Nations in Canada, and further research and publishing have centered around Plains Cree history, the history of the Canadian residential school system, the history of Aboriginal health, and the Canadian Federal/First Nations constitutional history. Milloy is a consultant on law cases related to issues of treaty rights and education.

Victor Montejo is associate professor and chair of the department of Native American studies at the University of California, Davis. He received his M.A. at the State University of New York in Albany and his Ph.D. at the University of Connecticut. A Mayan from Jacaltenango, Guatemala, he is author of the autobiographical *Testimonio: Muerte de un Pueblo Guatemalteco.* His other works include *The Bird Who Cleans the World and Other Mayan Fables* (1991), *Sculpted Stones* (1996), and *Las Aventuras de Míster Puttison entre los Mayas*, his first novel. His current research includes oral literature and traditional music of the Maya.

David Newhouse (Onondaga, Six Nations of the Grand River) is associate professor of Native studies and administrative studies at Trent University. Along with Don McCaskill (Trent University) and Peter Kulchyski (University of Manitoba), he is the editor of *In the Words of Elders: Aboriginal Cultures in Transition.* He is also editor of *CANDO, Journal of Aboriginal Economic Development* and author of a forthcoming text, *From the Tribal to the Modern: Reflections on the Development of Modern Aboriginal Society*. His research interest focuses on Aboriginal modernity in all its dramas and dilemmas. He lives and gardens on top of a drumlin in downtown Peterborough, Ontario, Canada.

Jean M. O'Brien is associate professor of history, American Indian studies, and American studies at the University of Minnesota. She is a member of the White Earth Ojibwe Nation. She is the author of *Dispossession by Degrees: Indian Land and Identity in Natick, Massachusetts, 1650–1790* (1997), and is currently working on a book about the construction of the myth of Indian extinction in New England.

Linda E. Oxendine (Lumbee) is associate professor and chair of the American Indian studies department at the University of North Carolina at Pembroke. She received her Ph.D. in American studies with a concentration in American Indian studies from the University of Minnesota. During her thirty-year tenure in American Indian affairs, she has held several educational, administrative, and cultural positions at both Tribal and national levels.

Robert E. Powless is professor emeritus, University of Minnesota–Duluth, from which he recently retired as head of American Indian studies. He is a full-blooded enrolled member of the Oneida Nation of Indians of Wisconsin. He was the 1995 recipient of the Jean G. Blehart Distinguished Teaching Award. Dr. Powless is married to Linda, and he has two children (Blair and Marcia) and three grandchildren (Key, Preston, and Yvonne).

Jay Stauss (Jamestown Band S'Klallam) is completing his tenth year as director of American Indian studies at the University of Arizona. He received his Ph.D. from Washington State University in 1971 and has served in seven different administrative roles in both higher education and the federal government in the past twenty-five years. He is the author or coauthor of more than two dozen articles on urban Indians, American Indian families, and the development of Indian/Native studies programs.

Blair Stonechild (member of the Muscowpetung First Nation in Southern Saskatchewan) has been a professor and administrator of First Nations higher education for more than twenty years at the Saskatchewan Indian Federated College. Some of the positions he has held include head of Indian studies, dean of academics, and executive director of planning and development. He is a nationally respected scholar, who received the Saskatchewan Book Award and was shortlisted for a Governor-General's Award in 1997. He has served as trustee of the Canadian Museum of Civilization from 1990 to 1998 and was a member of the organizational Saskculture Committee in 1996–1997. His various consulting projects include Indian land claims studies, storyline consultant for the Native People's Gallery at the Royal Saskatchewan Museum, and most recently the Treaty Four "Keeping House" Project. He lives in Regina, is married, and has three teenage children.

Stefano Varese is professor of Native American studies at the University of California, Davis, and director of the Indigenous Research Center of the Americas. He received his Ph.D. in anthropology from the Pontificia Universidad Católica del Perú, Lima, in 1967. His research encompasses indigenous peoples of the Americas, and he specializes in Latin American Indian diaspora; hemispheric and global perspectives; and Indian community development, agroecological and sustainable development, rural–urban and transnational migration, and human rights. He has served as consultant on indigenous issues to the World Bank, UNESCO, the International Fund for Agricultural Development, the United Nations High Commissioner for Refugees, and the Inter-American Foundation.